MATSUO BASHO AND HIS DISCIPLES

BASHO'S SEVEN ANTHOLOGIES

BASHO'S SEVEN ANTHOLOGIES

MATSUO BASHO was born in 1644 of a low-ranking *samurai* family in Iga, Japan. He began learning *haikai* poetry in his youth, and became a *haikai* master in Edo (modern Tokyo). He was a gifted creator of *haikai* (a linked verse jointly composed by several poets), and elevated the *Haik* (a first stanza of a *haikai*) to the simple and sweet art of literature. At the age of forty-one he began a life of travel, and thereafter wrote several travel pieces. The most famous work is *A Long and Narrow Road*, a piece of travel to the distant northeastern provinces in Japan. He traveled and wrote verses and had many disciples in various places of Japan. The chief works of Basho and his disciples were compiled in seven anthologies published as *A Winter Day*, *A Spring Day*, *Waste Land*, *Hisago*, *Salmino*, *A Charcoal Bag* and *Zok Salmino*—which have been admired as masterworks of Japanese literature. His last travel was a journey to Osaka in 1694, where he died of a stomach illness at fifty-one.

Copyright © 2019 Matsuo Basho

BASHO'S SEVEN ANTHOLOGIES

Translated by Jiro Fullset
Translation supervised by Richard Whitehead
Coordinator: Junko Rodriguez

Published by Babel Press U.S.A.
All rights reserved

ISBN: 978-0991478941

Babel Corporation
Pacific Business News Bldg. #208,
1833 Kalakaua Avenue, Honolulu,
Hawaii 96815

Haik is a traditional form of simple Japanese three-line poetry. Line one has 5 syllables, line two has 7 syllables, and line three has 5 syllables. Often focusing on images of nature and the four seasons and of Japan, Haiku is traditionally a mood poem written in the present tense that doesn't use any metaphors or similes.

MATSUO BASHO AND HIS DISCIPLES

BASHO'S SEVEN ANTHOLOGIES

Translated with
an Introduction, an Epilogue and Notes by
Jiro Fullset

TABLE OF CONTENTS

Introduction	11
A Winter Day	27
A Spring Day	43
Waste Land	57
Hisago	123
Salmino	143
A Charcoal Bag	185
Zok Salmino	225
Epilogue	271

INTRODUCTION

Before the Set-Out

The *Haikai* Master Matsuo Basho

The poet was born in the twenty-first year of Kan'ei (1644) as second son of the Matsuo, a low-rank *samurai* family in Iga. It was in the early Tokugawa Period, an era of the strong and stable Tokugawa Shogunate. The province of Iga, some thirty miles southeast of Kyoto, was the domain of the Todo, one of the great *daimyos*.

 Little is known about his childhood. As was often the case with a *samurai* boy those days, he changed his name as he grew up: Kinsack, Toshichiro, Chuemon, Munefusa, and somewhere in his teens he began serving Todo Sengin, a young high-ranking vassal of the Todo. As it happened, Sengin was a *haikai* poet of the Teimon School. The young *samurai* servant may thus have begun learning the *haikai* poetry of the Teimon under the guidance of his master, Sengin. The master, however, died young at the age of twenty-five when he was only twenty-three years old. It is not well known how the master-less *samurai* lived until he left Iga several years later. Just imagine his younger years from his words in his essay *Life at the Genjou-an*: 'I lived a life of failure, once envying men of high status and ambition, once trying to be a Zen priest.'

 At the age of twenty-nine he went up to Edo (now the metropolitan city of Tokyo), where, not the Teimon, but the new Danrin School had a strong appeal to the ambitious poet. He participated in a *haikai* meeting hosted by Nishiyama Sowin, a leading figure of the Danrin. And with Tosei as his pen name, he was gradually getting to be a popular *haikai* master. Among his disciples in this period were Kikack, Ransetz, Ranran and Sampou.

 And now, what did *haikai* masters do in those days? —They taught *haikai* poetry to their disciples, most of them merchants in the town; and hosted a *haikai* meeting, acting as judge in a *haikai* game. In that way they served town people who sought for intellectual pleasures. As time went by, he seemed to become reluctant to live like that; what is more, he began to regard the *haikai* poetry of the Danrin as merely witty.

 At the age of thirty-seven he moved from busy, noisy downtown to Fukagawa, a quiet village in the eastern outskirts of Edo, where he led a secluded life in a hut. One day one of his disciples planted one banana tree called *basho* in his garden; before long, his followers began calling the hut the Basho-an, and their *haikai* master the Reverend Basho.

The Land Alive with Words and Verses

Reading the said descriptions, you may wonder what the *haikai* is. What are the

Teimon School and the Danrin? To know the outline of the *haikai*, you're invited to see a brief, really brief history of Japanese poetry as follows:

The '*waka*' means a Japanese poem. The first *waka* is said to have been made by the legendary hero King Susanowo. Japan's oldest chronicle *Kojiki* (written in 712) tells us that, to save a daughter of a certain lord, the brave man fought and slew a huge snake-like monster with eight heads and eight tails. As a matter of course, he married her, and built a house for his new family, then making a *waka* of joy:

    The land of Izmo, where clouds are born, a hedge-shaped cloud;
    Now, let us build a house for my bride, let us set a hedge around.

Nobody knows when he composed it. He was a legendary figure at any rate. Yet in the *Kojiki* you can find some other *waka* poems in ancient Japan, one of which is a *waka* of Emperor Ojin's:

    Where are you from, crab? —I'm from the far seashore of Tsunuga;
    Where are you walking sideways? —The isles of Ichidi and Mi I pass;
    The lake's alive with grebes; The road runs along a stretch of ripples;
    And I go straight to Kohata; Where there appears a girl;
    The back view of her slender figure; The good shape of her white teeth;
    And lovely are her eyebrows; Not red, nor black, but dark and long drawn;
    She's what I've sought for; She's what I've long longed for;
    In this feast we meet, sitting face to face; And now, girl, will you marry me?

The emperor is said to have reigned over the Osaka Plains in the early fifth century. We may therefore say *waka* poems were made and sung at that time at the latest. Since then innumerable people have made innumerable *waka* poems. Ancient Japanese loved singing a *waka*. They never ceased to make *waka* poems even in the flood of Chinese culture. See the title 'The Land Alive with Words and Verses'; in praise of their country they called her so. Fortunately, we can read part of their 'Words and Verses' thanks to a *waka* poet in the eighth century, Otomo-no Yakamochi, who personally compiled the *Man'yo-shu* (or *Leaves of Ten Thousands*)—the oldest existing *waka* anthology that includes some forty-five hundred pieces of poetry: long and short, ancient and contemporary, noted poets' and unknown commoners', and many poems of various themes—love, wit, sorrow, joy, life, travel, farewell, bravery, death, nature, intrigue, jealousy. Let us see some of them:

    Princess Nukata-no Okimi:
      Being in love, I've been waiting for my sweetheart;
      Only hearing an autumn wind stir the straw blind.
    Great Poet Kakinomoto-no Hitomaro:
      The *take* trees whisper in breeze, dance lightly on the hill;
      While I think of my truelove left alone in my country.
    Lord Yamanoue-no Okra:

Let us go back, boys, hurry up toward Japan, toward our old white beach;
Where the green pine trees would wait for us with passion.
Poet Yamabe-no Akahito:
Sail out from the seashore of Tago, and you'll see a pure white peak
—The snowy summit of the great Mount Fuji.
Lord Otomo-no Yakamochi:
The spring garden, the red fragrant peach blossoms;
And on the sunny path appears a girl pure and lovely.

By the age of the *Man'yo-shu*, most of the *waka* came to be composed of five-seven-five-seven-seven syllables. For instance, the said *waka* of Otomo-no Yakamochi's is pronounced as follows:

Haruno-sono (5) Kurenawi-nihofu (7) Momono-hana (5)
Shitateru-michini (7) Idetaru-wotome (7)

Aristocratic Taste

In the early tenth century—it was in the midst of the stable and peaceful Heian Period (794-1192)—the *Kokin-Waka-shu* (the *Kokin-shu*), or *The Collection of Waka Poetry Ancient and Modern*, was compiled by Ki-no Tsurayuki and other poets under the order of Emperor Daigo. First of all, please see the sonorous beginning of its foreword:

The *waka* is made through the work of human mind, bearing thousands of leaves of words. People would sing of what they have in mind when they see or hear various things in the world. Listen to a warbler twitter among flowers or a frog chirp on a river, and you will find all the living sing a song. It does not show any power, yet it will shake heaven and earth, it will make a demon weep, it will go between man and woman, and it will console even a rough, tough warrior. That is the *waka*.

In this collection most of the verses are of court nobles, although in the *Man'yo-shu* there are not a few verses made by commoners. Such noble poets did not sing of sorrow and joy as simply and as frankly as the *Man'yo-shu* poets did. Sorrowful or joyful, they made elegant verses elegantly with their own sense of poetry. For such a purpose they removed vulgar language from the realm of poetry, and restricted poetic diction and themes to the extent of their aesthetic sense and taste. Their verses are subtle, sentimental and imaginative—the mirror of the nobles' mind and life. What was the most important was that their poetic style and method became traditional in the world of poetry to the days of Basho, thence to the modern age.

The collection consists of some eleven hundred pieces of *waka*, with themes such as spring, summer, autumn, winter, farewell, travel, celebration and love. Let us see some of them.

Lord Ariwara-no Narihira:
- Were it not for *sacra* blossoms in this world;

Spring would be a calm, serene, and easy season.
- We all shall pass away someday; I've always heard about that;
But never have I thought the someday is today or yesterday.
Lady Ono-no Komachi:
The fair and fresh hue has faded away from the flower;
While time passed by in vain, while I was lost in thought in rain.
Lord Ki-no Tsurayuki:
Hazy is the sky, the trees in bud, and spring snow falling in the meadow;
All this shows me a flowery scene in a flowerless village.

In the beginning of the eleventh century one of the greatest novels of the world *The Tale of Genji* was written by Lady Murasaki Shikibu. The refined taste of the novel, as well as the aesthetics of the *Kokin-shu,* set the tone for Japanese literature towards the succeeding centuries.

Great Decline

In the early thirteenth century the *Shin Kokin-Waka-shu* (the *Shin Kokin-shu),* or *The New Collection of Waka Poetry Ancient and Modern*, was compiled by Fujiwara-no Teika and other poets under the order of Emperor Go-Toba. By then, the power of the court nobles, and of the emperor, had been usurped by the warriors. The Kamakura Shogunate, founded at Kamakura in 1192, had already ruled over the land and people of Japan after fierce wars with other warriors. That was in a sense a natural course of history. In fact, the nobles had been nothing more than lazy tribute eaters in the flowery capital city for several centuries.

Having lost power, the nobles tried to keep up their cultural authority. Now powerful though they were, they were not able to make a single *waka*—those rough, vulgar *samurai!* In that way the *waka* became the symbol of the nobles, although their ancestors had composed *waka* poems in amusement.

Their verses are deep and sweet: delicate, elaborate, brilliant, visionary—the art for art's sake. They were inspired by the *waka* of the Heian Period. Many of their verses are associative with literature in the days of the *Kokin-shu* and *The Tale of Genji*—the golden age of the court nobles. When composing *waka* poems, they borrowed words, expressions, scenes and atmospheres from specific classical works, for example, the *Kokin-shu, The Tale of Ise*, and *The Tale of Genji* —the method to be employed in later times by *renga* and *haikai* poets, by the Teimon School, and by Basho and company.

The *Shin Kokin-shu* consists of some twenty hundred pieces of *waka* poetry. Let us see some of them:
Emperor Go-Toba:
Pieces of firewood burning at dusk, my old memories are coming back;
And lost in thought, I find myself coughing in the smoke with delight.
Lord Fujiwara-no Shunzei:
Sacra trees in bloom in the great Katano Fields; could I see this again?

At dawn in spring, the sky purple, the blossoms falling like snow.
Lord Fujiwara-no Teika:
The floating bridge has gone with a spring night dream;
And about the ridge lies a cloud, now leaving in a thin, gray line.
Lord Fujiwara-no Karyu:
Gentle is a breath of air from the oaks, blowing across the brook;
And a summer sight—people are making their ablutions at twilight.
Monk Saigyo:
Though not a man of poetry, I do feel sad and sweet when I see
A snipe rise from a stream at dusk in autumn.

Basho admired Saigyo, among others. A gifted man of poetry, Saigyo was originally a *samurai* and imperial guard, but quit, and lived a wandering life as a monk bard. Like Saigyo, Basho lived as a hermit. As Saigyo had traveled to the far province of Mutz, so Basho made a journey of *A Long and Narrow Road*.

The times after the age of the *Shin Kokin-shu* saw the court nobles gradually, sometimes drastically, on the decline through war, economic difficulties and land usurpation by the warriors, despite some attempts at restoration; and in the mid-fifteenth century the whole noble class ruined down to the bottom in a terrific civil war that burned down the city of Kyoto. During the period of decline, they continued making *waka* poems; however, they had very few gifted poets. Their day was already gone with a spring night dream.

New Culture

The age of the warriors continued. Though the Ashikaga Shogunate (founded at Kyoto in 1338) was an unstable ruler, the economy of the nation grew rapidly. This period saw various people—*samurai*, merchants, rich farmers, Zen monks, and just people—participate in cultural activities. Both in the town and in the country the many enjoyed watching the Dengack music and dances. Some had a tea party. Some held a *renga* meeting. Men of letters composed classical *waka* and Chinese poems (They composed Chinese poems as their own mode of literature just as contemporary European made verses in Latin). The Noh drama, the Kyogen comedy, the tea ceremony, the Zen garden, the monochrome painting, and the art of flower arrangement—all these were popular in those days, and have survived to the present day. Let us see some of them:

The Noh: Those days the Dengack was hugely popular with the many as said above; and then on the basis of it, the great playwright and actor Kwan'ami (1333-1384) worked out a refined form of musical drama, the Noh. His works entertained the *shogun, daimyos* and high-rank *samurai*. His son, Ze-ami (1363-1443) was a gifted dramatist; he created many wonderful Noh dramas, and also wrote a well-known treatise on the Noh—the *Kaden-sho*, or *The Book of the Flower*. In it he wrote, 'Know what is the flower; know what is not the flower; keep the flower within your mind; and do not show the flower on the stage; that is the very essence of art.'

Zen culture: In the Ashikaga Period (1338-1573) Zen Buddhism spread widely across Japan under the patronage of the *shoguns* and *daimyos*. Its temples and monasteries were something of a cultural center. What today attracts us in such a temple is a Zen garden that symbolizes Nature by the placement of a pond, a stream, rocks, trees and sand space. And in such temples and monasteries there were Zen monks engaged in cultural activities as well as ascetic training. Some of them composed classical Chinese poems. To modern Japanese the most famous poet among them would be eccentric but lovable Zen monk Ikkyu (1394-1481). And some of them drew portraits, landscapes, and religious scenes in ink and wash in a simple yet refined style; that is the monochrome painting. The most admired painter among them was Sesshu (1420-1506), whose works of art marked one of the heights of Japanese painting.

The Tea Ceremony is something of a synthetic art including a tasteful Zen garden, a simple tea house, a quiet tea room, a tea cup, tea tools, host and guest, rules and etiquettes, and tea itself. In a tea room the guest enjoys not only having a cup of tea, but also seeing a monochrome picture or a calligraphic work on the wall, a craft work or arranged flowers on the *tokonoma* alcove, and immersing himself in the silent space of light and shadow. The art of the tea ceremony was completed by the great tea master Sen-no Rikyu (1522-1591). He advocated the importance of sad and sweet taste in art, and his aesthetics has ruled over the various realms of Japanese art and culture to the present day.

Renga and *Haikai*

Remember that a *waka* consists of five-seven-five-seven-seven syllables. Divide it into two: the first five-seven-five syllables, one stanza; the remaining seven-seven, the other. Form a group of two, three or some more. The first one composes the first stanza of five-seven-five syllables; the second, the second stanza of seven-seven; and the third, the third stanza of five-seven-five—in that way a group of poets jointly make a chain of stanzas; that is the *renga*, or the linked verse. How many stanzas did they make? —Usually fifty or one hundred. Occasionally one thousand. On rare occasions, ten thousand. Basho and company liked a linked verse of thirty-six stanzas.

The *renga* was at first a mere amusement among *waka* poets, and yet in the Ashikaga Period won great popularity among high and low. Of such people, the commoners enjoyed the *renga* as a comical word-game, while the nobles and literati composed classical *renga* poems full of prosodic regulations. And some talented poets elevated *renga* poetry to the elegant art of literature. One of them was Iwo Sogi (1421-1502), a great *renga* master in the fifteenth century. Low-born though he was, the poet was a noted scholar of the *Kokin-shu*. He was not only respected as classicist by court nobles in Kyoto, but also welcomed fervently as great *renga* master by feudal lords in various places of Japan.

Although the highbrows composed *renga* poems of classical flavor, general people disliked its rigorism and enjoyed making their own linked verse full of vulgar words. And in the sixteenth century it was exalted to the linked verse of wit and humor thanks to Yamazaki Sokan (1465-1554) and Arakida Moritake (1473-1549). That was called the *haikai* (witty) *renga* or just the *haikai*. That was the root of Basho's poetry.

The Teimon and the Danrin

The weak and unstable Ashikaga Shogunate declined sharply during the Onin civil wars (1467-77), decidedly in the succeeding times of confusion, and fell in 1573. During the age of the warring states, many *daimyos* fought with one another across Japan—from which emerged some strong rulers (Oda-Toyotomi Period); and with the Tokugawa Shogunate (founded at Edo in 1603) ended the times of wars. Peace came. And the peace did greatly stimulate agriculture, commerce, construction, shipping, mining, manufacturing, arts and crafts, and entertainment. All became prosperous. How was our *haikai* poetry?

The Teimon School: With Matsunaga Teitock as leader, this *haikai* school dominated the circles of poetry in the early Tokugawa Period. Now the *haikai* took the place of the *renga* as the most popular genre of linked verse. The poets of this school introduced colloquialisms and Chinese expressions into linked verse, but many of their verses were dependent upon wordplay associated with Japanese classics. They were rather pedantic and particular about classical prosody.

The Danrin School was founded by Nishiyama Sowin. They disliked traditional rules. They enjoyed making parodies of classic works, and depicted everyday life of town people. They employed novel themes, playfully borrowing various types of diction from Noh dramas, Chinese literature, and colloquialism. Unrestricted poets, they composed verses easily and quickly, so their works are said to lack lyricism. The great novelist Ihara Saikack was a member of the Danrin. He was famous as a quick poem-maker who composed 23,500 stanzas within a day.

Basho's New Style

Remember that Basho was a Teimon poet in the beginning, was afterward attracted to the style of the Danrin. But in a few years, probably somewhere in the second half of his thirties, he came to dislike both of them. Teimon poets were particular about wording, but rather pedantic, and too rigid in prosody. Their works were no better than imitations of the classics. The Danrin School was free from trite rules, but their style was too loose, too easy. See his comments written in his letter sent to one of his disciples in that period:

- Stop making a stanza dependently upon the previous one; that is the way of the Teimon or the Danrin.
- Be moderate in employing colloquialisms; do not imitate the Teimon style.
- Do not make an elaborate verse.

- It is a manner of the Teimon to use a showy ancient wording—say, a white cloud about so-and-so.
- A hypermeter would be acceptable if such a word sounded in tune. The rhythm is all.

Basho began trying to establish a new style, not the Teimon nor the Danrin. In that period he seemed to learn the style of *waka* poets such as Saigyo and Teika, and of Chinese bards such as Li Bai and Du Fu. Yet that was but a quest on paper. In search of true poetry he set out on a journey. But that is to be told later.

Notes on Things Japanese

Months

Spring: Mutsuki (First Month), Kisaragi (Second Month)
          Yayoi (Third Month)
Summer: Uzuki (Fourth Month), Satsuki (Fifth Month),
          Minazuki or No-Water Month (Sixth Month)
Autumn: Fumizuki (Seventh Month), Hazuki or Leafy Month
          (Eighth Month), Nagatsuki (Ninth Month)
Winter: Kannazuki or No-God Month (Tenth Month)*,
          Shimotsuki or Frost Month (Eleventh Month),
          Shiwas or Busy Month (Twelfth Month)
          *In the Tenth Month all the gods are said to visit the province of Izmo, so that it is called No-God Month in the other provinces of Japan.

You may think Mutsuki (First Month), for instance, would be the same period of time as January; however, Japanese adopted the lunar calendar in those days, so that Mutsuki was roughly around February in the solar calendar; some year, a little earlier; some year, a little later.

Places

Iga: Go southeast some thirty miles from Kyoto, and you will reach the mountainous province of Iga. In its capital town Ueno, Basho was born and brought up. After moving to Edo, he visited from time to time his home country, where his siblings lived.

Ise: Go further southeast from Iga over the bordering mountains, and you will arrive in the coastal province of Ise, where there is Ise Shrine, the house of the imperial guardian deity, the Sun Goddess. The shrine has attracted high and low, old and young, men and women since ancient times. When visiting the shrine, Saigyo composed a *waka* as follows:

  I don't know, I don't know who lives in the sacred shrine;
  Yet its solemnity makes me simply shed tears.

Basho, too, paid a visit at the sacred shrine several times.

Yoshino: Go south over mountains from Nara in springtime, and you will find Mount Yoshino full of *sacra* blossoms. To see such a brilliant view, many *waka* poets of old visited there; for instance, Saigyo composed a *waka* on the mountain as follows:

  My soul has been lost and astray somewhere beyond;
  Since I found a *sacra* a bit in bloom on Yoshino Mountain.

Basho, too, paid a visit to the holy mountain on *A Lonely Journey* and on *A*

Sentimental Journey.
Kumano: Go further south from Yoshino over mountains, across ravines, through winding roads in forest, and you will reach the mountainous holy land of Kumano. There are three great shrines in the midst of splendid nature—rivers, gorges, ridges, falls, and a narrowed sky.
Suma: Go west from Osaka along the coast, and you will find the scenic beach of Suma, where Basho visited on *A Sentimental Journey*. It is a notable spot in Japanese literature. To this place Lord Genji was exiled from the capital city (*The Tale of Genji*); and on this beach young noble *samurai* Taira-no Atsumori was slain in battle (*The Tale of the Heike*).

Plants and Insects

tsubaki: A camellia. It blooms in red from winter to spring, and is loved as a garden flower.
mei: It looks like a plum or an apricot, but is neither of them. It blooms in red or white with a sweet fragrance in early spring. It came to Japan from China in ancient times. It is called *mei* or *mume*. The former would be easier to pronounce. It was loved by, among others, Sugawara-no Michizane, a learned statesman in the early Heian Period. See a *waka* of his (it was made when he was exiled from the capital city):
  When the east wind rises, *mei* blossoms, don't fail to raise your fragrance;
  Never forget spring comes when it does, though I will be not here then.
Since his death he has been worshipped as deity of learning at Tenjin Shrine, which is, naturally, alive with *mei* trees.
momo: A peach. It blooms in pale pink in spring.
nanohana: A rape flower or a canola flower. It blooms in yellow in mid-spring.
sacra: A cherry. It blooms brilliantly in pink-tinged white in the height of spring. Japanese like *sacra* blossoms very much. Narihira, Komachi, Tsurayuki, Shunzei, Teika, Saigyo, Sogi and Basho—almost all Japanese poets of old sang of *sacra* blossom. In the realm of Japanese poetry, the word 'flower' (or 'blossom') mostly means a *sacra*. In its season ordinary people, if not poets, enjoy seeing *sacra* blossoms or hold a *sacra* party under a flowering *sacra* tree.
yamabuki: A yellow rose. It blooms in bright yellow in late spring.
take: A bamboo. Note that it is pronounced *ta-ke* in Japanese.
nadeshico: A pink. It blooms in autumn, and is often compared to a little girl.
kick: A chrysanthemum. It flowers beautifully in the fall. A friend of Basho, Sodo was a lover of *kick* and made a *kick* garden in his hermitage. The word chrysanthemum is all right, but sometimes too long for a short verse like a *haik*.
kaki: A persimmon. It produces many fruits—some sweet, some sour—in high autumn.
hagi: Lespedeza. Unfortunately, I have not seen the plant Lespedeza. Do not think I am a botanist. Just think a *hagi* is a kind of clover. It flowers sweetly in

pale pink in autumn.

susuki: In the fall you can see in fields *susuki* (or silver grass) white with its soft ears. It looks like pampas grass in barren land, but Japanese regard it as a lovable autumn plant.

basho: A plantain. As said somewhere above, Basho was called so because a *basho* tree was planted at his hermitage.

As for insects, please note that, roughly speaking, Japanese think them to be something lovable. They love seeing a glimmer of a *hotaru* (firefly) flying gracefully at evening in summer. They like hearing a chirp of a *semi* (cicada) at eventide in autumn. Lady Sei-Shonagon wrote in the *Pillow Book* that a *mino-mushi* (bagworm) was a very pretty creature.

Rituals, Festivals and Customs

Seven-Herb Porridge: On the seventh day of the First Month people eat seven-vernal-herb (*nazna*, turnip, radish, etc.) porridge as a vegetable diet.

Hina Festival: On the third day of Yayoi people decorate their houses with Hina dolls of a prince, a princess, men and ladies in waiting, for their little daughters. It is also called Little Girl's Day or Momo (Peach) Festival.

The Changing of Clothes: Originally a court ritual. In the days of Basho people changed their clothes at the beginnings of summer and winter.

Tango Festival: On the fifth day of Satsuki, for keeping off evil spirits, people hang a bunch of irises or mugworts under the eaves; and as a ritual for health, they take a bath with iris leaves afloat on the water.

Tanabata Festival: It is said that, on the seventh night of the Seventh Month, two stars—Prince the Herdsman and Princess the Weaver (Altair and Vega)—cross the River Heaven (the Milky Way) to meet once a year. That night little boys and girls make a wish toward the couple of stars.

Bon Festival: In the midst of the Seventh Month the Buddhists, namely almost all Japanese hold a memorial service for the dead. The spirits of the dead, it is said, return to this world during the festival.

The Welcoming of Horses: An ancient court ceremony. In the mid of autumn horses were brought to the imperial court from the eastern provinces. The court nobles then held a ceremony of welcoming the horses at Ausaka Barrier, the eastern entrance to Kyoto.

The Beating of Bowls: A religious mendicancy. In late winter—from the death anniversary of the great monk Kouya to the end of a year—mendicant monks beat bowls as they walk around town asking for alms. Such monks are called bowl beaters.

The Sweeping of Soot: At the end of a year people clean their houses thoroughly, which is called the sweeping of soot.

The Beating of Cloth: In old times women used to soften hard cloth by beating.

It was done at nighttime; and at nighttime it resounded sweetly. See a poem of Chinese poet Li Bai:
> The City of Chang-an—in the sky, the moon.
> I hear women beating clothes at every door;
> And an autumn wind blowing ceaselessly.
> And that tells me what is in their mind:
> "When does my husband return from the wars?"

The *Kagra*: Theatrical dances with music performed in Shinto shrines. Its performance is highly stylized, and its themes come mostly from the Shinto mythology.

A Note on Religion: In the days of Basho almost all Japanese were devout Buddhists, and at the same time had great respect to a variety of Gods of Japanese Shintoism, somewhat like the ancient Greeks had worshipped the Olympians.

Japanese Classics

In the *haik* poetry of Basho and company there are not a few works associative with the scenes and episodes of Japanese classics.

The Tale of the Heike: An epic of the decline and fall of the Heike (or the Taira). The Heike was the first clan of warriors in power in Japan, was overthrown by the Kamakura Shogunate in 1185. Among its episodes are the battle of Kurikara Pass (Kiso Yoshinaka defeats Taira-no Koremori), the suicide of Koremori at Kumano, the defeat and death of Kiso Yoshinaka*, the battle of Ichinotani (Taira-no Tadanori and Atsumori are slain), the battle of Yashima (Minamoto-no Yoshitsune makes a surprise attack on the Heike), and the sea battle of Danno-ura (the Heike perishes).

> * After his death Kiso Yoshinaka was buried at Gichuji Temple in Zeze Town, Omi, a site where Basho's hermitage the Moumyo-an was to be built in later times, and there Basho, too, was to be buried.

The Tale of Yoshitsune: Minamoto-no Yoshitsune was a *samurai* commander of the Kamakura Shogunate. Although he defeated Kiso Yoshinaka, and then the Heike at several battles, he was suspected of treason against the Shogun Minamoto-no Yoritomo (his elder brother). He took flight to Hiraizmi, the city of the powerful Fujiwara Clan ruling over the province of Mutz, but was slain as the result of betrayal. Musashi-bo Benkei and other loyal warriors fought to the death at that time. Earlier, his wife Lady Shizka was arrested and taken to the city of Kamakura and forced to dance and sing (she had been a singing dancer originally) in the presence of the Shogun. She sang a song of defiance:
> Reel it, reel it, reel the wheel of time once and once again;
> Bring me back the days gone, please.

Chinese Poets

Tao Yuanming: A hermit poet in the Jin Dynasty. A lover of drink. He composed poems of country life and natural beauty. Died in 427 AD.

INTRODUCTION

Li Bai: A poet in the midst of the Tang Dynasty. He lived a wandering life except for a short period when he served the emperor as poet. His poems are sometimes dynamic, sometimes delicate, and almost always vivid and impressive. Died in 762.

Du Fu: A poet in the Tang Dynasty. He was a friend of Li Bai's, and the two bards are redeemed as the greatest poets of China. He composed poems of people in difficulty, and in his later years his poetry came to have a deep sense of humanity. Died in 770.

Bai Latien: A poet in the late Tang Dynasty. His plain, serene, sentimental poems were very popular with Japanese poets in the Heian Period. Died in 846.

Notes and Translation

The *haik* poems of Basho and company are of more than three hundred years old. There are many pieces of parody and of homage to ancient Japanese and Chinese poetry. There are not a few works associative with old tales, historic episodes, ancient rituals, and customs of those days. There are puns, jokes, witticisms in a Japanese context. Such poems you cannot understand without notes. However, it is irritating to read such poems with notes, especially linked verses, so I refrained from adding too many notes (please consider the translations are, in a sense, notes). You can also see the notes written by Kyorai and by Doho, both of them disciples of Basho. Their notes will be very helpful to you because they tell you what Basho himself thought and said.

Poetry will lose nine-tenths of its poetic value—rhyme, rhythm, syllables, composition, imagination or something poetic—through translation. The tones of the *haik* poems of Basho and others cannot be reproduced in English. Many of the wordplays are difficult to follow in English. I therefore focused my attention to what the poets had wanted to say. Reading the translations, you might feel as if you were reading very short pieces of prose. Nine-tenths of poetic value, let it be repeated, will be lost in translation. Enjoy the one-tenth.

A WINTER DAY

A Lonely Journey

The autumn of the first year of Jokyo (1684) saw the *haikai* master Matsuo Basho set out westwards from Edo together with one of his disciples Chiri, the travels to be described later in his first travel piece *A Lonely Journey*. Already one of the popular *haikai* masters in the metropolitan city, Basho, then forty-one years old, was to live as a wandering poet until his death at the age of fifty-one in the seventh year of Genrock (1694)—the miraculous eleven years of Japanese literature in which he was to become the most celebrated bard of Japan, far more celebrated than Saigyo, whom he admired most. Now then, let us go along the descriptions of *A Lonely Journey*.

Set-Out:
   A certain wise man of old said, 'Set out on a journey of a thousand miles, with no foods of any kind; you would go in cloudland at dawn under the moon.' Now in the fall—it was in the Eighth Month of the first year of Jokyo—cheered by such a word, I left my hut on a river in Edo. It was a chilly, windy day.

   As my soul is thrown in wasteland, so is my flesh blown by a biting wind.

   Ten autumns have passed in Edo; this town now feels like my hometown.

   It was raining when I passed Hakone Barrier. All the mountains hid behind a mist.

   The misty rain—it is rather amusing to imagine a view of Fuji Mountain.

And he traveled along the Tokai Coastal Highway.
—On a horse;

   It's been eaten by the horse—a white althea in flower on the roadside.

—At Sayo-no Nakayama;

   A nap on horse, a morning dream under a far moon, and tea smoke rising.

After paying a visit at Ise Shrine, he went to his hometown in Iga, then to Mount Yoshino.
   I trod alone into the heart of Yoshino, deep into the mountains. White clouds about the ridges, a misty rain over the vales, and there were some huts of loggers that looked rather small on the yonder mountainside. The sound of cutting trees in the west resounded in the east, and a peal of a temple bell, in the depth of my heart. In these mountains there had lived not a few people in seclusion, many of them poets. You might well call this place the Lushan of our country. That night I stayed at a lodging in a certain temple.

   A night at a lodging—if only I could hear the landlady beat clothes.

And he made a tour of the provinces of Yamashiro, Omi, Mino, and Owari.
—At Ogaki;

Autumn is passing by; I'm still alive, I'm still a traveler.

—At Kuwana;

The day breaks, and a tiny icefish glimmers an inch white.

—At Atsuta;

The night falls in the sea, and a wild duck cries faintly white.

And in the city of Nagoya he made some pieces of linked verse together with a group of poets—that is, *A Winter Day*. In the end of the year he left for Iga.

The year is passing by, while I'm putting on the hat and the straw sandals.

—On his way to Nara;

Spring has come; there is a light haze about a nameless hill.

—On his way to Otsu Town, Omi;

It touches a chord of mine—a violet in flower by the mountain path.

And he returned to Edo in early summer, the end of the travels.

The summer clothes—all the lice I have not yet picked out.

Linked Verse

A Winter Day is a collection of linked verses as said above. Linked verse is a chain of stanzas made by a group of poets, as said further above. Now then, how did they link verses?

In the Teimon School they linked stanzas by connecting a specific word in a stanza, say, a *'mei* tree', with another specific word in the succeeding stanza, say, a 'warbler'—the word-to-word method on the basis of classical diction. They were conservative in that respect. Such a method was therefore employed only by erudite people. In the Danrin they connected a stanza with another like a chain of witticisms—the wit-to-wit method by which a linked verse develops like a series of scenes.

Both the methods Basho and company regarded as trite or showy. They preferred a subtler way—the imaginative method that implies linkage of a sentiment, an atmosphere, a view, an image, and status of a thing. In making a linked verse, they sang of people or a thing or an event that suited the state (a sentiment, an atmosphere, a view, an image, etc.) of a previous stanza; however, it should not be told plainly. They hence changed scenes, seasons, characters, etc., etc. as they went from stanza to stanza—for example, from a young woman to an old nun, from a man walking in a withered field to a girl picking flowers, and from an old lady in the town in springtime to a character of an old tale living in the country in wintertime. In a sense, each stanza stands independent of its linked verse. That was the method of the Basho School.

Basho and company usually composed a linked verse of thirty-six stanzas. It seemed to be the number of stanzas appropriate to a single *haikai* meeting. It is divided into three parts: *jo* (the prelude; the first six stanzas), *ha* (the change; the next twenty-four stanzas) and *kyu* (the presto; the last six stanzas). In the *jo*, a poet who represents the guests first composes the opening stanza as a greeting verse, to which the host responds with the second stanza. The third poet changes the topic, and in accordance with it the fourth makes a verse in a soft manner. In the fifth stanza the moon is to be sung of. In this initial phase each verse should be, as a rule, mild and gentle in its tone and language. In the *ha*, the poets link the twenty-four stanzas by using various topics—spring, summer, autumn, winter, love, life, disease, death, nature, memories, Shintoism, Buddhism, and scenes of classic works. In the fourteenth and twenty-ninth stanzas the moon is to be sung of, and in the seventeenth stanza, the flower. In the *kyu*, the linked verse goes on to the end swiftly. The flower is to be sung of in the thirty-fifth stanza. And with the thirty-sixth stanza of a plain, happy tone ends the linked verse.

Linked verse is thus a work of collaboration. Its participants are at once poets and readers, jointly composing thirty-six lines through a keen but friendly competition under the guidance of a master. Its essence therefore exists in the process of making. "When it's finished," said Basho, "a linked verse will be but a scrap of paper."

Lastly, let me show you an episode from *Kyorai's Notes*. It tells us very well about the atmosphere of the making of a linked verse.

> When I (Kyorai) participated in a *haikai* meeting at Masahide's house, the Old Reverend Basho amended the third stanza I composed. And after the meeting—when we stayed at Kyoksui's house that night—the Old Reverend said, "You were the main guest of today's *haikai* meeting, so you should have thought you would be asked to make an opening stanza." He continued, "When you were asked to, you had to compose one at once, well-made or not. Night goes by swiftly. If you had delayed, it would have been a dull, boring party. That would have been no good, so I made the first stanza in your place." Still continued, "The host Masahide soon composed the second stanza of a stormy cloud, but it was followed by your third stanza of a quiet view. This in no way goes with that. A failed one." I got a good scolding all night long.

A Winter Day

As mentioned above, on his way on *A Lonely Journey* Basho visited Nagoya, where he met a group of *haikai* poets. They were old-fashioned *haikai* poets, but welcomed Basho, a noted *haikai* master in Edo, the capital city. Basho and his new disciples composed five pieces of linked verse, which were soon edited by one of them, Kakei, and were published with its title as *A Winter Day*.

Before going on to *A Winter Day*, let me introduce to you some of the poets in Nagoya.

Kakei: A physician, Yamamoto Kakei was a leading figure among *haikai* poets in Nagoya. He compiled not only *A Winter Day*, but also *A Spring Day* and *Waste Land;* yet, in fact, he felt sympathetic to the classical style of the Teimon, so that in later years he broke away from Basho.

Yasui: Okada Yasui was a wealthy kimono merchant and town official in Nagoya. Many of his *haik* poems were selected in *A Winter Day*, *A Spring Day* and *Waste Land*. However, he too parted from the Basho School in later years. They were unable to follow the new style of Basho after all.

Tokock: Tsuboi Tokock was a rice merchant in Nagoya. A young poet, he was the most favorite disciple of Basho's, but later he was accused of dishonesty in the rice trade, and was banished to Hobi Village in the province of Mikawa.

A WINTER DAY

(Linked Verse)

—On the long travels I had my straw hat torn in the rain, and from town to town my paper clothes worn in the wind. Though I knew what is sad and sweet, yet I did feel this journey really so. And now it hits me—long, long ago that wit of poetry paid a visit to this country.

Basho: My poesy's out of tune, my life's in a wild wind—O just like Chiksai! *

Yasui: Who's he? —bits of sasanqua blossom are whirling about his hat.

Kakei: There appears a morning moon; it's time to brew *sake*;

Jugo: And it shakes off dew from the head—that red pack-horse;

Tokock: And nearby are lean blades of Korean silver grass simply waving;

Shohei: The sun getting softer and softer, people reaping rice in the field.

Yasui: I'm living at a hermitage over there—where stays a heron at night;

Basho: And there she's going to stay until her hair has grown enough;

Jugo: So bitter is love, bitter indeed, she sighs in vain over her milk;

Kakei: And in front of a newly-built stupa she weeps sadly, sorrowfully.

Basho: A chilly shadow—there's a figure making a fire at dawn;

Tokock: And a bleak house—the owner is living in poverty;

Kakei: In the field stands the withered willow of Coman the Courtesan;

Yasui: And he looks like a lame—the man rowing a boat in the fog;

Tokock: Then I cast a side glance; in the darkening sky, a lean moon;

Jugo: I'm living in town—the noisy, gossipy neighborhood;

Yasui: Now then, madam, how are the flowers in the Konoe Garden?

Basho: There only flies a butterfly about the weeds, replies the lady in tears;

Jugo: And in the vehicle, a vague figure behind the blind;

Kakei: At it the arrow of vengeance is shot with a shout.

Basho: It's been blown down—the pine of an ancient bandit;

Tokock: Then, let us take a rest at the fount named after the poet Sogi;

Kakei: Take your hat off, let the winter rain wet us;

Yasui: And the withered winter fields—the lettuces alone green.

Tokock: There are pieces broken in white—Bones? Or something else?

Jugo: They might be squid bones used by barbarians for oracles;

Yasui: In no way are they able to appreciate the elegance of poesy;

Basho: And a long night—the clepsydra might run out of water;

Jugo: That is the hermitage of the Li Bai of Japan, and in the sky, the moon; **

Kakei: And he plays the *biwa* lute, a mallow flower on his hood;

Basho: And the grass field—he mourns for oxen at eventide;

Tokock: There appears a woman with fish in a sieve in hand;

Kakei: That is to pray to the morning star—May she have a baby;

Yasui: Today she goes to see her little sister draw the eyebrows;

Tokock: And bits of blossom—the bath water is filtered with a silk cloth;

Jugo: And along the corridor runs a shadow of wisteria.

(Note)
* Chiksai was a character of a popular tale of the day. A poet of vagrancy.
** Ishikawa Jozan, a monk in the early Tokugawa Period, was a good poet in Chinese poetry, was thereby called the Li Bai of Japan.

(Linked Verse)

—Being in the prime of life, I've not yet retired from service.
Yasui: The first snow of the season—I'm returning home in formal attire;
Tokock: See a frosty morning glory when you have an early breakfast;
Basho: Toward the wild aster flies a butterfly, weak in the wings;
Kakei: And a cart jolting on the road—chirp, quail, chirp;
Jugo: Then he plays the ancient tambourine to the elegant moon;
Shohei: He's poet Teitock, a man of wealth, a lover of peach blossom;
Tokock: And marshes in rainy Asaka—he's brought mud snails to town;
Yasui: Now in Kisaragi they cry toward the far homeland, crying out.
Kakei: Having a chat late at night, she finds her guest is her cousin;
Basho: Alas, we have been far from luck;
Yasui: Regret, regret, but I have no vigor to take away a single lump;
Jugo: And tomorrow I shall give my head to my foe;
Basho: Now giving a cup of *sake* to my page, now singing a song;
Tokock: While the peony thief wishes the moon to be late.
Jugo: The walls are fallen; the rope net on the roof is broken;
Kakei: In town a statue of holy Jizo is being chiseled in a tap, tap;
Tokock: And the flowery season—solemn is the wedding ceremony;
Yasui: Fairly pretty are the little attendant girls;
Kakei: And a subtly dark room—on the comb case, a piece of rice cake;
Basho: Now the paper lamp is lit—wake up, nightingale.
Yasui: The *take* trees—at the top of a *kaki* tree is a calyx alone;
Jugo: Then, let me use your *samisen* lute, keeper of Fuwa Barrier;
Basho: And on my way home from Mino I forget my tactics of the *go* game;
Tokock: Woke up, woke up again, and now as old as seventy;
Jugo: And for donation he goes to the temple, with a pack of gold in hand;
Kakei: So that people might follow the noble man.
Tokock: The lotus pond sees young herons playing about at eventide;

Yasui: Inside, I'm making up some sheets of window paper;

Kakei: And she stands in moonlight, her simple-style hair red dried;

Basho: Love's over; she beats clothes waiting for a virtuous monk to come;

Yasui: A quiet autumn day—you might hear a shell of a cicada chirping;

Jugo: And a dewdrop floats lightly on a wisteria fruit.

Basho: The shade of a hill—there's a lady taking out a pen;

Tokock: Such a woman would be a lady in waiting or a maid of honor;

Jugo: The third of Yayoi—the roosters and parrots compete in beauty; *

Kakei: In North Country the gray haired vie for wild carrots.

(Note)
* In the ancient court a cockfight took place on the third day of Yayoi as a seasonal event.

(Linked Verse)

—It happens before I could walk some ten steps.
Tokock: It fails to wrap the moon, then drops the moon—the winter rain;
Jugo: And I step on a patch of ice, making a crack of lightning.
Yasui: New Year Day—the arrow holder of a hunter is adorned with a fern;
Basho: And the north gate of the castle opens to spring;
Kakei: A hazy day, a breath of air, and they rake up horse dung;
Shohei: And a tea master gives a pleased look to *tampopo* in flower;
Jugo: Beside him sits his lovely daughter reading a letter;
Tokock: And their rivalry—she's got two lanterns from two men;
Basho: Now in the fall they too vie in beauty—a pearl of dew and a *hagi* clover;
Yasui: And at a lodging in Shigaraki the *soba* noodles too look green.
Tokock: At dawn he sets out in moonlight—the backgammon gambler in travel;
Kakei: Then the rouge merchant hears a cuckoo call;
Yasui: And a man in seclusion, I make Hina dolls to kill time;
Jugo: And he receives some food from a court lady;
Kakei: For there came a great tidal wave that broke down all the fences;
Basho: Slitting open a big fish, they find it having eaten a Buddha.
Jugo: In the country I'm well-known as a lover of blossom;
Tokock: And as owner of a six-acre field purple with violets;
Basho: And a skylark tweets, tweets, twittering very happily;
Yasui: The noontime—the horse looks rather sleepy;
Tokock: Quite long is Yahagi Bridge in Okazaki Town;
Kakei: And I send a letter with a poem of the Headman's Pine.
Yasui: He has grown to gather pieces of firewood—that abandoned child;
Jugo: And chilly New Year's Eve—my sword is now for sale;
Kakei: And here comes a lover of snow, wearing a snowy hat of Wu;
Basho: His scarf, a sleeve of Takawo the Courtesan's;
Jugo: Now then, let me drink to death a cask of *sake*, with a love of mine;

Tokock: Its flower having fallen, the poppy looks like a Zen bonze.

Basho: The crescent, a darkening sky in the east, and then a peal of a bell;

Yasui: And a faint note—on the autumn lake someone's playing the *koto* zither;

Tokock: And he has second thoughts, releasing the goby;

Kakei: Beyond the thicket, a sweet voice of chanting a sutra;

Yasui: The light is now feebly burning, yet he's hesitant to get up;

Jugo: And the night—there is a string of love between the two hearts;

Kakei: Lost in love, my soul flies into the shade of blossoms;

Basho: If only I could follow you on a full-moon day. *

  (Note)
   * This comes from a *waka* of Saigyo:
     If only I could die in spring in the shade of blossoms;
     If only it could be around full moon in Kisaragi.

A WINTER DAY

(Linked Verse)

—On the seashore of Naniwa rather sooty is a house where reeds are burnt; *
Jugo: And blackish is the wife of a charcoal maker;
Kakei: And for someone else he polishes a mirror in the chill;
Tokock: White frost, horse-bone white, and brambles too bloom in white;
Yasui: And from the window I can see a crane in dim moonlight.
Basho: A windless autumn day, a day when you find your *sake* bottle empty;
Uritz: And in the market he sells reed-woven hats;
Kakei: And the River Kamo—Coma Chiyo Fair is coming soon;
Jugo: Then we would see our daughter's family in Iwakura.
Yasui: She loves him, she loves him—the women are singing merrily;
Tokock: I'm as old as twenty; and this round head, a grief to me;
Uritz: And a sulky mandarin duck—are you living alone?
Basho: Sitting by the now fireless warmer, she's thinking of the deceased.
Jugo: He sleeps, wrapped in a paper blanket given by the old guard;
Kakei: His bloody sword sinks in the moonless darkness;
Tokock: And in the fog he hears a temple bell ring out at Hongo seven times;
Yasui: Winter is coming, they are chopping up *natto* beans.
Basho: A lover of flowers, I have had enough of *sacra* blossoms;
Uritz: And the monk drinks herb tea in silence;
Kakei: While a white swallow washes its wings with clear water;
Jugo: And on His Majesty's demand the craftsman casts a hairpin.
Yasui: He serves his mother heartily—the man of three past seventy; **
Tokock: And the nice reward—he marries a Princess the Weaver; **
Uritz: That is when the moon buds in the southwest;
Basho: And a creak of a press pressing orchid seeds into oil.
Jugo: When returning, the lord sees a wise woman living in a shabby house;
Kakei: While she's washing a bowlful of millet at twilight;
Tokock: The houses are decorated with pinks for driving away plagues;

Yasui: And they play the hand drums at Benkei Shrine;

Basho: And the day of the Tiger—the blacksmith gets up early at daybreak;

Uritz: Now fragrant smoke rising in the South City of Nara;

Kakei: Behind the hedge stands a statue of someone I know not;

Jugo: And in the muddy pond bloom dropworts in white.

Yasui: Eating a cup of gruel at dawn, he feels tensed in front of a flower;

Basho: And the spring wind sees a suit of armor under his robe;

Uritz: Now the dame in tears and tears pushes up the blind;

Tokock: And the night—she's dreaming a sleepless dream in the rain.

(Note)
* This preface is the first half of a *waka* in the *Man'yo-shu*, and it runs: 'Yet my wife's always white and beautiful.'
** This comes from a Chinese tale of a man of great filial piety.

(Linked Verse)

—A country view;
Kakei: The Frost Month—there stand storks in line in silence in the field;
Basho: A winter day—fairly touching is a pale morning sun.
Jugo: The oaks, the cedars, and their leaves are falling in the garden;
Tokock: And an ox passing by, from which salt is spilling down;
Uritz: A soundless suit of armor, a soft light of the moon;
Yasui: And the page steps out to shear an orchid.
Basho: Now in the fall there are noble travelers holding a simple *renga* party;
Kakei: The rain is over; they can see Mount Fuji from the temple;
Tokock: So quiet is the garden that you might hear a *tsubaki* blossom fall;
Jugo: A mirage shimmers in green, the scent of tea sails in breeze;
Yasui: And with a long hat on, scores of maids chase pheasants;
Uritz: In the garden there is a miniature rope bridge, and a lovely girl in silks.
Kakei: Now deep in summer—a wild citrus blooms like a *sacra* tree;
Basho: And I compile a *waka* selection, with its name as *Flax Reaper;*
Jugo: Alone on a river, happy in a hermitage;
Tokock: My shadow is in a mist; May my moon emerge.
Uritz: Flowers are falling, a traveler is playing the flute;
Yasui: A *boke* blooms by the roadside; he's allowed to get off the palanquin;
Basho: And looking at the bones, she collapses in tears;
Kakei: The day breaks; a beggar gives him a straw raincoat;
Tokock: And he gets a carp by chance in the mud;
Jugo: Now a cup of holy water is presented to the emperor in travel.
Yasui: Quite a hot season—the pea flowers look dull;
Uritz: There are some sedge-roof houses, where people pounding charcoal;
Kakei: Among a lively flock of little boys, a lovely little girl;
Basho: There are lotuses in fruit; some are crooked, some straight.
Jugo: Silent is the night, the moon is peeping at the dinner table;

Tokock: A fox is wet with dew in the wind of sorrow;

Uritz: And *kaki* fruits are hung from the eaves like a screen;

Yasui: And he fixes a *tofu* meal to mourn for his mother;

Basho: So sorrowful is Monk Gensei that his robe might be torn; *

Kakei: Fushimi, Kohata, flowery villages, and a peal of a temple bell.

Tokock: I'm at a loss; my boy cat has fallen in love;

Jugo: And she calls a sweeper; the sand garden is covered with spring snow;

Yasui: And here comes a gifted poet bright in silks;

Uritz: Then a winter wind—fragrant are sasanqua flowers about his hat.

(Note)
* Gensei was a monk poet in the early Tokugawa Period, famous as a man of great filial piety.

Addendum (Linked Verse)

Uritz: Unfriendly is the rain of hail pattering against the ox;
Kakei: And they warm a cask of *sake* in the withered pine wood;
Jugo: Now in rough hair and clothes they begin to weed;
Tokock: And the morning dew sees a noble man wearing a simple hat;
Basho: The moon is up over the sea; can I buy clam by silver?
Yasui: Look left, and you can find Mount Gifu beyond a bridge.

Published by Izutsuya Shobei, Kyoto, in the second year of Jokyo.

A SPRING DAY

It was in the early summer of the second year of Jokyo (1685) that Basho returned to Edo from the travels of *A Lonely Journey*. He lived there for two years, during which time, he strove to build up a new style of *haikai* poetry. Below are some excerpts from letters he wrote in those days in which he expressed his thought on the state of *haikai*.

The letter to Hanzan in Iga:

> Looking through some of the anthologies published in Edo, you will find many of the verses insufficiently composed or poorly expressed. Should you use them as a model, you would lose your way. The anthology *A Shriveled Chestnut*, for instance, has quite a few absurd *haikai* poems. Pray learn poetry from fine pieces of classical poets such as Li Bai, Du Fu, Teika and Saigyo.

The letter to Toto and Toyo in Atsuta:

> The thing is what to do in the future. What is important is originality. If every line were about scenery, such a linked verse would look old-fashioned. If it were too quaint, such a linked verse would soon be looked upon as tiresome. If there were an elaborate stanza, the succeeding line would be awkwardly positioned. In making a linked verse, you should make a variety of verses, with some lines of scenery here and there. That is all I should like to say.

New Disciples

This period also saw Basho have two new disciples—Kyorai and Sora. Below are two pieces of writing about them:

Basho's foreword to Kyorai's *Travels to Ise Shrine*

> The art of poetry of nowadays, it is true, looks like a rootless grass—flowerless, fruitless, tasteless and meaningless. Once in Kyoto, Kikaku met Mister Mukai Kyorai. They talked over tea and *sake*, and then Mister Mukai Kyorai expressed his deep appreciation of our *haikai* poetry. In it he found something sweet, bitter, sour, simple—as if taking in the taste of a hundred rivers in a single sip. This autumn he paid a visit to Ise Shrine together with his younger sister Lady Chine, then sending me a piece of travel that depicts an autumn wind on the River Shirakawa, silver grass on the sea of Ise, and other beautiful views on their way. Reading it once, I was moved; twice, calmed; thrice, I found they were nice and safe. What a perfect writer he is!
>
> You're in the west, I'm in the east, and there blows sweetly an autumn wind.

The Snowball

> Sora is living in my neighborhood. We exchange visits almost every morning and evening. He lays a fire when I fix a meal, comes to my hut when I make tea at night. A gentle man in seclusion. My closest friend. And one snow night —when he visited me—I made a *haik* for him.
>
> Pray lay a fire; I will show you, my friend, your good old snowball.

Haik

In making a linked verse, a guest of honor was usually asked to make its opening stanza (five-seven-five syllables). Most of the *haikai* poets may therefore have always thought what to compose in such a case. In course of time such an opening stanza was regarded as an independent form of poetry. That is the *haik*.

The *haik* (pronounced like 'hike') was thus an offshoot of the linked verse (*haikai*). Though modern people may think the *haik* represents *haikai* literature, to the *haikai* poets in the seventeenth century, inclusive of Basho, the main form of *haikai* poetry was the linked verse. When they had a *haikai* meeting, they composed a linked verse, not *haik* poems.

The *haikai* is a cooperative work, whereas the *haik* is personal. With the *haik* in hand, the *haikai* poets began singing of what they saw, what they heard, and what they felt personally—just like a *waka* poet. And by Basho, the *haik* was elevated to the simple and sweet poetry that could match the elegant *waka* in poetic value. Basho is called a poet of travel. He established the style of the newly-born poetry as he traveled in solitude over mountains, across rivers, through stretches of wasteland.

Now then, how did Basho make such a new type of verse? Please see his words:

'If you can read it smoothly from head to tail, it will be a good *haik*.'

'A *haik* is a combination. Well-combined, well-composed; badly-combined, a failure.'

It goes without saying that a work of poetry should be smooth. And as for a combination, let us take as example a *haik* below, one of the famous poems of Basho's (with this, it is said, he grasped the soul of *haik* poetry).

> An old pond—there sounds water as a frog leaps in.

Please note that in this *haik* the things eternal are combined with the things momentary—the old pond, with the leaping frog; the scene of Nature, with the little creature; and the silent atmosphere, with the sound of water. Very well-combined, very well-composed.

A combination of things is created by cutting a *haik* into two or three parts, and the cutting of a *haik* produces a blank space in poetry. A blank space can take in everything. Reading a *haik* of Basho's, you may feel as if you were seeing a picture rich in blank spaces that allow you various imaginations.

It says in *Kyorai's Notes* that, although the poets of other schools compose artificial verses, Basho's followers sing of a view as it is. According to the method of Basho, an illiterate man, or even a little boy, could sometimes make a good poem, while in other schools poets are limited to men of letters. And now, you may say it would be easy for us to compose a *haik* in the fashion of the Basho School. Indeed we can freely make a chain of words in a specific number of syllables, but the simplest, the hardest. "If you made three or five pieces of good *haik* in your life," said Basho, "you might well be called a good poet; if some ten pieces, a great master."

A Spring Day

The *haikai* anthology *A Winter Day* was very well received in the circles of poets, which pleased Kakei and other poets in Nagoya; so much pleased, they published another anthology—*A Spring Day*. It consists of three pieces of linked verse and a selection of *haik* poems. The linked verses were made only by the poets in Nagoya; yet, among them, you can find a new participant Etsujin.

Ochi Etsujin was a leading figure among *haik* poets in Nagoya. A lover of *sake* —so much so that he got much drunk on a horse when he accompanied Basho to Hobi, where Tokock was living in exile. Basho seemed to like him very much, calling him 'my friend'. See a *haik* given to Etsujin by Basho:

> Have you seen snow this winter—the snow we two saw last winter?

A SPRING DAY

(Linked Verse)

—The eighteenth day of Kisaragi. To see an early-morning view, we woke ourselves up before dawn by tapping on one another's doors, and set out toward Atsuta Shrine. While people on the ferry getting noisy at twilight, we saw a line of pines run. A calm, serene day. And a little way from there—at Jugo's cottage—we had a *haikai* meeting, with such a lovely view as the first topic.

Kakei: Spring has come; these people and those are on pilgrimage to Ise;

Jugo: The *sacra* blossoms falling softly, the horses going on slowly;

Uto: On the hill there's a new house stands in hazy moonlight;

Rifou: And at a fire there's a shadow in armors;

Shokei: Then a gust of sea wind—he can possibly hear a faint note of a seagull;

Scribe: Today, a cloudy day, it looks black—the rock off the beach;

Jugo: Now then, let's change our sweaty clothes at Suma Temple;

Kakei: Where we see that flute of his, every one of us in tears. *

Rifou: King Wen's words of cheer, and people carry packs of soil; **

Uto: And the rain—thorn-less blades of grass are dripping wet;

Kakei: It's chilly to the bone, although all of us shall once be dead and gone;

Shokei: Now at dawn—the fair lady covers her breast with the sleeves;

Uto: For she found a shadow on the mirror when the blur was cleared;

Jugo: And the village carries a divine palanquin on their shoulders;

Shokei: For a mile, through the shrine gate, along the sacred road of sand;

Rifou: A flowery day—good men are flying kites;

Jugo: And the nice shade of a willow—don't you have a *kemari* ball?

Kakei: The sun is setting, butterflies are being busy.

Rifou: They are threshing sheaves of wheat, I'm waiting for my friend;

Uto: Yet he's listening to an oracle, his head covered with his sleeves;

Kakei: And her beautiful black hair is cut short;

A SPRING DAY

Shokei: He's merciful, he's an acupuncturist, as high as the fifth royal rank.

Uto: Toward the pine tree tilts the gate of the shrine priest's;

Jugo: The winter rain—my barefoot steps have disappeared;

Shokei: And the daybreak—the *tofu* has been taken by a kite;

Rifou: Today, an autumn day, someone's chanting a chilly sutra;

Jugo: That is a grassy warehouse—where he's living alone;

Kakei: The moon is up; that bridge is named after mine, you know?

Rifou: Under the same umbrella, in the rainy twilight;

Uto: Monk after monk coming down from Mount Asaguma.

Kakei: Cuckoo, cuckoo, I would make a *waka* if I were a Saigyo; ***

Shokei: And one well-bucket two of us share;

Uto: She's in tears—the old court lady of bad luck;

Jugo: Yet luckily she's inherited a *chisa* field in Saga.

Shokei: Spring is passing by, people are busy between blossoms and *take* trees;

Rifou: And the boys, big and little, go for hunting birds.

(Note)
* Young noble *samurai* Taira-no Atsumori, an expert flutist, was slain in battle near Suma (*The Tale of the Heike*). His flute was enshrined in Suma Temple.
** King Wen was a legendary king of benevolence in ancient China.
*** This comes from a *haik* of Basho's: 'A woman washing potatoes on a river—I'd make a *waka* if I were a Saigyo.'

(Linked Verse)

—At Yasui's house on the sixth day of Yayoi;
Tanko: The road to Nara—the hills and fields alive with *sacra* double in bloom;
Yasui: In a haze resounds a temple bell sweetly far and near;
Kakei: And a spring traveler sees people dress up for Hina Festival;
Etsujin: Let us wash out our mouth; there flows clear water;
Uritz: Drunk, yet not so drunk as to stumble in a pine wind;
Scribe: And bright moonlight—the unsold insects are released.
Yasui: People wear a white hat; Uzmasa Festival has ended;
Tanko: Behind the chrysanthemum hedge sits a lovely little girl;
Etsujin: Let us hand over our shop, let us become monk and nun;
Kakei: And a sound of a cart on the street at dawn;
Tanko: It carries codfish, heading toward the port of Otsu;
Etsujin: Where I can hear some talk with an accent of my home country;
Uritz: And the cheap inn—for the guests there is only a single mosquito net;
Yasui: The *hagi* flowers are trodden; people chant a sutra in the fields;
Etsujin: And the autumn shower—straw raincoats are given to people;
Uritz: The flood, a moonless night, and people putting stones on the bridge;
Yasui: And the driftwood—there might be young sweet fish;
Tanko: Now in spring—I've had enough of a mountain spa.
Etsujin: A peaceful day—some wear Tukshi sleeves; some, an Ise girdle;
Kakei: A variety of eye shadows, court ladies' selections;
Uritz: And the day of battle—she refrains from being in love;
Yasui: Then the old man says, it's a chestnut of good luck.
Tanko: New Year's Eve—he chants a prayer to the Yebis altar;
Etsujin: He's far from avarice, he's a good neighbor;
Kakei: To plant a *kuco* tree is to enjoy its verdure at dawns and evenings;
Uritz: In these parts they can get flour good twenty days earlier than in Kyoto;
Yasui: Wonder if the temple I stay at tonight keeps a pack-horse;

Tanko: Strangely, they hold a Bon Festival around full moon in Kisaragi.

Etsujin: It looks like man and wife—the shimmering of a mirage;

Kakei: And a festive verse—their sleeves wet with a spring rain;

Uritz: And the flowery village—I was born a field owner;

Yasui: The most vigorous is my second son;

Tanko: And Lake Land—he has become the heir of a branch of Mi Temple;

Etsujin: And high up above lies snow-capped mountains;

Kakei: Tonight, the twenty-ninth night; in the sky, a chilly moon;

Uritz: And I trudge on an icy path to do my duty.

(Linked Verse)

—At Tanko's villa on the sixteenth of Yayoi;

Yasui: They woke me up beautifully—the frogs singing, singing merrily;

Tanko: Nay—from the ceiling fell a raindrop on your brow.

Etsujin: The inn smells peat; they are simmering brackens;

Kakei: And a colt is looking deep—deep at us;

Tobun: And the moonlight—I stand up on a ferry;

Scribe: The edge of my umbrella touching the reed ears;

Tanko: On the strand stand some monks praying for the drowned;

Yasui: Beyond the rocky shore are villagers' warehouses;

Kakei: They might be baking jars; a breath of smoke rising in the rain;

Etsujin: Now on a journey; hunger is my business;

Yasui: Calling on a certain monk, I find his house locked and empty;

Tobun: So that I untie a cord binding the pine tree.

—The meeting broke up because it was late at night, and restarted at Kakei's house on the nineteenth day.

Etsujin: It's wet with sweet dew—the *kick* flower of a new variety;

Tanko: And Shitago goes into Part of Autumn in his compilation; *

Tobun: Ignites a fire, hearing the seasonal honks of wild geese;

Kakei: And the good-bye moon—let me see tears in your face;

Tanko: In Shinomiya, far from the flowery city, women wear a simple hairstyle;

Yasui: For, on a spring path, they would feel rather hot with a hat on.

Kakei: So long a day that I might take things this morning for yesterday;

Etsujin: And the Satsuki rains—there grow mushrooms on the verandah;

Yasui: Jowo's bottle I've got; only a bowl of rice I have not; **

Tobun: And busy is the host of a *renga* party;

Etsujin: First of all, put some pieces of wood under the falls to quell noise;

Tanko: And a rock-laver picker is suspended in a cage on a cliff;

Tobun: While in the town people are eating, drinking, and walking in silks;

A SPRING DAY

Etsujin: Two straw mats are too many for my hermitage, though.

Tanko: Sweet is morning dew; people begin seeding the fields with wheat;

Yasui: And I see off a *go* player under the morning moon;

Kakei: Today, a windless autumn day, we get ready for fishing;

Tobun: Now let's go and see dances at Toba Town;

Yasui: Zakone and Tukma Festivals, we have seen already;

Kakei: Yet all—all in my life I have not had a family;

Etsujin: And New Year Day—he gets up late at noon to draw New-Year water;

Tanko: Then celebrates His Great Reign, eating a piece of rice cake.

Tobun: The whole village wine and dine all day in the hills full of blossoms;

Kakei: Not very cloudy, not very sunny, and then tweets a skylark.

(Note)
* Minamoto-no Shitago was a scholar in the Heian Period. He compiled the oldest extant Japanese dictionary.
** Jowo was a noted tea master in the Ashikaga Period.

Addendum (Linked Verse)

—At Shusen's villa on the nineteenth of Yayoi;

Etsujin: On the steep cliff is a yellow rose clumsily in bloom;

Shusen: In search of water a butterfly comes down on the rock;

Chosetz: Still chilly in Kisaragi—you can cool rice cakes with snow;

Shushi: We are washing cups and dishes; Our Majesty will be coming soon;

Kakei: And the first day—the blacksmith looks stern with his falcon on his arm;

Scribe: And a moonless sky—the gate is opened earlier.

Spring

Rijou: The pine of Shorick is long alive, and so is His Great Reign.

Jugo: New Year Day—horses trot, trot along a row of pine decorations.

Shokei: New Year Day—no oxen are seen in the far village.

Uto: A spring morning—there stretch wheat fields unto the far sea.

Shusen: The pine decorations at the gate, and the herb garden chilly with snow.

Uritz: The sound of a carp—the water is dark, the *mei* in white bloom.

Tanko: Punts and boats are moored, their pine decorations white with snow.

Tokock: The misty daybreak—people's faces look like a peony in bloom.

Saiseki: New Year Day—the whole village take a nap in the afternoon sun.

Donka: The starry, starry sky, a sight of nocturnal hues before a hazy morning.

Chosetz: Today, a holiday, yet the ox may dream a dream of bearing pine wood.

Kakei: The soft morning sun—the willow swaying slightly, and its sweet scent.

Kakei: The day breaks, and over the fields flows a low mist.

Tanko: The empty *sake* bottle—I stumbled when I picked a parsley flower.

—When visiting a certain hermit;

Etsujin: The sunset haze—turning back, I find a white wall unfit for the air.

Basho: An old pond—there sounds water as a frog leaps in.

Jugo: The umbrella craftsman napping; and on the umbrella, a butterfly.

Kido: The hill is filled with flowers; and shop after shop, a sign of new *sake*.

Etsujin: Being buried in blossoms, I should like to pass away in a dream.
   (Note) This comes from a *waka* of Saigyo:
      If only I could die in spring in the shade of blossoms;
      If only it could be around full moon in Kisaragi.

—In a spring field;

Tokock: There are footsteps turning at a *sacra* tree; ahead, two hermitages.

Rifou: On the foothill stands a temple—where you can see a *sacra* in full bloom.

Kakei: The *sacra* tree late in bloom, and the *enoki* tree now in bloom.

—A farewell *haik*

Etsujin: The wisteria simply hangs down; it's time to say good-bye.

Jugo: The sunset—in the tea field, women shade their eyes with their hands.

Jugo: A busy mosquito, a sleepless night, and spring is passing by.

Summer

Kyuhack: Cuckoo, cuckoo, the night is as long as the tail of a mountain-fowl.
  (Note) This comes from a *waka* of Kakinomoto-no Hitomaro:
    Long is the trail of the long tail of a mountain-fowl;
    Yet still longer is the night when I sleep alone all night long.

Rifou: Cuckoo, cuckoo, I drink a cup of hot water and sleep at night.

Etsujin: Lonesome bird, behind the shabby house is a mile mound.

Tokock: Amusing is a *mei* fruit alone in fruit in the leafy *mei* tree.

Kido: The lean young *take* trees sway, tree by tree, as sparrows perch and go.

Shusen: I leave my umbrella open, fireflies glittering in the dark.

—At the site of Benkei's House;

Shoro: The *suzcake* flowers, the path of death, and in the sky, the River Koromo.
  (Note) Benkei was a brave monk warrior who fought to the death in a fort near the River Koromo in Hiraizmi in the province of Mutz (*The Tale of Yoshitsune*).

—The day was beginning to break at Ausaka, so I could see people around me.

Chosetz: I've changed horses, being late to see the summer moon.

—The Chinese sage Laozi said you would be always satisfied if you knew you were already satisfied.

Etsujin: A moonflower in bloom, I'm having a bowl of gruel in a thatched hut.

Ryuwou:
    The broom herb wet with a light rain, mosquitoes buzzing with refrain.

Jinko: The broom herbs in flower, the day is getting darker.

Kakei: A summer day—rather hot is the hue of a *forget-me* in flower.

Kakei: They make me forget the depth of water—the lotus leaves over the pond.

Shokei: A summer morning—the tea house opens too late.

Jugo: A summer night, a lodging in Kiso, I'm listening to the whisper of a river.

—It says in the Lotus Sutra that the world is like a burning house, there's no comfort.

Etsujin: The lofty hall—I wipe off the late-summer sweat.

Autumn

Tanko: The back garden, yellowish egg plants, and there chirps a cricket.

—At a poor house on a Bon-Festival day;

Etsujin: Bon Festival—I face right against the pillar at evening.

Uto: The honks of wild geese at night, and I take a second sleep.
Basho: It gives a rest to the moon viewers—the occasional curtain of a cloud.
Etsujin: A bright moon night—they thresh rice in a temple in the mountains.
Yasui: Rather amusing is the tiled roof bright under an autumn moon.
—Seeing a picture of the Battle of Yashima;
Yasui: The moon, a battle ship, and there are many men in arms.
—A woman waiting for her sweetheart;
Kakei: He's come not yet; if only I could look down from a maize-high place.
—In solitude in love;
Kakei: A sleepless autumn night—I feel lonely, the *koto* zither being out of tune.
Shusen: A morning glory in flower; that is the last and single one.

Winter

Tokock: The winter shower—horses dripping wet, cows bask in a sunset glow.
—When the Old Reverend Basho staying with us;
Joko in Ogaki: A chilly frosty night—please use this mosquito net as bedclothes.
Shoheki: The morning glories are gone, and the *susuki* grass, and all is snow.
Basho: A fine view—now at dawn a horse is walking in the snow.
Etsujin: It makes me feel chilly—a sooty paper lamp in the snow twilight.
—When returning home after seeing off the Old Reverend Basho;
Tokock: This winter day—I do feel lonesome as I step on pieces of ice.
—Setting up a room for a certain hermit;
Kakei: Let winter go by; here's a new tea bag.

Published by Terada Shigenori in the autumn of the third year of Jokyo.

WASTE LAND

A Sentimental Journey

The early winter of the fourth year of Jokyo (1687) saw the *haik* poet Basho set out westwards again, the travels to be described later in a travel piece *A Sentimental Journey*. It begins as follows:
  There is a spirit in the flesh. You can call it, say, Monk the Wind-Clad. It might be called so because it would be easily torn even by the wind. For years he has composed *haik* poems out of tune, and has hence lived as poet. Sometimes getting weary of making verses, sometimes trying to outpoint others, he always debated in his mind whether to go on or not—a life of unrest. Being a poet prevented him from succeeding in life and from learning philosophy, and yet this man of failure, with no virtues nor gifts, has at last found his way in this sole line.
  Saigyo's *waka* poetry, Sogi's linked verse, Sesshu's painting, and Rikyu's art of tea—all these have a common spirit of art. That is, art goes with Nature, always with the four seasons. All you shall see, the flower; all you shall think of, the moon. Who finds no beauty in Nature would be but a man of barbarity; who imagines no beauty in Nature would be akin to a beast. You should be neither a barbarian nor a beast. Go with Nature. Go back to Nature.
  One early-winter day. The sky was not clear. I felt like a leaf whirling in the wind.

  Basho: The first winter rain—call me a traveler, let me be a traveler;

  Youshi: And from inn to inn you could see sasanqua in bloom in white.

Going westwards along the Tokai Coastal Highway, Basho arrived at Narumi Town, where he stayed at his disciple Chisock's house. Before long Etsujin came from Nagoya, and they visited Hobi Village in the Atsumi Peninsular, where Tokock was living in exile. That must have been a very happy reunion. And at the Cape Irago, the end of the peninsular, Basho composed a *haik*:

  The Cape Irago—I've found with delight a hawk of passage flying high.

In the end of the year he reached his hometown in Iga, and in the beginning of the next year visited the ruins of an old temple in the province.

  It's like a statue of Buddha—the mirage high above the stone foundation.

And after a tour to Ise Shrine—when he was about to set out, this time, to Mount Yoshino—there came Tokock. How joyful they were! The two poets began a spring tour of poesy.

—At Hatsuse Temple;

  A spring night—there's a gentle pilgrim in a corner of the temple.

—On Mount Yoshino;

  The spring rain—on the mossy tree is pure and fresh water trickling down.

—On the seashore of Waka;
   The seashore of Waka—we have just caught up with the passing spring.

On being a traveler:
   My heel being torn, I think of Saigyo's trouble on a ferry on the River Tenryu; riding on a horse, I remember the episode of High Priest Shokou, who got angry with the horse-keeper when he was thrown off a horse. I travel to see splendid sights of creation in land and sea, to visit sites of ancient great monks, and to view places sung of by poets of old.
   On a journey I need no special belongings. No belongings, no worries. I do not ride on a palanquin, but walk on so easy a pace that I can have supper more deliciously. I go as far as I can; I set out as late at morning as I want to. All I wish for in the daytime is a nice inn at night, and straw sandals fit to my feet. My soul is renewed from time to time; my mind is refreshed from day to day.
   If I met a man of poetry by chance, I would be highly pleased. Even if I saw an old bigot who I would usually keep away from, I would feel as though I found a gem among gravel, or gold in mud. That is what I should like to take a note of or talk of. That is a virtue of travel.

—At Osaka;
   Talking of an iris—that is a good memory of travel.

—On the seashore of Suma;
   The cry of a cuckoo has gone away; over there, a lone island.

A Moonlight Journey

After the travels of *A Sentimental Journey*, Basho visited Kyoto, Omi, Mino and Nagoya (Tokock returned to Hobi), where he may have been busy teaching *haik* poetry to his old and new disciples. And in the mid-autumn of the first year of Genrock (1688) he returned to Edo together with Etsujin via the Nakasendo Inland Highway; that was *A Moonlight Journey*. Let us see some parts of it.

Set-out:
   Go and stay overnight in the County of Sarashina, and you would see the moon bright up over Mount Obasute—thus stirred by a gust of autumn wind, I set out northwards, together with Etsujin, a man of poetry. Kakei was so worried about the steep mountain roads of Kiso, that he had his servant accompany us as a guide.

Kiso:
   The night. At the inn I tried to compose *haik* poems of the fine views I had seen in the daytime, and to finish some pieces of verse. Closing my eyes beside the light with the writing tool in hand, I tapped on my head and gave a groan in thought.
   Looking at me, that monk seemed to guess I might be being depressed by hard travel. To cheer me up, he talked about sacred places he had visited in

his youth, about miracles of the Holy Amida, and about mystical events he had heard of.

Irritated, I could no longer make a single piece of verse. Yet that was when I found the rays of the moon shining among the trees, twinkling through the crack of the wall. The sounds of clappers, the voices of people who tried to keep deer away here and there—and then did I feel a lonely yet sweet taste of autumn. I said, shall we drink together with the moon?

We drank. The cup was rather large with showy lacquer painting, a vessel that would be, in the town, looked upon as akin to bad taste. But now in the country it looked fairly amusing like a gem of a cup.

—At the foot of Mount Obasute;

A sad scene of yore—an old woman weeping alone, with the moon as friend.

—In the province of Shinano;

The autumn wind—it passes over my flesh, the bitterness of long radish.

It tosses pieces of gravel—the blast blown down from Mount Asama.

And Basho arrived in Edo in late autumn, the end of the one-year travels. Many of his *haik* poems composed on *A Sentimental Journey* and *A Moonlight Journey* were to be selected in a new anthology *Waste Land*.

Waste Land

Compiled by Kakei, this anthology—a selection of *haik* poetry (Part I-VIII) and ten pieces of linked verse (Addendum)—was published in the second year of Genrock (1689). In it there are approximately a thousand *haik* poems of various poets: some are ancient poets, some are *renga* poets, some are of other *haikai* schools. Of course, there appear many disciples of Basho's—not only the followers in Nagoya, but also those in Iga, Mino, Omi, Kyoto and Edo. Let us see some of them.

Sodo: A friend of Basho, Yamaguchi Sodo was born as a son of a brewer in the province of Kai, and lived as recluse in the outskirts of Edo after learning Chinese classics. He was a man of letters, an authority of Japanese and Chinese literature, and a lover of lotus and chrysanthemums.

Kikack and Ransetz: Takarai Kikack and Hattori Ransetz, both of them *haikai* masters, were among Basho's oldest disciples in Edo. A man with a prodigal disposition, Kikack seemed to avoid a man of effort Basho more or less. Furthermore, he may have had a feeling of rivalry toward the great master. On the other hand, Basho praised Kikack highly, saying: "he is a Lord Teika; he makes a prosaic scene poetic" (*Kyorai's Notes*), although, in his letter to another disciple Kyorick, he called the two disciples an 'old fox'.

Rotsu: A monk poet, Yasomura Rotsu was something of an eccentric. 'Rotsu is a recluse,' wrote Basho. 'A lover of *Essays in Idleness*. Living next door to me. A good poet.' Rotsu, however, got on bad terms with other disciples of Basho and made several troubles. When Rotsu quit the priesthood—it might well be called a scandal in those days—Basho defended him in his letter to another disciple Kyoksui, saying: "Rotsu is not a Monk Saigyo nor a Monk Nowin. He is just commonplace; a commonplace one would always do a commonplace thing; therefore, I'm not going to refuse to see him." A very thoughtful master.

The death of Tokock: In his letter to Tokock in the beginning of the third year of Genrock (1690), Basho worried very much about him. What happened to him? Trouble or sickness or another bad thing? Basho hoped to meet him again in Iga. Tokock, however, seemed to be seriously ill at that time. In the late spring of the same year Basho's most beloved disciple died young.

WASTE LAND

Foreword

It is the poet Kakei in Nagoya, west of Atsuta Shrine, who has compiled this anthology *Waste Land*. And why did he name it so? Let me say what he must have had on his mind. It was a few years ago in Nagoya that we composed some pieces of linked verse, which were later compiled and published as *A Winter Day*; and it was followed by another anthology *A Spring Day*. Both were well received in the circles of poetry, but I guess they cover brilliant and beautiful views alone—for example, willows, *sacra* blossoms, birds, butterflies, and skies in Kisaragi and Yayoi. They lack reality and simplicity. People might thereby be astray like a mirage, alone like a princess lily, and at their wits' end like a skylark in an endless firmament. That was what he thought of. That made him compile this anthology as a signpost that may guide people in this boundless wasteland of poetry.

                              Written by Basho in Yayoi, the second year of Genrock

Part I Sacra Blossom; Cuckoo; the Moon; Snow

Sacra Blossom

—At Yoshino;

Teishitz: O blossom, blossom, the *sacra* trees in blossom on Yoshino Mountain.

Rotsu: A *sacra* party—the guests are willful, the host is thoughtful.

Shintock: A hazy sky—the *sacra* trees are in bloom in dignity.

Shinpou: The mountain filled with blossoms—then what should I first sing of?

Yougo: The solitary eventide—beyond the blossoms, a tile of a tutelary goblin.

Shohack: A village in the mountains—some force some to eat in a *sacra* party.

Kyorai: His tastelessness—he's watching the blossoms with a long dagger on.

Yasui: A cloud sails across the ridge; in it there would be some blossoms.

Kido: The *sacra* trees in bloom; who's drunk not carries who's drunk much.

Etsujin: The *sacra* bloom at night; you may well call me the worst guest of all.
  (Note) This comes from an epigram of the *haikai* poet Yamazaki Sokan:
   'The best *sacra* viewer goes back soon; the next-best, within the daytime; and the worst stays overnight.'

Issei:
  The hill being full of blossoms, we can't break off the branches for firewood.

Shunji: I used to look up at them; yet now the blossoms fall like falls.

Sodan:
  The *sacra* trees in bloom; the little brothers have learned to write letters.

Shusen: The falling blossoms—you are a *sake* thief, indeed a *sake* thief.

Kokyu: The flowery shade—it's nice to eat cold soup, a blossom as topping.

Choko: Good annoyance—he's seeing the blossoms with his umbrella open.

Bokshi in Tsushima: The evening rain—in the boat, a *sacra* branch in bloom.

Oho in Gifu: It gets away before I could take it—the branch of a *sacra*.

Kakei: Amusing are *sacra* blossoms—when I walk with my funny cousin.

Sanka: There are *sacra* trees in bloom, there's a man with pock marks.

Hakshi: Ill-timed is a pinwheel seller—when *sacra* trees in bloom.

Lady Tatz: Blossom, blossom, you make me feel sweet indeed.

Shinbyo: The shade of a hill—I've found *sacra* blossoms in the sinking sun.

Etsujin: There is no reason, no logic, yet amusing is a cloud of blossom.

Yasui: The *sacra* trees in bloom, everyone's absent-minded.

Tosho: Alone have I come to the hill full of blossoms, to find people friendly.

Tobun: The ridges are roofed with blossoms, the birds are singing in happiness.

Kakei: Abalone diver, why don't you see the land filled with blossoms?

—On a picture of a drinker;

Basho: No moon, no bloom, and yet there's a man drinking alone.

—At a certain hermitage;

Basho: Highly lofty is the oak tree calm among *sacra* blossoms.
(Note) This *haik* is written in *A Lonely Journey* with a preface: 'In Kyoto I visited Mitsui Shoufou at his villa in Naltaki.'

Cuckoo

—Bought and released a cuckoo that had been kept in a cage.

Kigin: Cuckoo, cuckoo, you have lived a gloomy life in a cage.
(Note) Kitamura Kigin was a noted *haikai* poet of the Teimon School.

Sodo: See the leaves green, hear a cuckoo call, and taste the bonito in season.

Chosetz: Cuckoo, cuckoo, I always am busy when you have to sing.

Etsujin: Cuckoo, cuckoo, the candle light is too bright to hear you call.

Shoka in Tsushima: Cuckoo, cuckoo, the baby in my back imitates your song.

Jugo: Cuckoo, cuckoo, where are you singing, backward or forward?

Ryofou: Cuckoo, cuckoo, where are you in this long and wide meadow?

—When a certain one asked me to make an opening stanza of a linked verse;

Sodan: Cuckoo, cuckoo, I'm the crow-like poet of all.

Racgo: A very fine day—a cuckoo's flying in the blue sky, singing, singing.

Ippatz: Half-awake, half-asleep, I smell the mosquito net, then calls a cuckoo.

Ippatz: Cuckoo, cuckoo, hearing you call thrice makes me smile.

—At Yodo;

Fusen: The tenth night, the first boat, and I hear you cuckoo call in the dark.

Kyowou in Gifu: Cuckoo, cuckoo, it's nice to hear you call before going to bed.

Sanka: No sooner had I awoken than, happily, sang a cuckoo.

Sanka: Cuckoo, cuckoo, you are singing strong even in the dark.

Donka: A horse calls, another neighs back, and then cries a cuckoo.

— Seeing an old *waka* of 'the morning moon fading in the sky';

Nun Chigetz in Otsu: The *waka*-card game — where are you, cuckoo?
    (Note) This comes from a waka of One Hundred Poets' One Hundred Poems:
    Cuckoo, cuckoo, I'm looking up at where you sang;
    Only to find the morning moon fading in the sky.

Rito: Quite careless was I, looking downward — when you cuckoo sang.

Shizan: Quite careless am I, spring-minded — when you cuckoo call.

The Moon

Baizetz, a boy of twelve:
    It goes lightly over the *take* trees — the bright-night moon.

Tansui: Tonight, a bright night, I, too, am one of the moon viewers.

Issetz: Tonight, a bright night, everyone seeks after one and the same moon.

Etsujin: The full-moon night, a rainy night, a somewhat bright night.

Shoheki: A sight of sanctity — I look a little aside from the bright-night moon.

Shiryu in Tsushima: Lonely is an evening moon — when I have just moved in.

Ippatz: You are praiseworthy at any rate — the bright-night moon.

Choko: Bright is the moon; there spread fields shining as far as I can see.

Ninta: Bright is the moon; I've come to the heights, a pen in hand, but in vain.

Kido: A solitary house — I have had enough of the moon tonight.

Etsujin: So bright is the moon, I've failed to perceive the coming of dawn.

Bunrin: Tonight, the brightest, though we have twelve full-moon nights a year.

Shoheki: Bright is the moon; the boat is moored with the oar as a stake.

Sanka: Bright is the moon; I'm walking barefooted in the lawn.

Nisui: The note of a hand drum, the bark of a dog, and yet bright is the moon.

Yasui: Bright is the moon; people see what they are supposed to see.

— When being impatient for a bright moon;

Kakei: Do nothing today, and we will have a bright moon.

Kakei: You may forget the past moons — when you see a moon tonight.

Kyorai: Bright is the moon; I neither think of the sea nor see the mountain.

Kokyu: The bright moon — drunk or not, people are friendly with one another.

Chosetz: The bright moon — I walk through woods, feeling it's not enough.

Ippatz: The evening moon — lonely is the shadow of a bridge.

— On the thirteenth night;

Sampou: Tonight, a moon night, yet two nights short of full-moon bright.

—On the first night;

Kakei: The eventide—there's not a bit of moonlight as far as ends the sea.

—On the second night;

Kakei: Evening has come, yet there are few people see the moon.

—On the third night;

Basho: It beggars all simile and metaphor—that crescent moon.

—On the fourth night;

Bokshi: Blow out the fire, let us see the evening moon for a while.

—On the fifth night;

Issen in Iyo: True, that is the evening moon, but what night tonight?

—On the sixth night;

Kaksei in Okazaki: I've got used to seeing the Silver River; in the sky, the moon.

—On the seventh night;

Ippatz in Gifu: Began early, talked nicely, and returned promptly in moonlight.

Snow

—At Otsu Town;

Kikack: A snow day—take a look at the dark face of Mister Boatman.

Basho: Let us go, let us go see the snow, then slip and fall down flat.
   (Note) This *haik* was composed with a preface as follows:
      There is a bookshop named Fougetz (Wind and Moon). A very refined name it is. One day—while I was taking a rest at the shop—it began to snow.

Jinko: Sparrows chirp at night as snow falls, leaf by leaf, from the *take* tree.

Kasei:
   Behind mountains are mountains; the farther, snowy; the nearer, gloomy.

Shoshun in Kaga: A winter morning—there's no snow on the road.

Etsujin: Woke up, saw the first snow of the season, and then washed my face.

Zeko:
   The first snowfall of the season, and yet no one in the house, the door shut.

Shoho: A snow scene—there is not a stir of any shade.

Nisui: Dark is the night, yet there are shades of snow in white.

Fusen: The falling of snow, and in the stable sits a sparrow.

Jofou in Gifu: A snow night—I'll take a snow-covered branch as is snow-covered.

Rotei: A snow day—the river alone flows in a thin, narrow line.
Sanka: The first snowfall of the season—even my fist looks clean.
Hosen: Ships are covered with snow; the smaller it is, the whiter it looks.
Tobun: A snow morning—there's a piercing voice of a dried-salmon vendor.
Keiseki: A snowy twilight—there's a sweet tinkling of a falcon bell.
Kakei:
    It snows lightly, softly, and white flakes falling on the thickly steamy rice.
Rotsu: The first snow of the season—first, I put on sandals to visit the neighbor.
Yasui: I'm at my wits' end in a snowy sight; all is not nice that is white.
Hosen: The deep green sea—I'm on a ship at port on a white snow night.

Part II New Year; Early Spring; Things Vernal; Mid Spring; Late Spring

New Year

Basho: Next day, the second day, yet attention is all; it's a flowery spring day.
  (Note) This *haik* is written in *A Sentimental Journey* with a preface as follows:
    When the old year passing by, I drank so much at night that I was in bed all the New Year Day.

Monk Kobon: Nobody has helped flowers, but here comes the season of theirs.

Fourin-ken: Young is the water of New Year, old is the rope of the well-bucket.

Kikack: The pine decorations—wonder who buys Lady Ise's house.
  (Note) This comes from a word 'selling my house'—the preface to Lady Ise's *waka* written in the *Kokin-shu*.

Bunrin: They are neither in the *waka* nor in the *renga*—the food decorations.
  (Note) This means that the New Year's food decorations are not mentioned in the classical *waka* nor in the *renga*, but in the *haikai*. That is all. Nothing else.

Kyorai: They would look nice with the moon and snow—the pine decorations.

Issho: Happily, it has not been used for decorations—that old oak tree.

Rotsu: The New Year morning—I feel like a *sacra* late in blooming.

Issho in Kaga: New Year Day—it's fairly hazy, hazy like a spring haze.

Joko in Ogaki: A nice fragrance—I bite a bit of *mei* blossom as a rite.

Racgo in Gifu: Spring has come; I'm two years short of the good age.

Kido: The snowy *mei* tree—try pouring young water.

Kido: New Year Day in Ise, a day off from the carriage of the sacred logs.
  (Note) Logs are carried to Ise Shrine to build its divine house every twenty years.

Shoheki: A *mei* tree in bloom in my garden; I call you Felicity.

Genko: Potato, potato, you used to be rather small last spring.

Shusen: The chestnut and tangerine—let's pick them from the pine decorations.

Shusen: He has learned a festive song—the man of the year.

Jugo: The cooking stove—there are some green ferns among pieces of firewood.

Chosetz: The lofty pine—a decorated horse is drawn by the man of the year.

Chosetz: A piece of wood fit for a *biwa* lute; that is the beginning of art.

Issei: New Year Day—a boy is brought out, is performing a festive dance.

Kokyu:
   They're eaten by the horse, scattered—ferns adorned in the shrine stable.

Choko: Let us remember this scene of the New-Year sea, crisp and refreshing.

Sodan: The New Year morning—I get up to unknot the cord binding the willow.

Sodan: Princess Saho, vernal goddess, don't you wear an old-woman mask?

Tansui: They're like wood shavings of a shipwright—the New-Year decorations.

Lady Tome in Kyoto: The spring morn—the Gods more esteemed than Buddha.

Bokjou: Wonder if it would be lively this New Year Day—Nonomiya Shrine.
   (Note) This comes from a forlorn scene of *The Tale of Genji* at Nonomiya Shrine, where Genji tries to see a love of his. For further details please read the great novel.

Tobun: The dried foods—who thought them fit for New-Year decorations?

Sanka: New Year Day, a charcoal bag, and the head of a fish.

Tosho: It is more quiet than lonely—the New-Year morning.

Ryufou: Amusing are gates, here and there, with no pine decorations.

Bosen: The tea time—I feel a green scent of tea leaves last year.

Shosho in Inuyama: Being a man of the year, you go and hear a warbler sing.

Sekido: They are touching my umbrella—ferns adorned on the sacred shelf.

Baizetz: My sleeve touching pine needles—an auspicious sign on a spring morn.

Yasui: The New-Year rice cake—try putting it upright to mirror a haze.
   (Note) A New-Year rice cake for decoration is called a 'mirror' rice cake from its round, flat, mirror-like shape.

Yasui: Spring begins with dawn, the full tide of a vernal season.

Etsujin: *Katzwo* fish—it's a happy name on a happy New-Year day.
   (Note) The word *katzwo* (bonito) means a fish of victory.

Etsujin: The first dream of a year—where has Hamana Bridge gone?
   (Note) There was a bridge in Hamana in old times but it fell down in an earthquake.

Kakei:
   Reel it, reel it, and there are many bales of wheat on the shrine verandah.
   (Note) This comes from a song of Lady Shizka (*The Tale of Yoshitsune*):
   Reel it, reel it, reel the wheel of time once and once again;
   Bring me back the days gone, please.

Kakei: New Year has come; there are entertainers in the house next door.

Kakei: The year of the Snake—the old seasons are gone with my dim memories.

Monk Bansai: The eyelashes are pricking my eyes; that is my spring.
   (Note) This is a pun: *matz-ge*, eyelashes; *matz*, a pine; that is to say, the *matz-ge* (eyelashes) are pricking the eyes like a needle of a *matz* (pine).

Teishitz: It has come to my poor house, too—this New-Year morning.

Early Spring

Etsujin: Men are cutting firewood, where women used to pick young herbs.

Yasui: A spring day—slow and easy are the people picking young herbs.

Shunji in Tsushima: A little boy's anxious to beat the Seven Herbs, crying out.

Shoshun: Cranes have gone, women come in the fields full of young herbs.

Tora: Picking sea herbs on the shore, she may feel her sleeves wet and heavy.

Soshu in Gifu: All the young herbs they picked—even in my backyard.

Gensatz:
  A spring day—I break off a budded *mei* branch with a string and stone.

Oho: With my falcon on my arm, I break off a *mei* branch quite awkwardly.

Etsujin: It seems not to be in a good mood—the *mei* tree in bloom.

Racgo: Remember the blooming *mei;* on my way back I'll break off its branch.

Ippatz: Breaking off a branch from a *mei* tree, I look around in the field.

Tosho: It looks promising—the long and lean branch of a *mei* with no blossoms.

Shoryu: A *mei* tree in bloom —Is that a twig? —Nay, a bagworm.

—Seeing a son of Poet Ajiro Mimbu;

Basho: It's fairly in bloom—the scion of a good old *mei* tree.

Jakfou in Nagara: It's blowing vehemently, a warbler is singing awkwardly.

Kyorai: It picks, eats, and then sings as a side job—that warbler.

Itto in Iga: The day breaks, and on the well-bucket sits a warbler.

Issho in Tsushima: Warblers are singing; we cannot cut their little bush.

Shiryu in Tsushima: Let me take off the hood, let me hear a warbler singing.

Moumou: Here come no warblers; they might pass by this new house.

Baizetz: A spring morning—I'm spilling water as I listen to a warbler singing.

Yasui: The village is in a haze, the pine is in its height at eventide.

Jinko: Walking on and on in a haze, I find myself still in the haze.

Tobun: A traveler is walking on, his straw raincoat covered with haze.

Basho: The withered lawn—over it lies a mirage afloat an inch or two high.

Sanka: The spring mirage—the horse looks very drowsy in its eyes.

Rotsu: Now in spring—I can see a narcissus at ease at last.

Kakei: They are waiting for birds and butterflies—those boughs and branches.

Things Vernal

—A cutting

Shusen: The cutting is pulled out by a little boy—has it rooted?

—A graft

Sanka: As yet it has not covered the verandah—the grafted tree.

—A *tsubaki* blossom

Kakei: At dawn I pull the bucket up from the well; on the water, a *tsubaki*.

—A *tsubaki*

Bokshi: The butterfly notices it not—a *tsubaki* being in bloom deep in the grove.

—Spring rain

Tansui:
  Simple but beneficial is spring rain like blind poet Moichi's paper string.

—Spring rain

Sodan: It rains, it rains, a spring rain, come on to me, brothers.

—A white-tailed falcon

Yasui: It looks like wearing a short skirt—a white-tailed falcon.

Kisei: The spring rain—there's a trickle trickling on a spider's web.

Kamesuke, a boy of eleven: An empty hut—on the mortar grows a young herb.

Shusen: Monotonous are the father and son picking horsetail shoots.

Kikack: Monotonous are the people picking something like a horsetail shoot.

Shoryu: Monotonous are the horsetail-shoot pickers taking away a scarecrow.

Ensha: The earthen bridge—on its flank grow horsetail shoots.

Tobun: A spring day—being on a punt, I hold out my hand to a horsetail shoot.

Seiko: A spring day—picking one by one, I've got a hoodful of horsetail shoots.

—The ancient Chinese calligrapher Wang Xizhi had geese in his pond, seeing them swim like a brush.

Sodo: No geese in my pond, yet the willow swings its branches to learn letters.

Yasui: They are swung to any direction—the willow branches in breeze.

Etsujin: There's a willow, there's a shadow passing by it as if nothing happened.

Issho: Rather amusing is a cutting of a willow standing upright.

Shoshun: It begins to bend this early—the willow of a foot high.

Issho:
   Catch it, catch it — the willow is trying to catch the wind with its branches.
Shoheki: It seems halted on the shore — a raft surrounded by willow branches.
Kyowou:
   Try rumpling it, but the willow would always hold the shape of its hair.
Shikyo: Short are the willow branches — swinging over the hedge and away.
Kyowou: The ox turns his face away; the willow is blown by the wind.
Shoho: The falcon dodges quickly; the willow is blown by the wind.
Koyou: A windless day — the willow is motionless as it is.
Kakei: It's looking indifferently at the busy blacksmith — that willow.
Kakei: The willow branches stir in moonlight — as a bat flies by.
Soshu: I lean against the green willow — as a cart makes its way.
Oho: A break of wind — the willow branches swing back all at once.
Seirin: I planted it myself, yet I've forgot what kind of *kick* it is.

Mid Spring

Fukai: It blows and blows, and the *nanohana* flowers lean against the wheat.
Choko: On the bank grow horsetails; here and there, *nanohana* flowers.
Sanka: All the *nanohana* in bloom, their shadows are reflected in the room.
Seido: The furrowed field — here and there remain *nanohana* flowers.
Kyorai: He looks motionless — a man plowing in the foot of the yonder hill.
Shoheki: They are back; the New-Year dancers now plowing the spring fields.
Etsujin: It is given as gift — not only a *sacra* branch, but a long-lived *tsubaki*.
Shoso: It stands alone in the wide and large garden — the *sacra* tree in bloom.
Jofou: The *sacra* in bloom; on its bough we've sometimes hung a straw raincoat.
Ikkyo: The *sacra* in bloom; its branches have been broken off within their reach.
Tosho: A *sacra* tree in bloom on the cliff; its back we can in no way see.
Ippatz: The *sacra* tree late in bloom, the mountain is now monotonous at dusk.
Yasui: Vigorous is a skylark — flying briskly against a gust of spring wind.
Jofou:
   The spring fields — lie on your back, and you'll see a skylark fly overheads.
Issetz: Its face turns red as it cries — that little pheasant.
Ensha: A mountain path — I set free a trapped pheasant I've found by chance.

Yamazaki Sokan: Sitting up on all fours, it dares to chant a *waka*—that frog.

Racgo: Singing, singing, the frogs singing, not hearing an evening bell ringing.

Etsujin: They seem not to be in a good mood—the frogs singing at dawn.

Kyorai: It tries to land but slips down repeatedly—a frog at the water's edge.

Racgo: Jumping in the water, it swims with a slow, smooth stroke—that frog.

Shoka in Tsushima: Jumping abruptly, it soon straightened up—that frog.

Issei: The eventide—there are frogs in the darksome casting net.

Ryufou:
    It makes us smile; a little boy has found the first butterfly of the season.

Baiji: It passes by a palm leaf and away—a waltzing butterfly.

Suigyok: It is astray about the blood grass—an elegant butterfly.

Hyaksai: Flying up from the dead grass, it goes to young leaves—that butterfly.

Late Spring

Tadatomo: It is found at a corner on the bank—a violet in flower.
    (Note) This is a pun: *sumire*, a violet; *sumi*, a corner; that is to say, a *sumire* (violet) in flower at a *sumi* (corner) on the bank.

Kakei: Too sleepy to ride on a horse; beside the path, a violet in flower.

Yasui: A large pit gapes open, and there flowers a violet.

Shusen: In the cave sunny only in the middle of the day flowers a violet.

Oho: He nicely picks up a violet—the boy cutting the grass.

Shok-you:
    Butterfly, butterfly, you've flied away after touching on all the thistles.

Tokock: People working in the wheat fields, I feel crisp spring air on the bank.

Shikishi in Osaka: Hazy is the moon, the bare hill is rather bright.

Basho: The roars of falls, and yellow roses are falling lightly, softly in flakes.
    (Note) This *haik* was composed at Yoshino on *A Sentimental Journey*.

Yasui:
    The hues of a night—the flare of a torch makes the yellow roses look dark.

Bokshi: A gust of wind—yellow roses and white butterflies are tossed in the air.

Kinsetz in Gifu: I look deep at a yellow rose at twilight—is it single-flowered?

Howou in Gifu: I look deep at yellow roses, clinging to a jutting rock.

Kyorai: Are you, swallow, playing around, or merely flying around?

Shunji: The swallow is back to its last year's nest, daubing mud again.

Choshi: The swallow looks busy—as though it would say it has just come.

Choko: Curious are the sparrow, peeping the nest of a swallow.

Sodan: It is shut out from the house at dusk—that swallow.

Tanko:
　　Their friends have gone north; the wild geese are calling in vain at night.

Shoritz: Without its antlers, the little deer looks soft and easy.

Etsujin: Rice and pickles in hand, a boy calls his parent clamming at low tide.

Sanka: Little Girl's Day—both mother and daughter are drinking peach wine.

Yujou: Hazy low tide—some are clamming on the shore; some, on a punt.

Kakei: It cannot open to bloom—the bud of an azalea covered with a cocoon.

Kensei: A hazy moon night—there hangs a long vine of a white wisteria.

Kido: A torch flares on a cormorant fishing boat; the wisteria all the more white.

Bokshi: A long spring day—it's rather white even after the temple bell rang out.

Yasui: A long spring day—the oil-seed press is creaking.

Yasui: Spring is passing by, with some salted mysid left behind.

Part III Early Summer; Mid-Summer; Late Summer

Early Summer

Rotsu: The changing of clothes—a white kimono makes me feel unsettled.

Sanka: The changing of clothes—I wear a new kimono merely casually.

Monk Sodan: The changing of clothes—what if I wore a sort of sword?

—The ancient poet Shohack's incense 'Arashiyama' was given to Etsujin by Bunrin as a farewell gift, was last year brought to me one snow morning. And this year, the season of young foliage, I sent a *haik* of gratitude to Bunrin.

Kakei: The changing of clothes—maybe you have an incense for the beard.
   (Note) The great *renga* poet Sogi, the master of Shohack, liked having an incense for the beard.

—On a mountain path;

Basho: Summer has come, yet the single-felt fern still a single leaf.

Issei: Is an iris a female? —if so, then a roof iris would be a male.

Etsujin: Fairly thoughtful is the persimmon tree—being full of young leaves.

Fuko in Gifu: There's a young leaf springs up from a stump—a *sacra* it is.

Tora in Gifu: The young leaves—before long they would be in winter appearance.

Kido: I don't know, I don't know why, but every tree has its own young leaves.

Chikdo: Flapping, flapping, fluttering, and then on a young leaf sits a butterfly.

Donka: Late afternoon—took a bath, went out, saw young leaves.

Moumou: Around the bare hill skirts a stream; on the shore, a white deutzia.

Gensatz:
   It has grown on the heap of soil before we could know—a stalk of wheat.

Seirin: The green summer fields—the wheat alone looks yellow.

Anonymous: All the wheat has been reaped; there remain mulberry trees alone.

Donka: The villager puts down a sheaf of wheat; below it, a mallow in flower.

Ranran: Pure white are the poppy flowers—which make butterflies look gray.

Racgo: Rather unsteady are the poppy flowers—when a bird flies by.

Rito in Gifu: Their flowers just fallen, the poppies are all in fruit now at evening.

Tojun: Rather stout is the poppy flower—enduring in a heavy rain.

Kichiji:
  The poppy flowers falling one by one, a little boy's picking up one by one.

—At a certain hermitage in Fukagawa;

Ransetz: A night at a hermitage—night has been getting shorter night by night.

Yasui: Lonesome bird—wonder what hue sadness has.

Mid-Summer

Sacrai Motosuke: They're flying drunk in *sasa* woods at dusk—the fireflies.
  (Note) This is a pun: *sasa*, a bamboo; *sasa*, *sake*; that is to say, fireflies are flying *sasa* (*sake*)-drunk in *sasa* (bamboo) woods.

Ippatz: It glitters about the hay in the stable—that firefly.

Fuko: It moves up on the paper window in darkness—a glittering firefly.

Futeki: It attracts a darksome figure from darkness—that glittering firefly.
  (Note) This comes from a *waka* of Lady Izmi Shikibu (a poet in the Heian Period):
    One shall go from darkness to darkness—O, Fair Moon!
    Shine on me from the edge of a far mountain.

Seiko: The narrower path—I shall give up seeing fireflies on the stream.

Ganten: They won't fly tonight—the fireflies on a rainy night.

Bokshi: There's a man cutting grass, and out from his sleeve comes a firefly.

Oho: There's a woman drawing water, and on her wet sleeve glitters a firefly.
  (Note) See a *waka* of Lady Izmi Shikibu:
    Lost in thought, I've found a firefly about the stream;
    It would be a gem light of my soul afloat in the air.

—When a certain poet visited my house for the first time;

Shuho: He takes a look in my hut; under the eaves, an iris.

Shoshun: It makes the hemlock look hazy—the pillar of swarming mosquitoes.

Kyowou: It makes the room look small—the smoke of mosquito incense.

Nisui: The rainy nightfall—mosquitoes are buzzing over my umbrella.

Issho: It looks somewhat skinny—a mosquito sitting on the armor.

Kokyu: It looks like a hair ornament of the woman diver—the seaweed flower.

Jichick: They are shrunk in heat—the seaweed flowers at low tide.

Shikitz: With a princess lily beside my leg, I'm taking a noon nap.

Choko: With a lantern in hand, I'm walking in quest of a *take* shoot.

Kyorai: It is marked as wood for a bow—that young bamboo.

Yasui: It seems to be not knocking, but crying—that water rail.

Ichiryu in Otsu: The Satsuki rains—it stands at bay on the shore, that willow.

Shohack: Its drops are getting small nowadays—the Satsuki rain.

Kido: It might well be a break from a Satsuki rain—if your umbrella silent.

—At Gifu Town;

Teishitz: Amusing is the cormorant fisherman, now handling several leashes.

—At the same place;

Basho: It's fun, then a bit of sorrow—the cormorant fishing at night.
   (Note) This *haik* was composed with a preface as follows:
     Highly famous is the cormorant fishing on the River Nagara in Gifu. It was really wonderful, beggared all description. It should be seen by a man of wit, said someone as we returned in the dark. Walking on, I remembered a line of a Noh drama: 'I'm going back to the darkness. How sad! How sorrowful!'

—At the same place;

Kakei: Pitiful are the cormorants—busy in a rain of sparks from the torch light.

—At the same place;

Etsujin: Pitiful are the sweet fish, too; you could hear them cry out.

Junji in Otsu: Busy is the cormorant fisherman, not looking at his father's boat.

Baiji: The winding river—the cormorant boats ahead of ours are out of sight.

Rotsu: It disappears, then appears, now down, now up—the nest of a wild duck.

Bokshi: The summer fields—the pine cones are still green.

Donka: It cuts off the foot of a rainbow—a huge bead tree in the meadow.

Donka: They have got muddy since the rain yester-night—the rush flowers.

Etsujin: A *nadeshico* in flower, but a lacquer painter would not satisfy her.

Tora: Dull and boring is the nightlight—still burning in the summer morning.

Tanko: A summer night in a village—beyond the bonfire, a reed screen.

—When a certain hermit was absent;

Kikack: Dull and boring is a charcoal bag in summer, let alone a charcoal chest.

Basho: The moonflowers—the fall would see them fruit into a variety of gourds.
   (Note) This comes from a *waka* in the *Kokin-shu:*
     Spring sees all the leaves grow in green alone;
     Yet in the fall all's in flower in a variety of hues.

Yasui: It withers while nobody sees it—a moonflower.

Kaisetz: It blooms in a mosquito-buzzing darkness—the moonflower.

Shiryu: I have come down from the mountains; in a meadow, a moonflower.

Choko: The poor name is *loofa*, the fruit of a moonflower.

Late Summer

Shoheki: The camphor tree would be shaken; the cicadas are chirping hard.

Yasui: It makes a good stool on the heights—a white cloud about the ridge.

Sanka: The afternoon shower—the umbrella hung on the hedge is dripping wet.

High Priest Genshi: It's cool; everybody's being in the shade of a nettle tree.
(Note) This is a pun: *enoki*, a nettle tree; *enoki*, to move out; that is to say, everybody does not *enoki* (move out) from the shade of an *enoki* (nettle tree). High Priest Genshi, or Hosokawa Yousai, was a *samurai* commander and *waka* poet in the Oda-Toyotomi Period.

Kyorai: The afternoon shower, the crisp air, and in the west, a sunny sky.

Kakei: It looks cool—a green reed screen at the entrance of an inn.

Kakei: A cloudy day, a simple garden, and the sand space looks rather cool.

Jofou in Narumi: The cool evening—I've had a fortuitous encounter.

Shunji in Tsushima: Below the stepping stone is a lizard enjoying cool grass.

Shunji: Fairly cool is the sound of a stream running below the villa.

Bokshi: Somewhat tasteful are the lanterns of a pleasure boat at cool evening.

Migack: It is getting far and dim as we go back—the cool of a river.

Shusei in Gifu: It's blown and drawn—a lotus afloat on the water.

Shinpou in Matsuzaka: The sun being in anger overhead, yet I'll go see lotuses.

Kobon: The shades of straw hats—we all have seen all the lotus flowers all day.

Fusui: The stream forks into two, and there flower water lilies.

Choko: Into the fountain fall dead pine needles—one by one.

Shunji: The low tide—fairly clear is the water of a spring off the beach.

Bunjun: Many attendants waiting, the master is enjoying cool water.

Ryogetz: The cool fountain—I force my horse to drink the water.

Shohack: With a light-yellow kimono on, I go for enjoying cool water.

Ippatz:
   With an elegant robe on, he's nicely enjoying cool water—that nobleman.

Bokshi: Giving a curtain an airing, I find a *sacra* blossom fall from it.

Rishin in Gifu: A horse passing by, all the dew drops from the hemp leaves.

Etsujin: A bell flower—it must have been named so after a bell was named so.

Sodo: As it happens, the cotton flower is looking like an orchid.

Part IV Early Autumn; Mid-Autumn; Late Autumn

Early Autumn

Etsujin: The hemp plants reaped, an autumn wind blows in no cheerful mood.

Enkai: The fallen paulownia leaves—I'll wear one of them in an autumn wind.
  (Note) The falling of a paulownia leaf is said to be a sign of the coming of autumn.

—At Monk Ungo's temple in Matsushima;

Senka: It's simply noisy—the falling of a paulownia leaf.

Hosei in Tsushima: The cool autumn evening—my light kimono would be shrunk.

Kyowou: Tanabata Festival—who in the world has offered that men's kimono?
  (Note) In Tanabata Festival, generally, little girls offered clothes with the wishes of improvement in their sewing skill.

Basho: People are drinking merrily, a morning glory flowering happily.
  (Note) This *haik* was composed when Basho set out on *A Moonlight Journey*.

Bunrin: It crawls slovenly over the hedge—that morning glory.

Kakei: It's dewy, but looks not dewy—that white morning glory.

—To a nursemaid;

Kakei: Do not give him a flower of a morning glory; the baby would eat it.

Oho: The morning glory of the neighbor—I've had it creeping into my *take* tree.

Kokyu: A morning glory in flower; below it, a puddle mirroring the moon.

Sodan: A dewdrop sounds as it drops, as if giving a word from leaf to leaf.

Kyorai: A gust of autumn wind—it's time to string a plain-wood bow.

Shocho: It's cool—really cool fishing seabass directly from the sitting room.

Rotei: The rice field, a cool breeze, and a palanquin on a halt in the path.

Ippatz: It chirps when you have passed by—a pine cricket.

Soshu: It chirps when you have put out a light—an autumn cricket.

Basho: It promises lightning—the darkness of a cloud afloat in the sky.
  (Note) In Japan lightning is called *inazuma*, the same pronunciation as rice (*ina*) and spouse (*tsuma*), so it makes one associate with good harvest and pregnancy.

Kikack: Flashes of lightning—yesterday in the east, today in the west.

Shusen: It's all the more beautiful—the trodden *hagi* flower.

Basho: A slender flower, a dewy, womanly creature—the *fair lady*.

(Note) This *haik* was composed on *A Moonlight Journey*.

Anonymous: It looks somewhat bleak at first—the grape-vine trellis.

Ninko: The leafy, grassy field—that fellow is not a cutter, but a bearer.

Kakei: Throwing away a dying paper light, I find *susuki* grass white with ears.

Kokyu: The *susuki*-grass fields—a passer-by might get caught in a ditch.

—From a word of the great monk poet Sogi;

Sodo: There are blades of nameless grass, there are wild asters in flower.

Shunji: Year by year it grows taller and taller—the silver grass.

Mid-Autumn

Basho: Now at dusk in autumn—on a bare branch sits a crow alone.

Shoshun in Kaga: Now in autumn I look deep—deep at the picture of my fan.

Ekion in Kaga: A stream in the vale—I'm washing a tea bag at dusk in autumn.

Sanka: Now at dusk in autumn—somewhere sounds the cutting of stones.

Bokshi: The sound of an ax, and there appears a bat at dusk in autumn.
(Note) This comes from a line of Du Fu: 'The sound of an ax makes the mountain more calm and sweet.'

Ippatz: The eventide—a deer calls, people look at one another.

Issen in Iyo: It takes charge of two fields—that single scarecrow.

Jugo: A village in the mountains—the plowman made a scarecrow, laughing.

Kikack: Burn red maple leaves to warm *sake*—yet who's taught us to?
(Note) This comes from a line of Bai Latien: 'In the woods we burn red leaves to warm liquor.'

Tojun: The fine view of red maple leaves—I'm talking with whom I know not.

Rinpou: It looks rather low—a maple tree red in the grove.

Etsusui: Somewhat pitiful is the ivy—crawling on the ground.

Sowa: They are a little in autumnal attire—blades of grass in the garden.

—When a certain poet coming to my hermitage;

Hokshi in Kaga: This villa is rich in autumnal atmosphere—I dare say.

—At Sodo's hermitage;

Etsujin: All their fruits having fallen, the lotuses now in simple attire.

Bosen: A river in autumn—beside the weir there only is a lean reed alone.

Shusen: An autumn butterfly in a gust—watch you don't hit against a pine.

Kokyu: The mosquito net put away, I'm sleepless in a somewhat wide room.

Gyogo: It brings the mood down—the sound of beating clothes in busy town.

—When Sogyu coming to me from Seki;

Kikack: The beating of cloth—imagine swordsmiths Shiz and Magorock of Seki.

—At Yoshino;

Basho: A night at a lodging—if only I could hear the landlady beat clothes.
   (Note) This comes from a *waka* in the *Shin Kokin-shu*:
      In the mountains of Yoshino blows an autumn wind late at night;
      And there sounds a chilly note of beating clothes.

Issho in Kaga: It looks very busy—a shooting star in the stormy sky.

Late Autumn

Hajo: Though it was planted merely simply, yet now it's a nice white *kick* flower.

Shoheki: A little unsatisfied that the white *kick* flower should hardly fall.

Etsujin: A *kick* looks brilliant—not only in a field, but by a mountain path.

Gyogo: All of them in one hue, the wild asters are in full bloom.

—When I stayed at Kakei's, he offered a lacquered cup of *sake* for me to remove the fatigue of travels.

Kikack: The chrysanthemum—let me take a look at the nice picture on the cup.

Kikack: It's like a graceful woman—the dewy chrysanthemum.

Nisui: A thing regrettable this morning—I should have grown a *kick* flower.

Senkack in Iyo: It's too frosty to pull off—the ivy creeping over firewood.

Roseki in Mino: A solitary moment—the sound of a falling acorn wakes me up.

Kasei (Boncho): Winterberry, winterberry, you should have all your leaves fall.

Rotsu: They wave happily, then fall sadly—the reed ears.

Part V Early Winter; Mid-Winter; Year-End

Early Winter

Koshun: Here comes a winter rain; the heaven and the earth stop talking.
  (Note) The sound of wind was believed to be a talking voice between the heaven and the earth, was interrupted by the winter rain.

—To a certain person in Kyoto;

Shohack: Come on some night, sing a Noh song of *Mi Temple* in a winter rain.

Tansui: The first winter rain—then what have you recollected this evening?

—At a ten-thousand-line *haikai* meeting;

Kakei: The winter rain—we all have gathered here as if to take shelter.

—Waiting for a certain person;

Racgo: The winter rain—this morning I looked skyward time and time again.

Suigyok: The winter rain—there remains a dry spot beneath the temple bell.

Sanka: The winter rain—on the ferry the boatman alone wears a raincoat.

Kakei: The ripping wind—the second-night's moon would be blown away.
  Kyorai's Notes:
    (Although Kyorai valued this *haik* highly, Basho was critical of it, saying) "This looks nice in appearance thanks to the word 'the second-night's moon'; and yet, except for that, this is a commonplace *haik*."

Ippatz: Leaf by leaf—the persimmon leaves turn red, then dead, then all gone.

Ippatz: Dead leaves aflame at the fire place, and all burned to sad ash.

Ippatz: Nobody knows it in its leafy shade, but the medlar is in bloom in white.

Rishin: An early-winter day—I see tea blossoms merely incidentally.

Yasui: It looks rather lonesome in a winter rain—the pear tree wet in bloom.

Shoheki: When did you, bagworm, find the trees blooming a second time?

Shoheki: It makes my hermitage look nice—the view of a wheat-sown field.

Issei: The changing of clothes—a mild season when they seed fields with wheat.

Racgo: Having folded a piece of sewing neatly, she warms herself at a heater.

Kokyu:
  Amusing is a silver leaf in flower—as if dividing the stone mortar in two.

Bunrin: Green though it is, the scouring rush is one of the winter grasses.

Bokshi: The new well-bucket—in it lies a *shinobu* leaf afloat on the water.

Dosetz: Lifeless weeds, restless wind—the winter wasteland.

Ippatz: The lotus leaves are all dead; you can see the pond as it is.

Shoho: My falcon on my arm, I stumble on a stone in the withered field.

Kyowou: They are blown off by a gust of winter wind—the falcon blinders.

Shoritz: The lord has finished falconry; people begin to pull out turnips.

—A cold moon

Yasui: Amusing is the moon when I see it each time I get out of a warm room.

Shunji: The wintry moon night—I'm washing radish to salt.

Mid-Winter

Shokichi in Tsushima: It hails hard, and yet silent is the bell put on the ground.

Juji in Tsushima: It hails hard, and white foams running on the beach.

Rinpou: A lump of stable manure is put aside, is dotted with hailstones.

Kyowou: It stops before I could open the door—the hail shower.

Soshi: A bundle of firewood is put down, is dotted with hailstones.

Tokock: A frosty morning—over the white ground, pale brown bead-berries.

Shokichi: A winter morning—greens are frozen on the shelf in the kitchen.

Shunji: The deep pond—I try looking down when it has frozen over.

Jofou: A winter morning—breaking thin ice, I rake up dead pine needles.

Yashu: Pick the icicle; it would be useful for something—something I know not.

Sledge

Sodan: It sleds down the hill—a sledge load of firewood.

Kakei: Displeasing is such a man as is dressed warmly on a sled.

Choko: She has come, a one-night journey—the bride on a sled.

Issei: A snow morning—I take the sled out from the stable.

Kido: He takes a rest standing upright—that sled bearer.

Ganten: They have slowed the snow sled after all—the quick ropes.
   (Note) This comes from a *waka* of Saigyo's:
     Without quick ropes on, the snow sled goes slowly;
     And it snows heavy in white in Koshi Country.

Tadatomo: Green is the sea, the gulls white, the ducks black, and redheads.

Kido: There is a light in a ship in the sea, and to it calls a plover.

Sonshun: A flock of plovers—some might have been to Korea.

—Well-diggers feel chilly in summer; brewing men are barely clothed in winter.

Tosho: Wet with sweat, they are making an icehouse in winter.

Rijou: The icehouse—if only I could keep a jar of sea-cucumber guts in it.
(Note) An icehouse was used as a freezer. The poet wished he could eat sea-cucumber guts—salty but tasty especially as a side dish to *sake*—in summer.

Kido: The smoke getting weaker, the charcoal burner quickly fills the kiln hole.

Ensha: When a little boy, I'd feel rather chilly, trying to lengthen my sleeves.

Issho in Kaga: The winter camellia—how many days have you been in bloom?

Kido: The toppled eaves—under it, a winter camellia in bloom.

Basho: Let winter go by, with this pillar as my friend once again.
(Note) This *haik* was composed at his hermitage in Edo when he returned from the travels of *A Sentimental Journey* and *A Moonlight Journey*.

Year-End

Rika: The making of rice cake—that fellow is out, drinking *sake* somewhere.

Shohack: The end of a year—there's an illegible memo, though written by me.

Yasui: It will get sooty and fall someday—the flower on the rice cake.

Kido: Spring is coming soon, bundles of firewood are taken out of the field.

Ippatz: People are sweeping soot, and from the *mei* tree hangs a gourd bottle.

—Having seen the moon in Kiso, Etsujin gave me an acorn as a present. I kept it until the end of the year, for it could be, I thought, useful for New Year's decorations.

Kakei: The end of a year—there's an acorn rolling, rolling.

Naishu: He goes home with a basketful of clams—the pine-decoration vendor.

Kido: The New-Year dishes—I have to keep mice away all cold night long.

Part VI Things Various

Monthly Court Events
—New Year's Spiced *Sake*
Kakei: Objection, Objection, the old shall be the first drinker of spiced *sake*.
—Kasga Festival
Kakei: It's always in bud year after year—the wisteria beside the shrine gate.
—Iwashimiz Festival
Kakei: Everyone's walking quietly; on their hair, a *sacra* blossom.
—The Birthday of the Holy Buddha
Kakei: Today, a holy day, the other divine statues are cleaned, too.
—Tango Festival
Kakei: Skinny are their faces, sparse is their hair with a mallow flower on.
—Rice Donation
Kakei: Open the rice bag, and you might smell of the bug.
—Tanabata Festival
Kakei: They're easier to learn than the vernal ones—the flowery autumn herbs.
—The Welcoming of Horses
Kakei: Their hair and nails have been left uncut—those poor horse bearers!
—The Catching of Insects
Kakei: The autumn fields, blades of grass, and a foot-broken grasshopper.
—The Changing of Clothes
Kakei: A flowery season has come back; the costumes are renewed gorgeously.
—Gosechi Festival
Kakei: Lovely is the dancing girl; how many times has she turned her sleeves?
—Tsuina Festival
Kakei: The ogre is chased and chased, with his mask left fallen.

On Some Lines of the Chinese Poet Bai Latien
—Today, this day, who has arranged this? Here come spring wind and water at once.

Yasui:
　　Spring wind—the ice thaws, the waterworks begin its seasonal clattering.
—White *mei* blossoms afloat on a stream.
Yasui: Pure white is a *mei* blossom sticking to the bill of a waterfowl.
—Spring has come, yet I have no friends to walk out with.
Yasui: He asks me to take care of his house, the flower vendor next door.
—The flowers are beautifully in bloom; I have forgot to return home.
Yasui: If I nap among the flowers, then pray put something over me.
—I try to keep back spring in vain; And then come lonely days when it is gone.
Yasui:
　　Spring has gone, yet that temple seems to know what has gone, has gone.
—My clothes fluttering in a light breeze; It is neither hot nor cold.
Yasui: It will be fit when we enjoy hearing a pine wind—the cotton-less.
—The pond now at dark; there float fragrances of lotus flowers.
Yasui: Fragrant is the lotus flower—as though she has just had a bath.
—You've come to this poor house in this hot season; I make a present of north breeze.
Yasui: Enjoy a cool breeze; I have made a window in the north.
—I feel sad almost all seasons; Among others, breaking my heart is an autumn sky.
Yasui: Traveling in snow? Nay, seeing an autumn sky is more heart-breaking.
—The storm last night is gone; And here comes autumn together with crisp air.
Yasui: The autumn rain has gone; no watermelon vendors are seen.
—A long night, a far peal of a bell; And nearly at dawn glitters the Starry River.
Yasui: I have got a little hungry; what a lengthy night!
—The wall shadows the shade of a lamp; The window reflects a ray of the moon.
Yasui: She sleeps alone in bed in tears; beyond the window, the moon.
—Everything looks white in the autumn frost.
Yasui: An autumn morn—I'd see a white *kick* as it is, only it's frosted all white.
—A balmy early-winter sky in the South; A fine view—it's just like a spring day.
Yasui: Today, a Little Spring day, the winter wind is taking a short rest.
—A silent night at a forlorn village; In the snow fields honk wild geese.

Yasui:
>The honks of wild geese in a snowy village where bowl beaters won't visit.

—A white-haired man chants a sutra at night.

Yasui: He holds himself in his arms as he chants a sutra—that white-haired.

On Lord Ichijo Kanera's *Songs for Craftsmen*
(Note) Ichijo Kanera was a noble statesman and scholar in the Ashikaga Period.

—Saw setter

Shusen: A heat haze, a late-afternoon sunshine, and then some headache.

—Stick maker

Shusen: Dark is the night in Satsuki, and that sound is not waterfowl's but his.

—Well-bucket-rope maker

Shusen: An autumn village—on his way home he drops in at a *sake* house.

—Starch vendor

Shusen: A dewy morning—the old woman is picking plantain lilies.

—Dung raker

Shusen: A gust of winter wind—the boy walks out with a pine-needle raker.

Lady Li

—His Majesty comes to the smoke of incense; where is the ghost of her? (Bai Latien)

Etsujin: I hold the shadow in my arms, but that is but my sleeve.

Princess Yang

—She came down as soon as she woke up; With her hair unkempt, her garland aslant. (Bai Latien)

Etsujin: Her face half asleep, her sash loose in a spring breeze.

Lady Zhao

—Her little shoes, her shrunk costume; And her eyebrows drawn in blue; All this would make people laugh. (Bai Latien)

Etsujin: She dresses as if in her spring day—that strange woman.

Princess Xi Shi

—The wise man has found the fair lady in the palace; But won't offer the woman of ill omen to the king. (an old Chinese poem)

Etsujin:
>The peony, a lovely flower that is to be transplanted from place to place.

Princess Wang

—She looks all the more beautiful in the blast of sandy wind. (an old Chinese poem)

Etsujin: It stands out among other trees—the winter willow.

One Day at Home

—Early morning

Chosetz: They're chased out by kitchen smoke—mosquitoes around the bed.

—Morning

Chosetz: Let's arrange iris flowers; the painter is to come today.

—Late morning

Chosetz: The listeners are feeling drowsy, the storyteller is beating the fan.

—Noon

Chosetz: Boys, don't step on the dried indigo plants; go out for bathing.

—Afternoon

Chosetz: The chirps of a cicada—supper is over at a *samurai's* home.

—Late afternoon

Chosetz: The Satsuki rain—a rooster is preening at roost.

The Living Have Pitiable Jobs Wherever They Live

—Animals

Jusui: Pity—that he should be a good whistler to lure the deer.

—Wild birds

Jichick: The sun is sinking, a snipe hunter walking with his shadow cast long.

—Insects

Ganten: He's carrying a branch of stinkwood—that insect vendor.

—Sea fish

Ganten: The Bon-Feast moon—they are happy drawing the net full of sardines.

—River fish

Ganten: An autumn evening—cormorant fishermen swing fires here and there.

—Ox and horse have four legs by nature, but man sets reins in the horse's neck, and a ring in the ox's nose. (Chinese sage Zhuang)

Etsujin: The *mei* branch is in bloom, a graft to the peach tree.

—Keep a ship in a vale or on a stream in mountains, but all will be useless because the almighty Nature can destroy it overnight. (Chinese sage Zhuang)

Etsujin: The turban shell feels cozy in its shell, being on sale in winter market.

—Were it not for the sages, the robbers would disappear. (Chinese sage Zhuang)

Etsujin: It must have begun long before one rents things—Tanabata Festival.

—A sharp one shall be soon useless. (an old Chinese epigram)

Keiseki: It has simply fallen and gone—the firework.

—A dull one shall be long useful. (an old Chinese epigram)

Shizan: It remains red until snow falls white—the cockscomb.

—Fujifusa

Issei: Cuckoo, cuckoo, you know very well when you should stop singing.
(Note) Lord Madenokoji Fujifusa (died in 1380) was a noble statesman, a character of the historical epic *Teihei-ki*. He tried to remonstrate with Emperor Go-Daigo, but failed; and before long became a recluse.

—Moronao

Choko: Beautiful is the rose, so beautiful a flower that it may have thorns.
(Note) Kono Moronao (died in 1351) was a *samurai* commander, a character of the *Taihei-ki*. He made approach to a celebrated beauty of the day, but failed; and before long got killed in a power struggle.

—Ikkyu

Tansui: Amusing are various shapes of clouds afloat about the moon.
(Note) Ikkyu (died in 1481) was a Zen monk and poet, famous for wit and eccentricities. What he did was sometimes against the rules and customs of Buddhist monks (he had a love, for instance), although he himself warned his disciples not to imitate him. He lived long and died as old as eighty-eight, with the last word: 'I want to live a little longer.' The name Ikkyu means 'a rest'. See a *waka* of his:
  To live, to take a rest between birth and death;
  Let it blow as it blows, let it rain as it rains.

—Honen

Sodan: It sounds high—the chirp of a quail, and its simplicity.
(Note) The Great Priest Honen (died in 1212) was the founder of Jodo Buddhism.

—Rocks on a mountain

Tansui: It is hailing in the mountains; the rocks might be a little worn.

—Rocks on a beach

Tansui: All the laver has been gathered; no taints of soil about the rock.

Part VII Scenic Spots; Travel; Recollections; Love; All Ends Dead That Exists

Scenic Spots

Tokock: It is simply hazy to the depth of the scene—Mount Tatsuta in spring.
(Note) This comes from a *waka* of Monk Jakren in the *Shin Kokin-shu*:
Sacra trees in bloom on the heights of Mount Katsuragi;
And a white cloud cuts off the depth of Mount Tatsuta.

Kakei: Mount Oyea—the wit of Lady Shikibu, the bones of whitefish.
(Note) This comes from an episode of the daughter of the celebrated poet Lady Izmi Shikibu, who made a witty *waka* against the rude remarks of a certain court noble. Lady Izmi Shikibu was said to live in Mount Oyea.

Basho: It looks more flowery than a *sacra* in bloom—the misty pine of Karasaki.
Kyorai's Notes:
(When Kikack, Rogan and Kyorai made various comments on the prosody of this *haik*, Basho said) "All you are saying is just an argument; I just felt more amused with the pine in a mist than a *sacra* in bloom."

Tansui: The Awate Woods—I borrow a straw mat to see *sacra* trees in bloom.

Kakei:
I have cheerfully come to Saga, where there are *sacra* trees in full bloom.

—A view from Biwa Bridge

Ganten: Now in Yayoi—still chilly is the snowy holy mountain.

Monk Poet Sogi: Passing Seki, I see a wisteria in bloom in white on a hill.

(It is said the poet Sogi composed this *haik* when he found a wisteria in bloom at a temple on a hill in Seki Village, Mino.)

Tokock: The changing of clothes—I'm hesitant to sell what I wore in Yoshino.
(Note) This *haik* was composed when Tokock accompanied Basho on *A Sentimental Journey*.

Jugo: The ancient capital of Shiga—people are threshing wheat far and near.
(Note) This probably comes from a *waka* of the *samurai* commander Lord Taira-no Tadanori, which was given to the *waka* master Lord Fujiwara-no Shunzei for an imperial *waka* selection when the warrior ran away from the capital city, due to the defeat of the Heike (*The Tale of the Heike*):
A stir of waves—desolate is the ancient capital city of Shiga;
Yet it looks as lovely as it used to be—the wild *sacra* in bloom.

Basho: All disappears in the Satsuki rain; and in the rain appears Seta Bridge.

Kyorai: The Satsuki rains—Lake Biwa has a lakeful of rainwater.

Ippatz: There are no shade of any oxen—the Toba Plains in the Satsuki rain.
(Note) This comes from a *waka* of Fujiwara-no Teika:
There's not a tree to halt the horse, nor a shade to clear the snow;
There only spreads a white twilight view of the Sano Plains.

—The River Sumida

Teishitz: Come on, city birds, come on; Saga is alive with your sweet fish.
(Note) This comes from a *waka* of Ariwara-no Narihira:
City birds, city birds, do you know of my old city?
How is my beloved one? Let me hear, let me hear.

Haritz: The heavy note of a conch shell—Mount Yoshino now in the fall.

Basho: The sixteenth night, a moon night—I'm still in the County of Sarashina.
(Note) This *haik* was composed on *A Moonlight Journey* in the vicinity of Mount Obasute, a spot famous for a nice moon view. See a *waka* in the *Kokin-shu*:
I feel sad, I cannot soothe a feeling of sadness when I see
The moon shine over Mount Obasute in Sarashina.

Etsujin: The River Sumida—I beat with the cane a floating moon on the water.

—On the thirteenth night of the Ninth Month;

Sodo: Should you have a Mount Fuji in China, see the moon tonight.

Kokyu: The Tobata Wetlands—a snipe hunter is waiting for a horse to go by.

Enshi: They might be descended from the diver of Kayaz—those snipe hunters.

Shusen: The great Musashi Plains—there fall winter showers far and near.

Shohack: A winter shower—why don't you see Lake Biwa from the roof?

Zuiyou in Iyo: The first winter rain—as it happens, I'm in Karasaki.

Sen-ak: The great Musashi Plains—there goes swiftly a winter sun.

Shunji: Distant Ono Village—they eat sea cucumber, not raw, but grilled.

Issho in Tsushima: A winter day, distant Ono Village, a craftsman's making a pot.

Tansui: It is cut off by a thatch-roofed hut—the snow-white Mount Fuji.

Yasui: Mount Yoshino at dusk, a never-ending stretch of snow white.

Basho: Behold the darkness, cries a plover, about the Cape Star.
(Note) This *haik* was composed on *A Sentimental Journey* at Chisock's house in Narumi Town, a spot famous for plovers.

Joko: A bright moon night—they are sweeping soot off in Fuwa Village.

Travel

Basho: I'm taking a rest in a mountain pass, and below me tweets a skylark.
(Note) This *haik* was composed on *A Sentimental Journey* at the Hoso Pass on his way from Nara to Yoshino.

—At Hirao Village in the province of Yamato;

Basho: The shade of blossom—I'm in bed at night as though a traveler in a Noh.
(Note) This comes from a Noh scene where Taira-no Tadanori acts as main character. See a *waka* of his:
Now at twilight—I shall stay overnight in the shade of a *sacra*;
Blossoms, blossoms, be my host tonight.
And this *haik* was composed with a preface as follows:
When wandering in the province of Yamato, I stayed one night at a plowman's house. He was very kind and hospitable.

Sekifou: I was taking a nap on a horse, passing by a village full of blossoms.

Ippatz: The sunset—I'm on a boat down a river; on the shore, peaches in bloom.

Kakei: A calm, serene day—fish are left on the ground in the mid-day wharf.

Basho: The changing of clothes—I take one off, carrying one more on my back.

—As a farewell verse;

Jofou: Cuckoo, cuckoo, I hold in my tears, smiling.

Tosho: A sleepless night at an inn—they are now preparing breakfast.

Shoheki: A night at an inn—I'd continued killing mosquitoes until the sun rose.

Shuho: The Satsuki rains—there's a sprout on the pillar in a hut in the town.

Sanka: They are a little wet in the afternoon shower—those *daimyo's* men.

—To the Reverend Basho;

Chosetz: I'm all in a flurry, you are leaving like a flash of lightning.

Issei: The autumn cicadas crying out, we are holding on to your sleeves.

Yasui: I can't say anything—a sad farewell in the autumn wind.

Shusen: I can't say anything; farewell is sadder than autumn.

Sodan: The mist be gone, show us that esteemed figure as far as that pine.

—To those who are going toward Sarashina;

Kakei: It will be seen by the two poets—the moon of Sarashina.

—Hearing Etsujin would set out to Sarashina, I sent a *haik* from Kyoto.

Yasui: An autumn moon—you should wear a shorter dagger on a horse.

Basho: You are seeing off, I'm seen off; far ahead, Kiso will be in high autumn.
(Note) The eight *haik* poems above were composed when Basho and Etsujin set out on *A Moonlight Journey*.

Rotsu: Autumn has come to my hermitage, a web blown by the wind.

—Giving a cup to Kikack as a farewell gift;

Kakei: Autumn has come; in the mountains, try taming deer with this cup.

Lady Chine: They sing various thresher songs—as we go from village to village.

Gensatz: The moon is low in the west, I'm going a town farther.

Issei: Listen carefully, you can hear someone beating clothes in a ship off shore.

—Seeing off a certain person at Shinagawa;

Bunrin: The autumn sunset—now, we say good-bye before Monk Tak-an's tomb.
   (Note) Tak-an was a celebrated Zen monk in the early Tokugawa Period. He was buried at a temple in Shinagawa Town, Edo.

Basho: A traveler at night—somewhere whines a dog in a winter rain.
   (Note) This *haik* was composed at Nagoya on *A Lonely Journey*.

Joshu: No good traveler, I'm irritated with my long dagger in the rain.

—Seeing the Reverend Basho at Narumi;

Kakei: Many leaves have fallen, yet your sleeves look rather neat.

Yasui: Dreamed a dream—a dream where my kimono was wadded with cotton.

—Saw off Kikack;

Kakei: O he has left at last, left alone on a winter day.

Etsujin: A traveler at snow twilight—you might be beaten in the River Tenryu.
   (Note) This comes from an episode of Saigyo being beaten with a whip when he crossed the River Tenryu.

Sanka: Plovers are flying high, I'm going on a low-rate horse.

Nishiyama Sowin: The frosted bridge—those would be villager's footmarks.

—Staying at Yoshida Town together with Etsujin;

Basho: Chilly is the night, yet I'm blessed with a good companion.
   (Note) This *haik* is written in *A Sentimental Journey* with a preface as follows:
   Tokock was under confinement at Hobi in the province of Mikawa. To meet him, I joined Etsuin and went back from Narumi to Yoshida, a distance of some fifty miles, where we stayed that night.

Basho: Being a traveler, I merely simply see people very busily sweeping soot.
   (Note) This *haik* was composed on *A Sentimental Journey* when Basho left Nagoya in the end of the year.

Recollections

—When leaving my hermitage;

Rotsu: The ice will thaw when it does, running away.

Kaisen: The widow is plowing alone, with her only child right aside.

Racgo: One will keep off frogs from other rice paddies; that is life in this world.

—At the holy Mount Koya;

Tokock: Blossoms are falling, my laymen hair unfit for the sanctuary.

(Note) This *haik* was composed at the holy city of Koya on *A Sentimental Journey*.

Baizetz: There are *sacra* trees in bloom, there are beggars among people.

—At the holy Mount Koya;

Basho: It draws me into memories of father and mother—the cry of a pheasant.
(Note) This *haik* was composed at the holy city of Koya on *A Sentimental Journey*.

Kakei: It's been given by chance—the iris under the eaves.

Kakei: Tango Festival—happily, I have got a tubful of hot iris water.

Kyowou: It has too many fruits for a man living alone—that eggplant.

Sampou: An old man in summer—allow me to wear a thin coat.

Kido: It is well fit for the white-haired to sell—light firewood.

—On the tenth of the Ninth Month at Sodo's hermitage;

Ransetz: A man in seclusion—among the wife asters, your old *kick* flowers.

Gyogo: The rental house—around the site flower your old chrysanthemums.

—Visiting a certain person;

Basho: You are nicely living in a grassy, frosty hermitage, a simple home.
(Note) This *haik* was composed when Basho visited Tokock in Hobi, Mikawa.

—Sent a letter to a certain person in my hometown.

Tokock: A winter blast, whirling leaves, and on my little finger, a cut.

—At Kenchoji Temple in Kamakura;

Etsujin: Let me sweep off the dead leaves, let me serve the temple.

—A certain person sent me a basketful of dead leaves.

Kakei: Thank you, sir, it would be amusing to grill garfish with the dead leaves.

—The dawn found me remembering my hometown.

Sodan: The peal of a bell—the foot warmer of my mother would get cold.

Kyorai: A calm time—father and son sleeping by a fire, their legs stretching out.

Saim: The end of a year—my eyes going farther, your ear coming nearer.

Basho: The end of a year, my hometown, I'm weeping at the navel cord of mine.

Jofou: The end of a year—what have I seen, heard, and said this year?

—Imagine the surprise when I found a white hair in my hair.

Etsujin: The year is passing by, I'm hiding my white hair from my parents.

Love

Lady Sonome in Ise: The spring meadow sees a woman in love—as she really is.

Jofou: The morning good-bye—I first listen to a cuckoo call.

Choko: Getting out of the mosquito net, I peep at her sleeping in bed.

Bunjun: Conspicuous are a pair of pillows being aired in the sun.

Tobun: The airing of clothes in summer—she tries wearing one of them.

Shinkyok: The rice and cowpea, and desolate is the garden of my sweetheart's.
   (Note) This comes from an old *waka*:
   Desolate is the old garden of my sweetheart's;
   With a violet in flower in vain in the weeds.

—Every woman of the Palace lost their color before her (a line of *The Song of Princess Yang*, written by Bai Latien).

Choko: It drives away flashes of lightning—the face of an evening moon.

Shohack: The dance in a ring—when is she coming around?

—In solitude;

Kakei: When a bachelor, I would receive from the landlord a *fair lady* in flower.
   (Note) This probably comes from a verse of Bai Latien:
   Don't wither, rose, don't die;
   My garden alive with things spring;
   I'm a bachelor, a lonely man;
   When you flower you'll be my wife.

Shoshun: Not that I don't know the shadow is nothing but that of *susuki* grass.

Etsujin: The great Gods, delete the name of my wife when you go to Izmo.
   (Note) All the gods are said to meet once a year in the province of Izmo to discuss who is to marry whom. In this *haik* Etsujin asks them not to choose a wife for him. Was he a misogymist?

Shunji: The winter rain, a wedding parade, and the bride is under a pine tree.

Shusen: A man in love, I'm worried, so worried as to lift the *kotatsu* warmer.

Ransa: We meet in a dream, but part as the *kotatsu* warmer gets cold.
   (Note) This comes from *waka* poems of Lady Ono-no Komachi:
   - Yearning for my sweetheart, I slept and saw him in a dream at night;
   Had I known I was in a dream, I never would have woken at dawn.
   - A time of joy—I dreamed a dream of seeing my sweetheart;
   Ever since I have counted on such a time of illusion.

Shoho: He would be soaked all alone in love—the turnip picker in a field.
   (Note) This comes from a *waka* of Saigyo's:
   If only I could live far from people, somewhere between rocks;
   If only I would be soaked all alone in love.

Tosho: Good morning good-bye—yet it so hails that I turn back to her.

Shoheki:
   Terrible are the bowl beaters beating bowls when I say good-bye to her.

All Ends Dead That Exists; All's Reborn That Is Gone

—The last verse:

Arakida Moritake: Flowers falling, I'm chanting a holy word at dusk.

—Time goes by quite swiftly.

Sanka: They are busy flowering and falling in the fields—those poppies.

—The last verse:

Genjun in Sakai: All is in vain; there only is a cuckoo calling at dawn.

—Sent a *haik* when Fuhyo in Matsuzaka passed away.

Kakei: It always reminds me of your face—the scent of citrus.

—In memory of my sister Chine;

Kyorai in Kyoto: A firefly's on my palm, yet its light has been dead in vain.
   (Note) Lady Chine's last verse:
      It gleams soon, and goes out soon—a light of a firefly.

—Sent a *haik* to a certain person who lost his little son.

Kakei: Pitiful—so pitiful is a gourd flower falling down fruitless.

—When my wife died young;

Yasui: The paulownia leaf fell early, fell down too early.

—The last verse:

Kosai: Pitiful is my name Kosai on a lantern in Bon Festival.

—Sometime after my son was dead;

Racgo: Little children are dancing; is there anybody like him?

—At a temple in the Ichihara Fields;

Chosetz: Dewy are the fields, splendid are the bones of Lady Komachi.

—In memory of my wife;

Jietz: A *fair lady* in flower; May the villagers take care of her to the other world.

—To console Rika when his wife passed away;

Kyorai: A gust of north wind—you might be sleepless beside the chilly bed.

—When Kosai passed away;

Kikack: An autumn evening—yet now, that snore of his cannot be heard.

—On a child whose mother was dead;

Shohack: An autumn evening—the little child is having supper alone.

—In memory of a certain person;

Basho: A tear drops in the dying charcoal fire, and the fizzling sound of it.
—When a certain person was dead in travel;
Sodan: It goes out before it could come down—a flake of light snow.
Shoshun in Kaga: The winter moon—people are chanting a sutra in Toribeno.

Part VIII Buddhism; Shintoism; Festive Verses

Buddhism

—At Ise;

Basho: The sacred hedge—and it rather surprises me, an image of Nirvana.
(Note) Basho seemed to be surprised when he saw a Buddhist ritual on Nirvana Day in the Shintoist city of Ise. On *A Lonely Journey*, for instance, he was rejected to enter the precincts of Ise Shrine because of his Buddhist-monk-like attire.

Sodan: The image of the Dying Buddha—I take my mother down from my back.

—On the five hundredth anniversary of the great Saigyo's death;

Kakei: Here below the clear morning moon are *sacra* trees in full bloom.

—On the same day;

Kokyu: It withers on the full-moon day—that forsythia flower.

Shoho: The statue of King Nio—hung from his wrist is a bee nest.
(Note) A statue of King Nio is generally set up at the gate of a temple as guardian of Buddhism.

Tokock: The blossoms wet in the rain, a monk is walking in wooden clogs.

Tosho: The temple is alive with flowers; I try striking the bell with my fan.

Kikack: A cup of *sake*, a pinch of salt, and a monk and I drink among blossoms.

—On the first day of Yayoi in the fifth year of Jokyo, in memory of the ancient great monk Jiyea, a large-scale lecture on the Lotus Sutra was given by a prime priest at a temple in the Great Tosho Shrine, an esteemed event in which I heard the essence of the holy sutra.

Etsujin: The flowers are falling, we are talking of the old days.

—In the room there was a lady who, behind the blind, heard the monk lecturing on the Lotus Sutra. She seemed to weep when it came to the episode of Lady Dragon becoming a Buddha.

Etsujin: Down drop her tears one by one like a jewel of the Snake.

Shunji: Beyond Kwannon Temple are *sacra* trees in bloom at the top of a hill.

Issei: A desolate temple, the bell on the ground, and beside it, a violet in flower.

—At the Isle of Yashima;

Senkack in Iyo: Now in flowery Yayoi—a fisherman calls in a mendicant.

Issei: The poor temple—there's a red peony richly in bloom.

Buyo: The summer hill—here and there in leafy shade stand Zen-monks' cots.

—At Nara;

Basho: Little fawn, you are born today, the Holy Buddha's birthday.
(Note) This *haik* was composed on *A Sentimental Journey*.

Shohack: The birthday of the Holy Buddha—people wear clean white clothes.

—At Koya;

Issetz: The cool, holy mountain—courteous but useless is my fan.

Issho: A memorial service, supper with monks—a day like a clear stream.

—On the words of truth in the Lotus Sutra;

Kakei: Truth flows like a clear stream; that is the truth.

—On being a living Buddha;

Gueki: A summer shade—I might be something of a Buddha when I take a nap.

Sodan: The summer clothes—a monk is sewing his torn vesture.

Kakei: Imagine the surprise—when I saw a man carrying a Bon-Feast altar.

Tangan: Bon Festival—pitiful are insects flying into a fire in a lantern.

Bunri: On the shore is a broken Bon-Feast altar caught on the stone hedge.

Kido: Bon Festival—being on a boat, I offer *sake* to the souls of the drowned.

Bokshi: Bon Festival—I'm making my way among wild asters.

Chosetz: The shade of a pine—let us offer passers-by some cups of tea.

—Serving passers-by;

Shunji: People strolling along the street, I offer some of them some cups of tea.

Kakei: A streak of lightning flashes in the fields, I pray to the Great Buddha.

Bokshi: It peeps at a monk saying a requiem—the *basho* tree behind the hedge.

—A certain person said he would eat neither quail nor water rail because he enjoys seeing them in every season. Likewise, I shall quit eating wild goose.

Kakei: I will no longer eat wild goose; not that I'm a man of piety.

—At a *haikai* meeting in a certain temple;

Kikack: Swallow, swallow, turn and beat the drum of this temple.

Issei: The boat in moonlight—a monk is talking, with fun, fun, fun.

Bokshi: He accepts a lump of cotton with his bowl—that mendicant monk.

—It began to rain before I could leave a certain house.

Sodan: Another winter rain—I have another talk, with the coat on.

—At Ankockronji Temple, Kamakura;

Etsujin: Great is the esteemed life of his, and my tears soon to freeze.
(Note) Ankockronji Temple is noted as a temple of the great priest Nichiren (died in1282), who founded Nichiren Buddhism in the Kamakura Period.

—At an old temple;

Kakei: The snow dawn—the monks make the round from hall to hall.

—At an old temple;

Shunji: The heavy snow—against the King Nio's arm leans a broken branch.

Issei: It is left as it is—the snow statue of a Buddha.

Bunjun: Quite irritating are bowl beaters when I'm still in bed at morning.

Kikack: The end of a year, busy days, Monk Sengan's horse, too, would be busy.
(Note) Sengan, a monk in the Heian Period, helped people as a pack-horseman.

On the Seven Benefits from the Lotus Sutra

—Give a fire to a man in chilly air.

Kokyu: The south garden—there blooms a *mei* tree full of whiteness.

—Give clothes to a naked one.

Kokyu: A snow day—a fisherman picks up a cask of *sake* on the shore.

—Give a customer to a merchant.

Kokyu: The rainy season—I call in my fellows to play the dice game.

—Give a mother to a child.

Kokyu: An upright stick of bamboo—onto it creeps a cowpea vine.

—Give a boat to a traveler on a river.

Kokyu: A bright moon night—the neighbor has kindly cut the nettle tree short.

—Give a doctor to a patient.

Kokyu: I felt thirsty—just when I found a fountain in the mountains.

—Give a light to a man in darkness.

Kokyu: An autumn night—someone wakes me up from a nightmare.

Shintoism

Chosetz: An old shrine—meltwater dripping on the statue of a guardian dog.

—Votive verses offered to Tenjin Shrine on the twenty-fifth day of Kisaragi:

Kakei: A *mei* in bloom in moonlight on the twenty-fourth night of Kisaragi.

Kakei:
   Silent is the flare, and *mei* blossoms are waltzing over the sacred bonfire.

Kido: The sacred *mei* tree—warbler, warbler, make your ablutions.

Shoheki: The sacred *mei* tree—May my sleeves touch it not.
(Note) The four *haik* poems above were offered to a Tenjin Shrine in the province of Owari, a shrine where Lord Sugawara-no Michizane, a celebrated scholar in the Heian Period, was deified as god of learning. The twenty-fifth day of Kisaragi is the anniversary of his death. Michizane is also noted as lover of *mei*.

Chosetz: Faint is a light among the *mei* trees—full of blossoms.

Etsujin: The *mei* merely in flower, I'm simply looking up in chilly air.

Shusen: The sacred *mei* trees in bloom, I feel something pious.

Uto: Dewy is the *mei* tree, and I feel chilly in the forehead.

Jugo: The shrine gate being closed, I pray to a *mei* tree by the sacred hedge.

Gensatz: It peeps from behind at people gazing at votive tablets—that *sacra*.

Donka: I've come see *sacra* blossoms, to find fern decorations still in the shrine.

Rito: Visited a shrine, crossed a river, saw *sacra* blossoms.

Koyo: It sits on a leaf in the basin for ablutions—a little frog.

Gensatz: Cuckoo, cuckoo, you have flown through the night-*kagra* dance.

Kido:
   A sacred bonfire—from it the Shinto priest gives a fire to the hunter's torch.

Migack: The purification service—I had a chance to throw away my broken fan.

Kakei: The purification service—I had a chance to cool down an ague on a river.

Shohack: A gust of cold wind—boys are peeping into the portable-shrine house.

Shoho: The great Yebis—are you still around here in this No-God Month?
(Note) Yebis the God is said to have been unable to walk until the age of three.

Racgo: A cold winter day—a Shinto priest is carrying an oil pot.

—A *haik* offered for Wakamiya Shrine

Rijou: The *kagra* music and dances—the songs are unknown yet graceful.

Yasui: The night, the *kagra* music, and in the bed I turn toward the note.

Shoheki: They are crossing the River Suzka at dawn—the *kagra* strollers.

Sonshun: Too bright is the bonfire—especially for the God of Katsuragi.
(Note) The God of Katsuragi was famous for his shyness from ugliness.

Bokshi: The sweeping of soot—there's a duster caught about the bridge pile.

Festive Verses

Tobun: A calm, serene day—how old is that tea-leaf jar?

—In celebration of Kakei turning forty;

Jugo: Many springs have passed, but you look like an evergreen *take* tree.

Etsujin: It is like an ever-bright camellia—His Great Reign.

Sanka: Truly inexhaustible is the green laver on a rocky seashore.

Kido: Old father and mother—May two of you live long.

Kido: The nice scent of new rice—May our country be eternal.

—To a man living in seclusion;

Basho: If winter comes, first think of merry *mei* blossoms.
  (Note) This was to encourage Tokock when he was under confinement.

Addendum (Linked Verse)

—Who cares not for the flower? Who wants to see a morning view in the town? I am living at the foot of Ueno Hills, always thinking of the flower, so much so that I do feel it reasonable that Sagawada Kirock says in his verse he thinks of Mount Yoshino every morning.

Indeed you've eaten much wheat in the field, yet I miss you, wild geese.

This *haik* had been composed by good Yasui in Owari, said my old friend Basho. I made light of it at first; however, when I moved to the countryside, its poetry touched a chord of mine. Once upon a time someone talked about a tiger. Among many listeners, a certain man alone lost color; he had once been chased by a tiger. Truth thus comes out by itself. Remember a line of Du Fu, a man of true poetry: 'The cries of a monkey really make me weep thrice.' Now then, let me make a piece of verse after Yasui's.

Sodo: The wild geese are gone, all the wheat and flowers left behind;

—Kakei, Etsujin and I recited this verse of Poet Sodo's several times.

Yasui: And it makes a farewell—the mirage on the hill.

Kakei: Spring has come, the snow path now a band of mud;

Etsujin: And rather quiet is a rice-sweets vendor;

YS: He takes a rest at a corner stone while the moon rises;

KK: Observing the wind as early-autumn clouds move.

EJ: In the mountains a *samurai* hunter walking around to capture a hawk;

YS: The sign says this way, and he finds a waterfall roaring;

KK: On the lawn sits a monk picking out a sutra from his bag;

EJ: A shower has just run through; he's dripping wet;

YS: Then he goes back to the village to buy a torch;

KK: And North Hill—a *haikai* meeting to be held at a temple;

EJ: Where *old ladies* and single *sacra* still in bloom;

YS: And the evening—the moon is up merely simply.

KK: Life's like a pearl of dew, love's like a muddy intoxication;

EJ: And now in autumn she sighs deep—the wife of a thief;

YS: At dawn the temple bells ring out east and west;

KK: And a boat on the River Tone—it's getting cold.

EJ: A winter day, a sunshiny day, but it darkens all at once;

YS: And I go out for Boar Feast in a formal coat;

KK: It's swinging from my hand—the salted yellowtail I bought last night;

EJ: Such a one might be looked upon as fox mad;

YS: And he walks like a Kashiwagi, getting worse in beriberi; *

KK: And all is heard that they talk in whispers;

EJ: Now watching a *sumo*-wrestling match in moonlight;

YS: And in autumn people make up *sake* casks.

KK: A dewy evening—a fisherman is walking to the river with his cormorants;

EJ: He enjoys secret love, he's Mansack of Fuwa; **

YS: One weeps, the other remonstrates;

KK: He might have touched something like red hot tongs, I daresay;

EJ: That happened when he stood up, saying: let me see, let me see;

YS: He may have found something when they dredged the pond.

KK: The capital city full of blossoms, everything is unsettled;

EJ: Spring is going by, donation is called off;

YS: And hence every new year I do without charities;

KK: Anyway I'm busy drying chopped radish.

(Note)
* Kashiwagi is a character of *The Tale of Genji*.
** Mansack of Fuwa was a brave page and homosexual love to Toyotomi Hidetsugu, a *samurai* commander in the Oda-Toyotomi Period.

(Linked Verse)

Kido: Off the shore people picking clams, a pole put up in the shallow waters;
Kakei: There come no ships in spring, not a single cask of *sake* in the village;
Shoheki: And the calm, serene sound—I enter a lodging earlier;
Yasui: Yet in the room I have to smoke out centipedes;
Shusen: At twilight a white lump of cloud afloat in moonlight;
Chosetz: At cold night I draw nearer my straw raincoat.
Scribe: There rustle blades of silver grass—where am I?
Kido: With another load of old cotton, another horse passes by;
Kakei: On the path stands a Shinto priest, a ritual stick in hand;
Shoheki: For such a job he looks too old;
Chosetz: To do so, to build a warehouse;
Shusen: To make cotton clothes, to pay a visit to the Holy Mount Yudono.
Yasui: Cool is the air; I'm on a mat on the shore of a river;
Kakei: The moon up in the sky; he might be fooled;
Kido: And an autumn wind—there comes a woman cart; but in it, a hairy man;
Chosetz: Dewy are her sleeves; she's visiting Horinji Temple in Saga.
Shoheki: Flowery spring has come; the young are so lovesick as to lose appetite;
Yasui: A double yellow rose, a woman of twenty;
Shusen: The sun has risen, a mild day, and what should I do today?
Kido: And then he readily gives me a pack of soil;
Kakei: He's on a small punt, a distance of a pole;
Shoheki: And the ablutions—I'm watching over their clothes.
Chosetz: He's learned how to dry fish—the nobleman in exile;
Shusen: Singing a song in a low and feeble voice;
Yasui: Got up, ordered an odd thing, slept again;
Kakei: And the servant calls an eggplant vendor passing by the gate.
Kido: Foot Soldier Street, a bushy area, a little away from the main street;
Chosetz: They are followers of the Takata Sect, thoughtful men and women;

Shoheki: Their cups left at hand, the non-drinkers are seeing the moon;
Yasui: Nay, he's just a convalescent this early autumn.
Shusen: The window of a monk dormitory—the swallows are mostly gone;
Kido: And salty is the water—the port of Kominato in Awa;
Kakei: Now in the summer daytime—the mud will be dried soon;
Shoheki: That will be while he repairs a hooped pail;
Chosetz: And he goes seeing blossoms—like a good man—with a dagger on;
Yasui: He eats sardine; he has just quit a vegetarian diet.

(Linked Verse)

Shusen: Sweet is the spring water where mudfish are swimming around;
Shoho: And on the branch of a willow lies a mantis' spawn.
Tobun: The sunset haze—there's a shadow going home, dyed goods in hand;
Kakei: And it looks as if feeling bad in smoke—the hazy moon;
Shoho: Full of shapes and colors, the autumn herbs beautifully in bloom;
Shusen: And the sumo wrestler roughly takes the winner's bow.
Kakei: As usual he goes out to pick things—anything left on the ground?
Tobun: As it happens, he finds a chip of wood on the sandy beach;
Shusen: As a matter of fact, he has been looking for a fire-rat hide; *
Shoho: Smiles in appearance, tears in mind;
Tobun: As a matter of fact, he missed his step, falling from somewhere high;
Kakei: What is more, the meal is taken away in the middle of drinking.
Shoho: A pilgrimage I haven't made for years; that is the great vexation;
Shusen: And an illustrated story—what I see first is the illustration;
Kakei: A woman in love—her face flowery, yet her mind melancholy;
Tobun: And a hazy moon—she must be a Princess Askai; **
Shusen: Then a gust of spring wind—she covers a light with her hand;
Shoho: A rosary in hand, a lump of sorrow on the armrest.
Tobun: A gruff voice—a Ryutatz is singing with false teeth; ***
Kakei: That is a nice but stale song like a *kick* flower on the tenth day; ****
Shoho: And rare is raw sardine at a village in autumn mountains;
Shusen: Today, a somewhat cold day, I buy and bring a chest home;
Kakei: And the shade of the moon—we wade across a stream gallantly;
Tobun: A horse neighs as another passes by.
Shusen: Lonesome is a winter rain at a lodging in Tarui Town;
Shoho: On a straw mat they are threshing buckwheat;
Tobun: And quite disgusting is the gorgeous attire of mine;
Kakei: Now deep at dawn I read out a Deva Sutra;

Shoho: And a poppy petal falls while I'm arranging flowers;

Shusen: And rather noisy is the neighbor grinding *miso* paste.

Kakei: They are in my way, checking firewood at the gate at twilight;

Tobun: Day by day it's getting warmer and warmer;

Shusen: And a spring morning—a little boy is walking on ark-shells;

Shuho: His father has come home to see him, now setting out among flowers;

Tobun: And now in Kisaragi—before light he goes out to buy cotton cloth;

Kakei: The sky's getting white when he's at a house in front of a hill.

(Note)
* A fire-rat hide is mentioned in an episode of *The Tale of Princess Kagouya* (written in the Heian Period) as an imaginary thing. When she is wooed by several court nobles, the Princess asks one of them for a fire-rat hide—which, as a matter of course, he can never find out.
** Princess Askai is the heroin of *The Tale of Sagoromo* (written in the Heian Period).
*** Ryutatz was a song writer in the Ashikaga Period. See one of his works: 'Amusing is a spring rain; let it rain, let it rain softly, for the *sacra* now in bloom.'
**** *Kick*-Flower Day is the ninth of the Ninth Month.

(Linked Verse)

Kakei: Cuckoo, cuckoo, I'm not always waiting for you to call;
Yasui: The rain is beating against the young leaves—shut the door;
YS: The cart is left on the road, is made of hard *biwa* wood;
Kakei: There are fault finders, there are teasers;
KK: And an autumn moon—I set out on a journey as I please;
Yasui: With a load of cloud-ear mushrooms wet with dew.
YS: In the roars of wind are monks of Hatsuse Dormitory;
KK: To them people shout—keep out of the field!
KK: That is where they have composted evening after evening;
YS: And awkwardly, I have lost my seal somewhere;
YS: It was on my way to my love that I ran against an obstacle and away;
KK: That was quite a failed affair when I was young and low.
KK: The pilgrimage—I'm too ready to visit a sacred place in one's place;
YS: All I've got is only a bundle of money and a piece of dried bonito;
YS: And the morning moon—he goes out for his warbler to learn a warble;
KK: Thoughtful to tell us flowers bloom when they do;
KK: And the spring twilight—he eats rice and fresh vegetables;
YS: Lock the door when you peruse a sutra;
YS: He's an ordinary man, a casually clad recluse;
KK: And at evening I give him a busy cup of *sake*.
YS: Here come tributary horses, yesterday from Shinano, today from Kai;
KK: Outside, autumnal stormy weather; inside, an old storyteller;
YS: And happily, the old man is invited to Bon Feast;
KK: It continues until the eighth night's moon has set.
YS: Hazy is the view of firs and pines on the yonder ridge;
KK: And a very heavy tobacco—you might feel dizzy and giddy;
KK: A very hot day—I'm simply thinly clothed;
YS: And you are going upstairs to drum, aren't you?

KK: Being a traveler, he lies down cozily, lazily in a cheap inn;

YS: He's a nice guy, he is wanted to wed their daughter;

YS: Without the knowledge of secret love—say, one or two years;

KK: Hence the annex is built for the newlyweds.

KK: The noble man burns an arithmancy tablet, for it is rather ill-omened;

YS: And his attendants sweep the sandals down to the vale;

YS: To Koshio, to Ohara, to Saga in search of blossom;

Scribe: And people help them cross a spring river.

(Linked Verse)

—As the moon rose up, the heat of the day cooled down. A good evening. We chanted the ancient monk Sokan's poem of 'a nice fan'. Etsujin then composed a *haik* of 'a good summer night'. And with them as the opening and second lines, we made a piece of linked verse.

Yamazaki Sokan: It would make a nice fan if you fixed a handle to the moon;

Etsujin: And without flying mosquitoes, it would be a good summer night.

Sanka: I've stumbled—who placed a *sake* bottle here?

SK: It was unexpected—that sudden gust of wind;

EJ: And against the pillar leans a lady feeling something sad;

EJ: So wait here for a little while, messenger;

Scribe: The fact is, she's hesitating which kitty to choose;

SK: The thing is, he's old enough and fool enough;

SK: Perhaps he's thinking about what the fortuneteller said;

EJ: And her eyes deep wet with tears;

EJ: That is because people speak ill of the Hokke Sect;

SK: And he braids a rope calmly in evening moonlight.

SK: This and that and any others—all the *kaki* fruits are sour;

EJ: And the guest gives a look at the field, now in autumn attire;

EJ: He wishes he would be a hermit someday, I daresay;

SK: Yet his writing is all aslant—did he lie down when he wrote it down?

SK: Being congratulated on his long life, he begins to weep at last;

EJ: A spring wind blowing, his clothes hard starched.

EJ: The low tide—let us go to that small cot on the shore; *

SK: Inside the cot is a dog barking at us;

SK: Drunk deep, I just want a cup of water;

EJ: And it begins to rain simply calmly.

EJ: A *waka* competition—those two monk poets begin arguing;

SK: It goes on as usual; hence the meal will be delayed;

SK: And he spills kerosene from a lamp stand, which he hides behind;

EJ: Then a grasshopper hops out as he lifts the mortar;

EJ: And blades of bristle grass sway and wave as the wind blows;

SK: The autumn garden—the mound is left half broken.

SK: He's looking at the moon quite sullenly, the picture of his father;

EJ: Tut-tut, he never will be a guarantor;

SK: Busy and noisy loading gourds and clothes;

EJ: And in the street some *tatami* mats fall down flat.

SK: Lunchtime, Komoro Town, travelers are walking around;

EJ: Chanting prayers all in chorus;

SK: And flowery spring—Lady Hyakman would go mad; **

EJ: The *tofu* cakes sold out, the blossoms look sad.

(Note)
* This comes from a *waka* of Fujiwara-no Teika:
  Looking around, I find neither *sacra* blossoms nor red maple leaves;
  Only seeing a small cot on the shore at dusk in autumn.
** Lady Hyakman is the heroin of a Noh drama.

(Linked Verse)

—One night at Fukagawa;
Etsujin: It would sound sad and husky if I'm sober—the honks of wild geese; *
Basho: And an autumn moon—I've got used to offering you a drink; *
BS: A lovely *formal-coat* is in flower, yet who loves it so formally?
Etsujin: And it beggars all logic—the beautiful autumn sunset.
EJ: A bottle gourd would sometimes weigh some five barrels; **
Basho: And the merchants go home, blown by the wind;
BS: Chang-an is the city of fame and money in every aspect of life; ***
Etsujin: And hence too many a physician to choose.
Basho: The Busy-Month sky—they are busy going here and there;
Etsujin: That is to seek a successor to a certain temple;
Basho: And he's taken over the name of a village chief, a good old name;
Etsujin: And it rains at dawn—stay with me a little longer.
Basho: The morning good-bye—she looks fair and slender;
Etsujin: She's had a cold, but her voice all the more sweet;
Basho: She feels sick, she does not eat much at lunch;
Etsujin: On the seaway everything smells fishy;
Basho: The moon, the flowers, and in the north, the great summit of Hira;
Etsujin: Skylarks are singing happily, people are clothed thinly.
EJ: Spring is passing by, I'm nailing the broken door;
BS: In the shop there is a lonesome figure grinding wheat;
EJ: And what is left is a mirror wrapped with a silk cloth;
BS: What a shrine maiden foretold, she's deeply thinking about;
EJ: The noble spirit is gone, the seat it sat on is still fragrant;
BS: That would be in a corner in the temple of Hatsuse;
EJ: Cuckoo, cuckoo, the mice are running about;
BS: And dew dripping from a cowpea plant in the hedge.
EJ: A woman is gazing, with a vacant look, at a twilight view;

BS: The tears are in a shroud of the glow of cloud—who's she?

EJ: And the moon going on, yet her mind somewhere beyond;

BS: The distant sound of beating clothes, and he's napping on a horse.

EJ: The lawsuit so drags on, the plowman cannot reap the rice;

BS: And from time to time he comes to ask him what the papers say;

EJ: The house roofed with ponderous tiles, the house of a druggist;

BS: Yet, for all the nice meals, his son is skin and bone.

EJ: A flowery season—they happily go and hear a sermon at a temple;

BS: His breath smells; he eats pond shell.

(Note)
* Please remember that Etsujin was a heavy drinker.
** This comes from an ancient Chinese episode: When a certain one told a bottle gourd weighing five barrels would be useless as a bottle, the wise Zhuang replied that it would then be used as a boat.
*** This comes from a line of Bai Latien: 'Chang-an (a capital city in ancient China) is an old city of fame and money; No gold, no resources, no connections I have.'

(Linked Verse)

—The Old Reverend has come to me, accompanied by good Etsujin.
Kikack: The letter of a wild goose—first take a look at Kakei's;
Etsujin: The three bright-moon nights—there's not a single lump of cloud; *
EJ: Now then, let's put a mat in the garden alive with *kick* and *hagi* flowers;
KK: And a cup of tea in hand has cooled down;
KK: Someone kindly put a summer blanket over me when I was napping;
EJ: He's grinding his teeth, a temple bell ringing out at dawn.
EJ: Her eyes wet with tears—and her resentment;
KK: That is because they force a Lady Shizka to dance; **
KK: And it may frighten you—that vengeful spirit of hers;
EJ: And the disease consumes a good twenty thousand of gold;
EJ: So that he has to part with his beloved son;
KK: And I feel sorry when I see his scar of a burn;
KK: And the odor of *sake*—he whispers in my ear;
EJ: The punt is on a moonlit river; not that he's fishing.
EJ: The autumn sun setting, Mount Fuji is dyed golden yellow;
KK: In the vase there are herbs in flower;
KK: And a little boy pockets a piece of sweet cake happily;
EJ: In this world death is a bad bargain;
EJ: Queen Xi, witty Dongfang Shuo, all passed away; ***
KK: Parrot, parrot, stop talking philosophy.
KK: Awkwardly, the hem of my sleeve is caught at the door;
EJ: Could you please make a chance of love some of these nights?
EJ: A sleepless night, a lovesick night, I lie down awake all night;
KK: That is close to the year-end; I hear someone polishing rice.
KK: There flies a crow at twilight, and rather irritating is this long street;
EJ: He bears a mountain of straw-woven hats, he's a tough carrier;
EJ: On the road there is a boy traveler playing the coin-putting;

KK: And in Ise they display Hina dolls not in spring but in autumn.

KK: The full-moon autumn night—let us see that ever-blooming *sacra;*

EJ: And yet that meticulous monk is like a fickle wind in the fall;

EJ: And a lodging at eventide—I feel bitter again with a paper blanket on;

KK: The window is propped up with a sooty dirty rod;

KK: On the roadside, the sacred hedge of a beggar-like shrine;

EJ: And there—rough pack-horsemen settle a dispute by lot.

EJ: Raw fish, green leek, and the scent of a flower;

EJ: Spring has come to the shore of Yobitsugi; let's spread a straw mat.

(Note)
* On *A Moonlight Journey* Basho and Etsujin stopped at Sarashina to see a bright moon.
** This comes from an episode of Lady Shizka—wife of Minamoto-no Yoshitsune, a *samurai* commander in rebellion—being forced by the Shogun Minamoto-no Yoritomo to dance in public (*The Tale of Yoshitsune*).
*** Queen Xi and Dongfang Shuo are long-lived characters of ancient Chinese tales.

(Linked Verse)

Ransetz: I won't offer you a drink; fresh *sake* would make you sober soon;

Etsujin: Chilly is the autumn night; I prefer a cup of *sake* to a bath.

EJ: A lodging in moonlight—I'm sleeping in a mess of papers;

RS: In the day I walked about to pick medical herbs;

RS: And my horse vies with a herd in a meadow, gamboling;

EJ: Crossing a rill, I hit a path down toward the castle.

EJ: There's a pimply woman with white teeth;

RS: Scatting in a low but clear voice;

RS: Her eyes wet with tears, and in the sky, clouds afloat going apart;

EJ: That fellow is told to remarry, but will not;

EJ: And the morning—he fries some *tofu,* with well-arranged clothes on;

RS: And after fixing a paper lamp, the master-less *samurai* goes home;

RS: He takes off his coat, asking for cloth beating;

EJ: And the moonlit evening—she's going to take the tonsure tomorrow;

EJ: The life of dew—a group of women are weeping in sorrow;

RS: And his heartlessness—the doctor is going back soon.

EJ: The flowers are falling, the sun setting, he's talking on;

EJ: Why is the calling bird called a calling bird?

> (Note) The second half (the remaining eighteen stanzas) of this linked verse is cut from the anthology. It is said that the second half was unsatisfactory to Basho.

(Linked Verse)

Yasui: The first snow of the season—the paulownia has grown high this year;
Racgo: The days getting shorter, I get up earlier these winter days;
RG: In the mountains the cormorants might be looking for fish in a stream;
YS: But you ought to see them fishing from a distance.
YS: Having hustled and jostled, we've got tired of seeing the moon;
RG: Rather showy are the *hagi* flowers in the chest; *
YS: And an autumn rain—people are sent out to a river as porter;
RG: His face gets distorted; a boil or something might be sore;
YS: And yet she has no choice but to hide her lover under the floor;
RG: That was when she was a girl learning the *koto* zither.
YS: Late at night—I drink not hot water, but a cup of water;
RG: And he tickles the roommate monk in slumber;
YS: That is because he has found a nice view of pines about the ridges;
RG: In that way you travel and learn;
YS: Raw or boiled, an egg sells at one coin;
RG: And a hazy moon—all the non-drinkers go out;
YS: The old can hear, can chew, but far from the flower;
RG: Today, the first day of the Ox, lovely little boys are bravely in arms.
RG: The forest revisited, a place where I heard a warbler sing some years ago;
YS: But there is a Shinto ascetic chiding people;
RG: Rattling, rattling, clattering, the wedge-less rice cart is running;
YS: And the lantern light fades away into the darkness of evening.
RG: Her tears, her tangled hair—what has made her so?
YS: And her silence, her distance;
RG: She's been forced to mount on a horse despite her shyness;
YS: And he leads the horse in the street, chewing candy.
RG: The rain is over, and amusing are clouds torn and ripped in the sky;
YS: The road is ready; the willow leaves are likely to fall;

YS: And it cuts off the moon—the eaves of fifty yards long;

RG: Now in lonely autumn—there are man and wife;

YS: They are the envy of us all; they are good fortunetellers;

YS: And tasty is the millet wine of olden.

RG: Every morning he offers dried fish to the sacred shrine;

RG: That is why he is the first to see the trees in bloom;

YS: And the spring rain—I have just come over the Dark Pass;

RG: Then a skylark airily sings you to take a rest.

(Note)
* This comes from an episode of Lord Tachibana-no Tamenaka, a poet in the Heian Period, who brought *hagi* flowers packed in a chest to the capital city from the distant province of Mutz.

(Linked Verse)

Issei: Wonder when a charcoal vendor goes home in winter;
Sodan: The morning—at the end of the conduit, in the jar freezes water;
Kokyu: And people ask him to bring some wood down from a mountain;
Choko: Yet he's drunk, dressing awkwardly;
Sodan: The moon setting shortly, he's walking along the bank;
Issei: And now in the fall they put *funa* carp in bales.
Choko: A distant village—he teaches people how to dance two or three days;
Kokyu: And he's in trouble; the wife of the shrine head falls in love;
Issei: She's weeping for his reply, but that is hard to reply;
Sodan: And she receives a wicker basket, picking a letter out;
Kokyu: Then she boils water, half-awake, half-asleep;
Choko: And a cold night in Koshi—the men clear snow from the roof;
Sodan: They work and they talk and they laugh;
Issei: And when it comes to clamming, the pickers are women;
Choko: Cool moonlight—her kimono is flapping in the sea wind;
Kokyu: And solemn is the sacred shrine of Ki.
Issei: In the flowery shade stands a young man doing the archery;
Sodan: And his smell of garlic—people keep away from him;
Kokyu: Now at dusk in spring he walks and walks at a drowsy pace;
Choko: In the hem of his paper clothes, a lump of cotton;
Sodan: And he washes his hands again and again as he talks;
Issei: Setting up a mosquito net, the size of a room.
Choko: The pine trees being pruned, the garden looks neat and clean;
Kokyu: And the gardeners weigh themselves on the scales merrily, noisily;
Issei: For all his age, he has no marks of moxibustion;
Sodan: And the moon—every night he sleeps sound soon;
Kokyu: On the paper screen, a cool shade of the moon;
Choko: And the *hagi* clover withers as if she had had a hard job.

Sodan: Pitiful is the princess—who has just become a nun; *

Issei: She covers herself with the hood as she hears someone approaching; *

Choko: She won't eat gourd, saying it's poisonous;

Kokyu: Then a gust of wind, then a white shower;

Issei: And the fences have been blown around; in the garden, no space to step;

Sodan: Yet it struts around, the old black rooster.

Choko: A warm, flowery, hazy day—I cannot have the time;

Kokyu: And all over the fields spread azalea blossoms.

(Note)
* This comes from a scene of *The Tale of Sagoromo*, a tale in the Heian Period. I have not read it, unfortunately; the readers are asked to imagine the scene reversely from these stanzas.

Published by Izutsuya Shobei, Kyoto.

HISAGO

A Long and Narrow Road

Basho is noted not only as a *haik* poet, but as a travel writer. You have already read some of them—*A Lonely Journey, A Sentimental Journey, A Moonlight Journey;* and most Japanese, if they were asked to name the greatest work of Basho, would answer it's *A Long and Narrow Road*, a piece of travel to the distant northeastern provinces in the second year of Genrock (1689). Let us see some parts of the *Road:*

Preface:
　Time's like a traveler going from age to age, and so are the years gone and to come. Who makes a living on a boat or who grows old as a pack-horse man does also live a life of travel from day to day. Likewise, many poets of old died on journeys. And some years ago I, too, stirred by the sight of a piece of cloud going with the wind, had an earnest wish to travel afar.
　I wandered about seacoasts in the western provinces, and last autumn returned to my old hut on a river in Edo. And then ended the year. Then came spring. The hazy sky found me longing to travel again—this time eastwards beyond the Barrier of Shirakawa. Under the charm of Far Country, I was now in no mood for anything else. The god of travel was calling me. I mended my torn travel clothes and straw hat, and took care of my knees by moxibustion, before long imagining the moon shining over the sea of Matsushima. I gave up my hut to another and moved to Sampou's villa.

　　Doll Festival has come; it's time to go away from your old grass hut.

Set-Out:
　The twenty-seventh day of Yayoi. I set out on a boat. At dawn the sky was hazy, the pale morning moon fading away, and there faintly appeared the great Mount Fuji. *Sacra* trees in bloom at Ueno and Yanaka—could I see it again? I felt a little lonely. My old friends had come the night before to see me off. We got out of the boat at Senju—ahead lay the road of thousands of miles! We parted. Everyone was in tears—one should wander from illusion to illusion.

　　Spring passing by, the birds crying, and the eyes of fish wet with tears.

In this travel Basho was accompanied by Sora, one of his closest disciples. The two poets headed north.
—At Nikko (Sunlight Shrine);

　　Holy is the sunlight that twinkles through the green and young leaves.

　　The early-summer falls—let's be here for a while like a monk in seclusion.

—Seeing a little girl at Nas;

　　Little Kasane—a pretty name like a name of a lovely double pink. (Sora)

—At Unganji Temple;

The summer grove—you've pecked a hole not in the holy hut, woodpecker.

And they passed the Barrier of Shirakawa into Far Country.

Now in the Far Country—my poetry begins with a song of rice planting.

Asakayama Hill:
We left Tokyu's house. Going northwards some ten miles, we passed Hiwada Town. And a little off from the road there was Asakayama. Nearby there were many marshes. Now in early summer it was a season when people would gather well-known *katsumi* herbs near water. We asked people where the herbs were in flower. Nobody knew, however. We walked from marsh to marsh, from village to village, in search of a lovely *katsumi*—*katsumi*, *katsumi*, where's it?—until the sun getting low in the west.

The Stone Monument 'Tsubo-no Ishibumi':
(Basho was very much impressed when he found a stone monument that had been placed at the ancient city of Taga in the eighth century.) Many brilliant poets have sung of many splendid views since ancient times; however, such mountains shall crumble, such rivers shall shift their flows, such roads shall be renewed, such stones shall be buried in the earth, and such trees shall grow old to be replaced by young ones. Time goes by, the ages change, which makes many such views disappear. But we found it, before our eyes we found the very stone monument of a thousand years before, an unquestionable memento of the men of old. That was indeed the virtue of a journey. The joy of life. Travel is sometimes worth troubling. Our eyes were wet with tears of delight.

Matsushima:
As you all are well aware of it, the sea of Matsushima is the nicest place of scenic beauty in Japan, is so beautiful as Lake Dongting or Lake Xi in China. The sea spreads southeast, and there flows a tide half a dozen miles like the River Zhejiang in China. There are innumerable islets. Peaked ones point skywards, flat ones lie on ripples. They look double, triple, left and right, so that some appear to have some others on the back or in the arms as if holding a baby. And on such islets grow pines green and tender. Their trunks and boughs and branches are twisted and winding, due to high sea-winds, as if they were by nature so. Her lovely, quiet expression, her sweet and graceful looks—the sea of Matsushima must have been created by the Great God of Mountain a long time ago. Who can fully describe this heavenly beauty?

Ojima Island is connected with land by the beach. In it there was an old site of Monk Ungo's hermitage and a sitting stone for Zen meditation. In the shade of pines there seemed to live a recluse at a hut; a breath of smoke was rising from a pile of pine needles and cones—who was he? Feeling somewhat friendly with him, we went to the hut, from which we could see the sea reflect moonlight —the splendid view of nocturnal Matsushima. And we returned to the shore, entering an inn. On its second floor I opened the window and lay down before the great scenery, with a joyful flutter of wonder in mind.

Hiraizmi:
   The glorious days of the Fujiwara are past and gone afar like a dream of old. The ruins of the Great Gate were a couple of miles away; Hidehira's Palace now a rice field. All we could see now was Kinkeizan Hill alone.
   We went up Takadachi Heights, the old site of Yoshitsune's fort, finding the great River Kitakami running from the direction of Nambu. Below us it meets the Koromo, which skirts the hill of Izmi's Castle in the upstream. On the other side of the Koromo is the old site of Yasuhira's Palace, which may have been to defend the country against the North.
   Once upon a time on the Heights those loyal warriors fought bravely to the death, and now the site was covered with green grass. What a great sight! It reminded me of a line of Du Fu: 'The country has perished, but there remain rivers and mountains; Spring has come to the city, and there grow green leaves.' I sat still for a while, with my straw hat off. I felt myself weeping.

   Here grows summer grass, here once dreamt the brave hearts.

―At Chousonji Temple, Hiraizmi;
   It stands still in the tail of the Satsuki rains―the Hall of Light.

Shitomae Barrier:
   Giving a glance at the road northwards toward the distant domain of Nambu, we turned to the southwest and that night stopped at Iwade Village. Then passing Ogrosaki, Mizno-Wojima and Narugo Hot Spring, we reached the Barrier of Shitomae, the gateway to the province of Dewa. The guard gave us a suspicious look; he seemed to rarely have travelers there. It was quite a job to get permission to pass through. Going up the large bordering mountain, we saw the sun set, yet fortunately found a keeper's house and asked for lodging, though we had to stay there three nights as it stormed hard.

   The lice, the fleas―and the horse passes water right by my bed.

Ryushakuji Temple:
   At a hill in the domain of Yamagata there is a temple called Ryushakuji. It was founded by the great priest Jikack, such a calm, peaceful place that we should pay a visit to―thus recommended by people, we set out toward the temple, though that was southbound from Obanazawa. It was a journey of some fourteen miles, and it was before sunset when we found ourselves at the foot of the hill. After reserving a room at a lodge, we went up toward the temple hall on the heights. On the rocky hillside there were old pines and cedars. The earth and rocks were wet and mossy. The monk houses on the rocks were all shut. Not a single sound was heard. We made our way around the cliffs, along the rocks, toward the main hall. We got there. The air was crisp and pure, the view wide and nice, which made me feel refreshed indeed.

   All's still on the hill; into the rocks seep the trills of a cicada.

The River Mogami:
To go down the Mogami, we waited at Oishida for the weather to turn better. In the village there had once lived some *haikai* poets, and the people, old-fashioned though they were, remembered such flowery days, now gone. Without a good master, they were ignorant about modern poetry, and should they follow the new style, or the old? —thus told, I hosted a *haikai* meeting. That was something of a virtue on our travels.

The River Mogami springs from the mountains of Far Country, running through the domain of Yamagata. In the course there are dangerous rapids such as the *Go* Stones and the Falcon. Skirting along the northern side of Mount Itajiki, the river meets the sea at the port of Sakata.

Now all round us were mountains. For us they got a boat ready on the water beyond the grass. It might be a so-called rice boat of old. Going downstream, we saw the White String Falls twinkle through green leaves, and Sen'nin Shrine stand on the shore. The river running high, we felt a fear on the boat.

It runs fast and high—the River Mogami, the mass of a Satsuki rain.

—At Mount Moon;

Mountains of cloud broken away, and there appears a moonlit summit.

—At Sakata Town;

The River Mogami—the red hot sun was put in the sea.

Kisagata:
We had visited a good number of scenic spots—rivers, mountains, land and sea; and now, all we had in mind was the sea of Kisagata. Northwards from the port of Sakata we walked over hills, along seashores, through a number of sand beaches—a journey of some twenty miles. We arrived there. The sun was low in the west, white sand whirled in blasts of sea wind, and a misty rain cut off the great Mount Chokai. We could do nothing in the dark, but the rain was good in a sense. The next day we could see a fine view. Hence at a fisherman's hut we waited for the rain to stop.

And the next morning. Rainy, windy, cloudy, fine. A beautiful day. The young sun rose cheerfully when we got on a boat on the shore of the lagoon. First, we landed on the Isle of Nowin, paying a visit at the site where the ancient monk poet Nowin had lived three years. Then, we got to another island across the water, finding the old *sacra* tree under which the great Saigyo had made a *waka* of 'rowing through the ripples of blossom'. On the shore there was a sacred mound—people called it the tomb of Empress Jingou—and Kammanji Temple. However, I have never heard of the great Empress having come to this place. What makes them say so? Anyway, from the sitting room of the temple I looked out. All the panorama of Kisagata was right before my eyes.

In the southeast Mount Chokai shoulders the heaven, with its shadow falling on to the lagoon. In the southwest, Mouya-Mouya Barrier blocks the way to the north, and in the northeast there is a dike and its causeway extending toward Akita in the distance. In the west lies the sea; the western border of the lagoon, where murmur the waves of the sea, is called Tide Break. In the lagoon there scatter islets over a couple of miles long and wide. The scenery of Kisagata thus looks like that of Matsushima, but there is a difference. Matsushima is merry, Kisagata melancholy. So lonely, so sad, it seems as a fair lady in sorrow.

The sea of Kisagata—that silk flower of Lady Xishi's asleep in the rain.

(The landscape of Kisagata has changed greatly due to an earthquake in 1804: the earth upheaved several feet, which changed the lagoon into land, and many of the islets into mounds and low hills. Thereby you cannot see the view Basho did.)

The Province of Echigo:

Having stayed several days in Sakata, we parted with friends and headed south toward the provinces along the Hokrick Coastal Highway. I had felt depressed before the set-out when I heard it is a good two hundred sixty miles to the city of Kanazawa—how far away! Anyway, passing Nez Barrier, we went through the province of Echigo on to Ichiburi Barrier in Etchu—a nine-day journey, hot and humid days. Feeling bad, I entered nothing in my diary.

Up over the rough sea, up over the Isle of Sado lies the River Heaven.

Ichiburi Town:

The Parent-to-Run, the Child-to-Run, the Dog-to-Back, and the Horse-to-Turn are the most dangerous coastal spots in the north provinces. We had so hard a day getting over the rough beaches that, arriving at an inn in Ichiburi, we went to bed at once. Before long I heard two young women having a talk in another room. There seemed to be an old man with them. According to their talks, the women were courtesans in Nihigata Town, Echigo, and now on their pilgrimage to the sacred Ise Shrine. The old man, who had accompanied them to this town, was going back the next day, so the women were asking him to convey their messages to their hometown. They had lived as harlot—a life of misery, an unknown fate, hard days—how sad, how sorrowful! Hearing the women thus sighing, I fell asleep.

The next morning we were about to set out from the inn when the two women approached us. "We don't know where to head for," they said in tears, "—so uneasy, so anxious, we would like to follow behind you at a little distance. Merciful monk, please let us be with you." For all my sympathy with the ladies, I answered that we had to stop at some spots on our way. "Follow people as they go ahead," I added, "and you will surely safely reach the sacred place under divine protection." Going on my way, I did feel pity for the women of misfortune.

A *hagi* blooms in moonlight, and courtesans too asleep under the same roof.

―At the seashore of Nago;

I go into the sweet scent of early rice; on the right side, the rocky beach.

Kanazawa:
Going over Deutzia Hill, then across Kurikara Vale, we reached the city of Kanazawa on the fifteenth of the Seventh Month. We saw a merchant from Osaka, Kasho. He and we stayed at the same inn.

A man in Kanazawa, Issho was known as a good poet, but last winter died young. In memory of the deceased, his elder brother held a *haikai* meeting― in which I joined.

The tomb be shaken―a whistle of autumn wind, my cry of sorrow.

―On the way;

Unfriendly is the sun glowing, glowing red, and then a gust of autumn wind.

―At Nata Temple;

It's whiter than the white stones of the temple―a gust of autumn wind.

Yamanaka Hot Spring:
Sora had somewhat of a stomach trouble, setting out alone to visit his kinsman at Nagashima Town in Ise, with a piece of *haik* left for me:

A wayfarer, I'd fall down dead somewhere―where *hagi* clovers in flower.

―At the Port of Tsuruga;

Bright is the moon, yet unstable are the skies of the North Country.

Ogaki Town:
Rotsu came to the port of Tsuruga to take me to the province of Mino. I rode on a horse to Ogaki Town, where came Sora from Ise, and Etsujin, too, in a hurry by horse. We got together at Joko's house. Zensenshi, Keico and his son, and many other friends visited me night and day. They looked happy and kind to me as if seeing a man restored to life. And on the sixth of the Ninth Month, though still tired, I set out on a boat for the province of Ise to see the renewal of the Great Shrine.

Now in the fall―we part as though a clam left its shell.

Thus ended the travels, an epoch-making event in his life of poetry. "When the Old Reverend returned from Far Country," wrote Kyorai, "the poetry of our school had already changed greatly."

Hisago

A wandering poet, Basho continued travel. He visited Ise Shrine, then his hometown in Iga.

―At his disciple's house in Ise;

The moon be sad and sweet; let me talk of that good wife of Akechi's.

And in the spring of the third year of Genrock (1690) he stayed in the province of Omi, east of Kyoto, where there were many close disciples of his: Kyoksui, Masahide, Chinseki and Shohack in Zeze Town, Otokuni and Nun Chigetz in Otsu Town, and Monk Senna in Katada Village.

Kyoksui: Suganuma Kyoksui was a senior vassal in the domain of Zeze. He helped Basho financially from time to time, and in the summer of the third year of Genrock (1690) recommended Basho to stay at the Genjou-an to pass the hot season (See *Life at the Genjou-an* in Part VI of *Salmino*). He was a man of bravery and frankness.

Toad, toad, why don't you say what you must say? (Kyoksui)

Calling him the Brave Man, Basho had great trust in the *samurai* poet. Dosui was his younger brother.

Masahide: Mizta Masahide was a physician and merchant in Zeze. He, too, was a financial supporter to Basho, a main contributor in building in Zeze a hermitage for Basho, the Moumyo-an (or the Nameless House). Basho praised him in his letter to Kyorick, saying Masahide was a fearless, daring poet.

Otokuni and Nun Chigetz: Kawai Otokuni was engaged in forwarding business in Otsu, the port town on Lake Biwa. Nun Chigetz was his elder sister, living with him. She was a very kind woman, at times taking care of Basho in his daily life. Their home seemed to be very comfortable for Basho; he made a long stay there several times. See two pieces of conversational verse between Basho and Nun Chigetz:

Basho: It snows softly in Shiga; I would talk of the fair lady, Shosho the Nun;

Chigetz: That is a lovely white sand beach, this is but a tasteless winter gust.

Chigetz: The winter snow—there only is a broom in this old one's house;

Basho: Yet your stove warms the heart of a man in monk attire.

Chinseki (Shado): Hamada Chinseki (later called Shado) was a physician in Zeze. The editor of *Hisago*. The *haik* below was composed by Basho when he stayed at Chinseki's hermitage in Zeze, the Sharack-do.

Lake Biwa—all over the ripples are *sacra* blossoms fallen in breeze.

Spring has come to Omi; and in the beautiful Lake Land, Basho and company make five pieces of linked verse, *Hisago*.

HISAGO

Foreword

A poet in South Lake Land, Chinseki sent me a gourd (*hisago*). It was neither a bottle for *sake* nor a vessel that could sail across the lake. I could hardly hit upon any idea of how to use it. And one day—when I was napping beside it—I fell in it by mistake and woke up to find a world of poetry: the sun, the moon, a bright autumn day, a snow dawn, and a cuckoo in the dark. And there appeared friends of mine. And fine pieces of verse. Where was I? I felt as though being thrown into another world, and since then I have visited there day after day.

Written by Ochi Etsujin in the Sixth Month of the Third Year of Genrock.

Sacra in Full Bloom (Linked Verse)

Basho: Under the tree are bright bits of blossom about the cups and bowls;

Chinseki: The sun a little low in the west, the day's fine and serene;

Kyoksui: And the passing of spring—there's a traveler enjoying a scratch;

BS: Yet he looks rather awkward with a long dagger on;

CS: In moonlight heading toward the Imperial Villa for investiture;

KS: And prompt is the logger when he makes a mortar.

BS: Autumn has come; there stands high a saddled horse of three years old;

CS: And it rains this way and that as the season goes on;

KS: Now at eventide in Suwa there are men and women in a spa;

BS: Among others, outstanding is an ascetic of great height;

CS: He's eloquent, yet rather arbitrary; he's always like that;

KS: And she's all the more in love for a small reason;

BS: Alas, in spite of being lost in thought, she's made to eat things; *

CS: And the moon—her face wet with tears, her sleeves with dew.

KS: Autumn wind, roars of waves, and she's scared of the rocking, rolling ship;

BS: And toward Shiroco and Wakamatz soar wild geese;

CS: In Isshinden a thousand sutras are chanted among blossoms;

KS: And the mirage—there's a pilgrim dead on the road;

BS: Nothing is more pitiful than a butterfly flits, flits, flittering in this world;

CS: Being in deep sorrow, I cannot write even a single letter of love.

KS: In the sun a lady veils her face gracefully with thin silks;

BS: And she sighs sadly—take me to sacred Kumano! **

CS: Yet at the Barrier of Ki stands a stubborn guard with a bow;

KS: He might have a wine-stricken bald red head, I daresay;

BS: And the sun is setting; he has devoted all day to gambling;

CS: At times making a wish to his amulet.

KS: Be on the dirt floor, and you will be free from lice;

BS: Yet mine's a bad name in the whole village;

CS: Yet, for all his poor reputation, he dares to manage a dancing event;

KS: Night after night, bright nights, we dance all night in moonlight.

BS: They wave and wave and in the end wither—those *susuki* flowers;

CS: Nice and dewy is that simple and square hermitage;

KS: Yet the hermit gives back a good pack of money, saying it's troublesome;

BS: He would not, wisely, take any pill of physician's prescription. ***

KS: The flowers now in full bloom; let us run around on Yoshino Mountain;

CS: Yet it might bite you—a gadfly droning in spring mountains.

(Note)
* In the realm of Japanese poetry, 'lost in thought' means 'thinking of a sweetheart' in most cases.
** This lady is said to be wife of Taira-no Koremori, who killed himself in Kumano (*The Tale of the Heike*).
*** Basho is making a joke about Chinseki (physician).

(Linked Verse)

Chinseki: Many a name the spring herbs have, and its complication;
Basho: Being surprised, a butterfly wakes up from a dream;
Rotsu: And a bat is calmly, happily looking outwards;
RT: It was a really narrow pass that I came over;
CS: And the eventide—people put *ciso*-berries in straw bales;
CS: And in moonlight the parent and child dine side by side.
RT: A hue of autumn—the princess looks up gracefully at the moon;
RT: And such a little figure is tickled into a laugh;
CS: Around his neck, a formal coat sweet with a scent;
CS: Humming a merry song on his way home from market;
RT: And the riverside—there's a little shadow of a fisherman;
RT: Chants a prayer, makes a bow to the sacred hedge.
CS: The end of a year—the medicine has not sold well;
CS: And it scares me—a howling dog in Shino;
RT: And there's a little boy travelling with his nanny;
RT: The flower is red, boy, and hazy is the moon;
CS: And serenity creeps up to the tide right below the verandah;
CS: And spring sees the sea alive with a romping shoal of seabream.
Kakei: Indeed this is a large village, but there is not a single doctor; *
Etsujin: Use an abacus, and you will be called a wise man;
KK: And in this monotonous world have I lived without boring;
EJ: Then he makes another burst of tears just before he could sober up.
KK: The sun is setting; an autumnal red spreads as far as I can see;
EJ: The flank of a hill is covered with *soba* flowers in pure white;
KK: And the moonlight—in the village there's a sound of kneading noodle;
EJ: And all the little boys have got plums in hand, all undressed;
KK: Let's take a rest, let's see cocoons being boiled;
EJ: Manjushree's wisdom, Cudpanthaka's grumbles; **

KK: As it happens, the *miso* paste is very well made;

EJ: As it happens, the hanging shelf drops by itself.

KK: The girl giggles when she meets her sweetheart secretly at night;

KK: And he says good-bye without seeing her face;

EJ: Left behind is his kimono with a faint scent of sweat;

EJ: It rains, it rains, it's a heavy rain;

KK: And a flowery day—we must prepare dishes for a hundred guests;

KK: Now in spring a traveler can travel easy.

(Note)
* The first-half of this linked verse was made by Basho, Chinseki and Rotsu in Zeze; and the second-half, by Etsujin and Kakei in Nagoya.
** Both Manjushree and Cudpanthaka were disciples of Buddha's. The former was a wise man; the latter was dull but endeavored very hard to become a great ascetic.

At the Castle Town of Zeze (Linked Verse)

Yakei: A cloudy early-summer day—there sounds a distant crack of a musket;
Rito: And in the lean, sandy field scatter stalks of wheat.
Deido: Let the west wind blow, let us gather little red shells;
Otokuni: Yet I'm hesitant to ask for a single cup of water;
Dosui: And on and on runs a row over the *go* game into dawn;
Chinseki: Then comes the watch—what are you doing late at autumn night?
Scribe: It might be dreaming a bad dream—a *fair lady* alone in flower;
Yakei: Her wet and heavy eyes, her worried looks;
Rito: Today and always—all he keeps in mind is the theater;
Deido: You may say he has a natural-born funny face, may you not?
Otokuni: Yet he's an enviably nice figure—that Shinto priest on a horse;
Dosui: And the whole village weed the sacred woods;
Deido: So they know where I am; I must leave this old rock; *
Rito: The winter rain, a weepy rain, and the world goes on;
Yakei: And she looks chilly on a sled—a courtesan in North Country;
Otokuni: With a hundred coins in a string at hand.
Chinseki: The moon, the blossoms—let's get the village chief to pay all;
Dosui: And yet rather salty is the simmered bracken;
Rito: Spring to come; unforgettable are beautiful days in Kyoto;
Chinseki: And out cries a bonze half-crazy;
Otokuni: That is a usual fuss at the tavern, where there are usual drunkards;
Yakei: And in Kamakura there are good old gamblers;
Dosui: From time to time there comes a plowman, too, in full attire;
Deido: That is to cook clam for a nobleman in exile;
Chinseki: And the eventide—the sea ghosts are sadly singing;
Rito: The fact is, every mate and attendant is a hairless man.
Yakei: The Taikoji Road—gusts, blasts, wild winds;
Otokuni: And an itchy stomach—where's a men's room?

Deido: On a small mat, with a hard-starched night blanket on;

Dosui: Sniffing out some food in evening moonlight.

Rito: She gives a cough when she reads a sutra;

Chinseki: Around forty, the age of mature beauty;

Otokuni: A shock of hair, a mark of the pillow—she turns around;

Yakei: Deep drunk, he opens the sliding door a little to enjoy a cool breeze.

Dosui: A sign of rain—the cedar forest alive with young leaves and blossoms;

Deido: And some seedlings are left at the edge of a rice paddy.

(Note)
* This probably comes from a *waka* of Saigyo's:
  If only I could live far from people, somewhere between rocks;
  If only I would be soaked all alone in love.

Things Various (Linked Verse)

Otokuni: The *suppon* tortoise, simmered in the pan, neither chirps nor chants;
Chinseki: And the wind whistles around the lumps of fuel.
Rito: Winter comes when people have reaped the cotton;
Tanshi: Let's sing in chorus, let's rotate the millstone with ropes;
Shobo: And in the broad room sleeps a traveler alone; outside, the moon;
Masahide: Into the candle light flies a mantis, then nothing but darkness.
Kyuken: Autumn *hagi* bloom in front of the lord, and a flock of monk servants;
Yakei: Calm and serene is water warming in the kettle;
Nisho: And a green warbler begins to give a chilly note;
Otokuni: The *kamasugo* in season—its fish dust is as white as snow.
Chinseki: Flowers begin opening, Hina Festival to come, casks of *sake* ready;
Rito: And in the depth of the heart there is love;
Tanshi: That is a flutist in disorder, is sweet incense from behind the blind;
Shobo: Talked in sleep, woke up, heard a rooster crow at dawn;
Masahide: And he goes out under the moon, a purse in his hand;
Kyuken: Tonight, a chilly night, Kamikyo Downtown can still be seen;
Yakei: And the street in Toba Town—on a bowl, a pile of fresh rice;
Nisho: In the cage of a peddler murmur sparrows.
Otokuni: A gloomy, cloudy day, not frosty, yet chilly;
Chinseki: And yet the lady's too shy to ask aloud for alms;
Rito: It is a grief to her—the gray-dyed cotton vesture;
Tanshi: Nothing given, she stands still at cold daybreak;
Shobo: And the dawn—in the dark she stokes up a fire under the kettle;
Masahide: In front of the shop someone's calling a horseman;
Kyuken: One with a spear in high spirits, the other with a box of carriage;
Yakei: An autumn day—a carp-monger is changing the water;
Nisho: And a soft touch of breeze—the tassels of a lantern are dancing;
Otokuni: The request of donation, the mention of a hazy moon.

Chinseki: What is most pleasing is, food has savor and flavor;
Rito: You sweep out the soot, I move to the next room;
Tanshi: And she pretends to be in tears—the girl in waiting;
Shobo: Yet he's a man far from romance—the country *samurai;*
Masahide: And he gets ready quickly, a twisted hand towel on his hips;
Kyuken: And ropes are collected to set up the roof of a temple.
Yakei: A flowery day—we are all in good attire waiting for a party to begin;
Nisho: And in spring breeze a lion-dancer is dancing crazily.

A Country View (Linked Verse)

Masahide: On a path along a spring paddy stands a talismanic pole;
Chinseki: At dawn the faces of wild rats would turn all pale;
CS: And a spring sky—a flock of ravens caw, croak, cry;
MH: The gate of a bijou villa—there's a sign or something;
MH: This is a Rikyu-style house—boasts the owner in moonlight;
CS: And yet he gives me sweet potatoes from time to time.
MH: Sew it, sew it—chirps every cricket;
CS: And everyone looks for his other shoe—where's it? where's it?
MH: And a hundred vows are given when he leaves her house;
CS: The *samurai* attendant's eyes a little wet with tears;
MH: In Suma the kitchen is ill-equipped indeed;
CS: So will you go and borrow a bow to drive foxes away?
MH: The River Heaven—the moon is frozen up in the winter sky;
CS: I have no appetite, though the meal is ready;
MH: So I give you my long dagger; now it's useless for me;
CS: My only child has grown away; I'm living with a bantam.
MH: I always care for good *sake* from Edo when flowers begin to open;
MH: And the spring twilight—let me play a tune of music;
CS: In the village sings a skylark sky high; on the ground, lumps of dung;
MH: And he's fanning a fire—an old man in monk attire;
CS: The main temple still unfinished, with walls and pillars alone set up;
MH: And she's in tears—a lady in soft silks;
CS: That is a sketch of a woman with a bad toothache;
MH: Lean blades of *susuki* grass sag down, covered with light snow.
CS: A sad and sweet night—at the wisteria window, a paper lamp;
MH: And he makes a speech of farewell that never ends;
CS: Then he counts gold coins with care—the *samurai* in good attire;
MH: And the fall has come to Kumamoto in the province of Higo.

CS: The traveling troupe would always see the moon on a boat;

MH: Chilly is the night; all I have at hand is a cotton blanket;

CS: And I'm always chided badly—bald head, bald head;

MH: And my cat has gone somewhere; where are you, kitten?

CS: The rain is over; in Attendant Street calls a cuckoo;

MH: And the maple trees are beginning to bud.

CS: The blossoms are falling, and the sound of clogs;

MH: And there shimmers a mirage over the riding ground in Kitano.

Published by Izutsuya Shobei.

SALMINO

Happy Days

The Satsuki rain—let us go see a nest of a grebe afloat in the lake.

From the third to the fourth year of Genrock (1690-91), Basho moved from place to place in pursuit of poetry.
- Stayed at the Genjou-an in the outskirts of Zeze Town in the early summer of the third year of Genrock (1690).
- Stayed at Boncho's house in Kyoto in late summer, enjoyed a cool breeze on the River Kamo, and made a linked verse together with Boncho and Kyorai at the Rakshi-sha in Saga, Kyoto.
- Held a moon-viewing party in celebration of the publishing of *Hisago* at the Moumyo-an in Zeze in mid-autumn.
- Visited Senna in Katada Village, Omi, in late autumn.
- Saw the old year out and the New Year in at Otokuni's house in Otsu Town.
- Held a *haikai* party to cheer Otokuni, who was leaving for Edo on business, in the beginning of the fourth year of Genrock (1691).
- Stayed at his hometown in Iga in spring.
- Stayed at the Rakshi-sha in early summer.
- Held a moon-viewing party at the Moumyo-an in mid-autumn.
- Left Zeze for Edo in late autumn.

Saga Diary

As mentioned above, Basho stayed at the Rakshi-sha in the early summer of the fourth year of Genrock (1691). It was Kyorai's cottage in Saga, northwest of Downtown Kyoto, a place where runs gracefully the River Owi, where there are pine-covered hills, green *take* groves, bijou villas and temples—beautiful scenery that ancient nobles had loved. At the Rakshi-sha he helped Kyorai and Boncho compile a new *haik* anthology *Salmino*, and kept a diary today called *Saga Diary*. Let's glance through it.

> The eighteenth of the Fourth Month of the fourth year of Genrock—After paying a visit at some of the scenic spots in Saga, I came to Kyorai's cottage the Rakshi-sha, accompanied by Boncho, who returned to town shortly before sunset. For me to stay here several days, Kyorai had had some of the paper screens repaired, the garden weeded and the bed arranged in the corner of a room. I put in the room a small desk, writing tools, and some books—*Bai Latien's Collection, One Hundred Poets' One Hundred Chinese Poems, The Tale of Flowering Fortunes, The Tale of Genji, Tosa Diary* and *Shoyo Waka Collection*. There was a five-tiered lacquerware decorated with a Chinese landscape; in it, a variety of confectionery; and beside it, a cup and a bottle of good *sake*. Also, my friends had brought here bedding and food enough for me. I could forget a life of poverty for a while; and for a while I would enjoy a time of calmness.

The nineteenth day—Visited Rinsenji Temple in the afternoon. In front of it runs the River Owi; across the river, on the right side lies Arashiyama Hill, its ridgeline going down on to Matsuo Village. There were many people heading toward Honrinji Temple.
(...) The sun being low in the west, I returned to the Rakshi-sha, where Boncho had come from town. Kyorai returned to town. I went to bed in the evening.

The twentieth day—Nun Ukoh came to see a festival to be held in North Saga. Kyorai too came. On his way from town he made a *haik*:

   They are tackling, grappling in the field—those wheat-tall boys.

Although the Rakshi-sha is in part left damaged and unimproved, yet such a house is in a sense more tasteful than what is newly built. The engraved crossbeams and the painted walls have been worn by wind and rain. The garden stones and pines hide themselves in thriving weeds. Yet in front of the bamboo verandah blooms a citrus tree fragrantly.
(...) Received some food and confectionery from the wife of Kyorai's elder brother.
 Ukoh and her husband Boncho stayed here over night. We, five in number, lay down sleepless under a mosquito net, then rose up at midnight and had a chat over *sake* and sweets until nearly dawn. We remembered that, last summer, the four people from the four provinces had slept in a mosquito net in Boncho's house, then someone saying those four men would dream four kinds of dream. We laughed. The next day Ukoh and Boncho returned to town. Kyorai remained.

The twenty-second day—It rained in the morning. No one visited all day. Feeling a little lonely, I put down in an idle manner a word of the wise Zhuang: 'one's in sorrow in mourning, with delight with a cup of *sake*.' Similarly, the great Saigyo may have been in solitude when he made a *waka* of 'one would live in melancholy were it not for a feeling of solitude.' And another *waka* of his:

   Lonesome bird, who do you call in the village?
   Don't you know I want to live alone?

I do like living alone. The *waka* poet Chosho-shi once said, "The host would lose calmness half a day when the guest enjoys calmness half a day." This word Sodo likes very much. Likewise, I once composed the *haik* below when I stayed alone at a certain temple.

   Lonesome bird, let the man in melancholy be more sad and sweet.

Received a letter from Kyorai. To it many letters were attached. They were from my friends and disciples in Edo, were brought by Otokuni, who just returned from the city. In them there was a letter from Kyoksui. It said he had seen Soha when he dropped in my old hermitage the Basho-an.

The twenty-fifth day—Senna returned to Otsu. Fumikuni and Joso came. (...) Otokuni came and we had a talk about Edo. He then showed me a piece of linked verse composed with Kikack in Edo.

The twenty-seventh day—Here came no one; I enjoyed solitude all day.

The twenty-eighth day—Dreamed of Tokock. Woke up at night, my face wet with tears.
When coming across a spirit, one dreams a dream. When darkness wanes, one dreams of fire. When light declines, one dreams of water. When a bird pecks one's hair, one dreams of flying. And when one sleeps with a belt on, one dreams of a snake. *The Sleepers' Stories*, *The Land of Dreams*, and *The Tale of a Dreaming Butterfly*—all these are reasonable stories, far from mystery. My dream, however, was not of the wise, but a sort of day dream or merely a wild fancy or just a dream. What I dreamed was a so-called dream of wishes. My friend Tokock—he had once come to my hometown in Iga, and we lived together, traveled together during the journey of a hundred days. He was just like a shadow of mine. Sometimes a joking guy, sometimes a man in melancholy. His nice wits did deeply impress me; the unforgettable one he was. And now, I found myself weeping again.

The second day of Satsuki—Here came Sora, who had been to Yoshino to see *sacra* blossoms, thence to Kumano to pay a visit to the sacred shrines. We talked about friends and disciples in Edo.
(...) In the afternoon we went up the River Owi on a punt along the foot of Arashiyama Hill to Tonase. It began to rain. At dusk we returned to the Rakshi-sha.

The third day—It continued raining all day, all night. We too continued talking about this and that until the next day broke.

The fourth day—Lay down all day. Dead tired from the overnight talk. It stopped raining around noon. I am going to leave the Rakshi-sha tomorrow; I looked around the house for my memory.

Salmino

Salmino is the most celebrated anthology of the Basho School. Kyorick called it the *Kokin-shu* of *haik* poetry. It is also an anthology that, unlike the preceding ones, Basho himself directed compilation. The selected works were examined, approved, and if necessary, amended by Basho, and Basho himself offered brilliant pieces of verse he had composed since the journey of *A Long and Narrow Road*. The editors are Kyorai and Boncho.

Kyorai: Mukai Kyorai was born in the city of Nagasaki as a son of a Confucian physician, and lived in Kyoto. Chine was his younger sister, but died young in the first year of Genrock (1688). A man of great learning, Kyorai was one of the disciples who very well appreciated the new style of Basho. And he was a critic rather than a poet, so keen a critic that he was called the Director General of *Haik* Poetry in the Western Provinces. After the death of his great master, he wrote *Kyorai's Notes*—a *haik* commentary that includes interesting episodes of Basho and his followers. See one of the episodes:

When a beginner of *haik* poetry, I (Kyorai) asked the Old Reverend how to compose a *haik*.

The Old Reverend replied: "Make a vivid and clear one."

Then I showed him a *haik* of mine:

> A cool-evening party—I had to go home because of stomachache.

"This is not that," said the Old Reverend with a burst of laughter.

And one more episode:

> The edge of a rock—here sits alone another guest of the moon. (Kyorai)

Kyorai: "Shado (Chinseki) told a 'monkey of the moon' would be good, though I myself think a 'guest' is better. What do you think about that, sir?"

The Old Reverend: "Monkey? It makes no sense. What scene did you imagine?"

Kyorai: "When strolling on a bright-moon night, I find another moon viewer at the edge of a rock; that is what I imagined."

The Old Reverend: "Think that you yourself are the 'guest'; that would make this verse more poetic. You should imagine like that."

Boncho: Nozawa Boncho called himself Kasei at first, then Boncho. Nun Ukoh (formerly Tome) was his wife. He was a gifted poet of vivid and clear taste, was also a man of self-confidence.

> The last day of a year—that is the very enemy in my life.

According to *Kyorai's Notes*, this *haik* was originally an unfinished work of Kyorai's, was completed by Boncho by adding the word 'the last day of a year'.

"Verily, verily," said Basho, laughing heartily. "The last day of a year (In those days the last day of a year was the date of repayment) is the enemy of a thousand years. A wonderful job Boncho has done."

Joso: Let me introduce to you another disciple, Joso. Once a *samurai* in the domain of Inuyama, Naito Joso became a monk and lived in Omi. He often stayed with Basho at the Moumyo-an in Zeze. A faithful follower of Basho. A poet of sad and sweet taste. Basho highly valued his talent.

Salmino consists of a fine selection of four-season *haik* poetry, four pieces of linked verse, and Basho's essay *Life at the Genjou-an* plus dozens of *haik* poems on it. Basho was particular about *haik* prose as well as poetry. By adding the essay to the anthology, he may have intended to make a joint work of prose and poetry. See his comment on prose (*Kyorai's Notes*):

> The works of *haik* prose nowadays are tasteless indeed. Some are bad translations of Chinese prose, some are unrefined compounds of Japanese and Chinese. Some stick to trifles in describing sentiments; Saikack (author of *Five Women Who Loved Love* and others) in particular is a writer of vulgarity. You should therefore describe things smoothly in a refined manner in harmony with Chinese words, with a clear motif in mind.

SALMINO

Foreword

Making an anthology of *haikai* poetry would provide an opportunity of showing the flag of our school among ancient and modern poets. The expression is all, and a lack of esprit would make verse look vague like a dream in a dream. The changing will remain unchanged, and such a poem alone would be sung forever. You should keep such an idea deep in mind, not to mention the five Confucian virtues.

Long, long ago the great Saigyo tried forming a skull and bones into the shape of a man, only to find it whistle tunelessly like a broken flute. He may have failed to inspire a soul into it. The bones of a man-like shape were unable to utter a cry of five vowels A-E-I-O-U. How sweet could it have sounded had a soul got well in it?

And now, our Old Reverend put such a soul into *haik* poetry. That happened when he passed through mountains toward Iga; he then threw esprit into poetry by imagining a monkey in a little straw raincoat. That did greatly move us all at once. Amazing is his power of expression. With such a *haik* as a starter, the anthology *Salmino*, or *A Monkey's Straw Raincoat*, was compiled. And at the request of Kyorai and Boncho, I have written this foreword with such an idea in mind.

Written by Kikack in late Satsuki, the fourth year of Genrock.

Part I Winter

Basho:
:   The first winter rain—the monkey too might want a little straw raincoat.
    (Note) This *haik* was composed on his way to Iga after the travels of *A Long and Narrow Road*, with a preface as follows:
    :   Hot summer was past, and sad and sweet autumn, and now I'm staying at a hut in early-winter mountains.

Kikack: A chilly rainy night, a peal of a temple bell—let us hear, let us hear.

Senna: Here comes a winter rain, and a broken line of fishing boats.

Monk Joso: The winter rain, Seta Bridge, and through it run some people.

Masahide in Zeze: The winter rain—a spearman in high spirits, a spear in hand.

Fumikuni: Alone in Hirosawa Pond swims a goose—wet with the winter rain.

Shohack: A boatman gets me to get into his boat, and then comes a winter rain.

—At the border of Iga;

Sora: The road to Nara—it rains, it rains, it makes me feel at home.

Boncho: The winter rain, a pile of firewood, and above it, a light at the window.

Otokuni in Otsu: The winter rain—I go on horseback through Takeda Village.

Nun Ukoh: A chilly rainy wintry night—I've been taken in by the stars bright.

Shobo in Zeze: The winter rain—a heap of husks smoking in the new rice field.

Kyorai: Off shore are busy ships in the winter rain; some in full sail, some half.
:   *Kyorai's Note:*
    :   "*Salmino* is the first anthology of the new style," said I (Kyorai). "The winter rain is its main theme, but this *haik* is a failure. It should have been composed like this: 'The morning moon—off shore are ships in half sail in the winter rain.' Had it thus been made, it might have included a 'busy' atmosphere and a 'full-sail' image, might have been a smooth and simple poem."
    :   The Old Reverend: "The original *haik* is well made, too, although the revised one seems far better."

Hyaksai in Iga: The first frost of the season—I'm walking toward the Polar Star.

Yasui: A frosty night—there's not a whit of hue alive.

—On the River Yodo;

Kikack: The first frost of the season—how have they slept in the chilly boat?

Kikack:
: Let us lay a straw mat in the garden; some flowers bloom unseasonably.

Boncho: An early-winter day—dead pine needles are fallen in the Zen garden.

Ranran: The early-winter field—there's a shrike shrieking on a log.

Basho: A blast of winter wind—his cheek swollen, his face distorted with pain.

Boncho: A fisherman's hut, a winter tree, and protections against a sandy wind.

—At Nara;

Doho in Iga: A winter day—the deer herd and sleep in the withered fields.

Kyodo in Zeze: Ten Holy Nights—I give a look at sour *kaki* fruits, walking by.

Etsujin: The tea blooms in pure white; Nun the Pure is far from being wooed.
: (Note) Nun the Pure is a character of an ancient Chinese tale, a woman of great filial piety.

Ensui : The tea tree blooms, I break off its branch together with a bagworm.

Boncho: Winter coming, green bamboo protections are set around an old temple.

—Hearing the Old Reverend stays in Katada;

Kikack: Let winter go by; your village is famous for porridge.

Sharai in Iga: Chilly is the air; nevertheless, the peonies are all bare.

—At Kusatz;

Shohack: The end of the No-God Month—let's eat that pig cake of Old Aunt's.

Chinseki:
: The Gods are back, the tinkling of horse bells coming from Minakuchi.

—At morning on the first day of the Frost Month;

Ryobon in Iga: A bowl of red rice—that is all I have on the table.

Fugyok in Sakata: It's grown with the water of No-Water Month—that daffodil.

Tanko in Owari: What is meek and weak—thou art the bee in winter.

Kyorai: The sea cucumber—where's your head? Which is your tail?
: (Note) This is a famous *haik* of Kyorai's, although you may not understand it without seeing a sea cucumber.

Tangan in Iga: They are getting colder night by night—those aired greens.

Shohack: It looks rather chilly on the roadside—the shrine gate of Taga.

Kiwo in Edo: A cold winter day—I begin practicing the art of tea as usual.

Boncho: A cold day—in front of the charcoal furnace is a wild boar fallen flat.

Basho: A winter day—there is a foot warmer, there is a mind of vagrancy.
: (Note) This *haik* is written in Basho's letter to Kyoksui with a preface as follows:

Though they tell him to go out, yet he continues to eat, feeling lonely and awkward ('he' seems to be Rotsu).
Also see a *waka* of Monk Jien, a poet in the Kamakura Period:
Just as one dreams a dream when he's dreaming,
So I travel while traveling this fleeting world.

Kikack: It is until the foot-warmer cover gets cold that I can sleep sound.

Boncho: A winter solstice—they enjoy pastime, a small shop beside the temple.

Kekyo in Owari: It looks rather dull and drowsy—an owl sitting in the daytime.

Hanzan in Iga: It's been shot and had a fall—the owl in its sleep.

—On friendship;

Joso: Exchanging some patches of paper cloth—that is our friendship.

Sora: It's broken up by a blast of sea wind—a swirling circle of plovers.

Kyorai: The rough seashore—the plovers are running rather smoothly.

Fumikuni: They might be treading off tracks of a wolf—those sea plovers.

Joso: They run, they step, they flock—the sea plovers in the back beach.

Senna: You're flying and crying in snow; how long do you go on, sea plover?

Boncho: It might be astray, crying—a lone plover flying in the Yata Fields.

Boksetz: A rapid stream—the raft man looks back at a pair of mandarin ducks.

Joso: It might have seen the river bottom—that little wild duck of a civil face.

Rotsu: Lake Yogo—birds, birds, are you sound asleep?
(Note) This *haik* was praised by Basho as 'subtle and sweet' (*Kyorai's Notes*).

Tanko: It will live in pride until its death—the hawk with sharp eyes.

Sampou: The winter moon—I have my head buried in the muffler.

Kikack: The wintry moon—the wooden gate is locked with the bolt.

Kyorai's Notes:

When *Salmino* was being compiled, Kikack sent us this *haik* with a comment that he had wondered if this should be the 'wintry moon' or the 'frosty moon'. Besides, the 'wooden gate' was read by mistake as the 'brushwood gate'. The Old Reverend told us either was good, so we chose the 'wintry moon'.

Afterwards the Old Reverend sent a letter to Boncho and me. "That is the 'wooden gate'," it said. "Even one word is critical in such a good verse. That should be amended even if the anthology be ready to be published."

Boncho: "I don't think there's a difference between the 'brushwood gate' and the 'wooden gate'."

Kyorari: "The 'brushwood gate' in moonlight, I think, is rather commonplace. Imagine a moonlit wooden gate of a castle. It would create a very tense atmosphere. It thereby was reasonable that Kikack wondered if this should be the 'wintry moon' or the 'frosty moon'."

Bonen in Nagasaki: Travel in winter—on a light-weight horse, a cushion alone.

Nun Chigetz: It's a fairly chilly sight—a traveler walking toward Mount Ishibe.
  (Note) The 'traveler' is said to be Rotsu.

—The Old Reverend gave me a blanket he used on his journey to Far Country. The details are omitted.

Chikco in Mino: I shall see the first snow of the season—with this blanket on.
  The 'details': When Basho staying at Joko's house in Ogaki after the travels of *A Long and Narrow Road*, Chikco, a blacksmith in Ogaki, massaged the great master; in return, Basho gave him the paper blanket he used during the long journey.

—On Chikco's blanket;

Sora: Note that it is the paper blanket I used to fold up during the journey.

Tangan: Fish swim below the ice, and on the ice is a cormorant in its chagrin.

Joso: Without a rosary, and in silence, the fisher watching the wickerwork trap.

—At the white-sand space in the Imperial Palace;

Fumikuni: I sit stiff at the entrance, the knee mat dotted with hailstones.
  (Note) Fumikuni was a *samurai* officer at Security Authorities in Kyoto.

Yado: It hails and blows furiously; the hemp palms are dancing crazily.

Jiho in Iga: They might fall from Magpie's Heavenly Bridge—the hailstones.
  (Note) The magpie is said to bridge the River Heaven on a Tanabata night for the lover stars to meet once a year.

Boncho: He disappeared before I could call back—the fish vendor in the hail.

Gako in Zeze: Let it sleet, let it sound high until breakfast is ready.

Kikack: The first snowfall of the season—who will be staying at home?

Fumikuni: The first snowfall—I take a look at the falcon house at dawn.

Nun Ukoh: The snow play—I give a blow to the hands of a little girl.

Tangan: The snow play—I've found bits of rouge in white.

Boncho: Shimokyo Downtown—now in the night it is raining over the snow.
  Kyorai's Notes:
  When this *haik* was still half-finished, the Old Reverend mentioned the word 'Shimokyo Downtown' after we made some failed suggestions. "Ah," said Boncho, but seemed unwilling to agree with that. "Boncho," said the Old Reverend, "you should have this word in this *haik;* if there's a better one, I would quit a poet."

Boncho: It's a fairly long flow—a single streak of a river in the fields of snow.

—Passing through the province of Shinano;

Basho: White patches of snow—some blades of silver grass left uncut for rites.

—Visiting a certain hermitage when the hermit is absent;

Kikack: The snow-covered hermitage of an old man—even the blind left closed.

Uritz in Owari: A snowy day—nothing is more useful than the bamboo hat.

Ushichi in Nagasaki: All would set out in the snow were they sound and healthy.

Kyorai: In the heavy snowfall I do start on a journey—with a short coat on.

—In lamentation of Seiya;

Shohack: My friend has passed away, his son still a baby, and the end of a year.

Basho:
    Dried salmon, lean Kouya monks—all will be gone when the cold is gone.
Doho's Notes:
    "In making this *haik*," said the Old Reverend, "I took great pains several days to express the state of mind in cold winter days."

Otokuni: The bowl beaters—the beat sounds pious, the faces look coarse.

Joso: Bowl beater, keep me a one-month portion of rice, will you not?

—A *haik* offered for Sumiyoshi Shrine:

Kikack: Night *kagra* dances—the dancers give out white breath in their masks.

Juntack in Iga: Here come beggar dancers; not that I have a special wish.

Youho: People sweep soot from their houses, dirty and sooty from top to toe.

—At Otokuni's new house;

Basho: Let one buy a house, let a year go by, and let me have an easy day.

Kikack: Beggar, beggar, pass by my house; I have no rice cakes now.

Chowa: New Year's Eve—how is grandfather? —just napping.

Kyorai: The thin walls of my house, and through it passes the year.

Kyorai:
    The year passing by, they will be busy at the shrines in Ise and Kumano.

Nun Ukoh: The last day of a year, a nervous day, everyone has no way out.

Kikack: The end of a year—all is given or done except a thin straw mat.

Rotsu: They tell me to go out, and again, go out, and the end of a year.

Sampou: The end of a year—there is good many a torn garment.

Part II Summer

Kikack: Cuckoo, cuckoo, you are singing in honor of the morning moon.
   (Note) This comes from a waka of *One Hundred Poets' One Hundred Poems*:
     Cuckoo, cuckoo, I'm looking up at where you sang;
     Only to find the morning moon fading in the sky.

Boksetz: Cuckoo, cuckoo, I've lost sight of you in a summer mist.

Basho: Turn the horse sideways; your cuckoo is calling in the meadow.
   (Note) This *haik* is written in *A Long and Narrow Road* with a preface as follows:
     I set out toward Death Stone from Kwandai on a horse by courtesy of the governor. On the way I was rather impressed with the horse-keeper's sense of poesy when he asked me for a piece of *haik*.

Shohack: Cuckoo, cuckoo, today of all days there's none.

Boncho: Cuckoo, cuckoo, there's nothing in the fields but a bijou villa.

Nun Chigetz: Cuckoo, cuckoo, you are being not in a hurry until noon.

Fumikuni: A cuckoo's calling among trees; over there, a turret.

Nun Ukoh: The eventide—a temple bell is resounding, a cuckoo's answering.

Joso: Cuckoo, cuckoo, where are you? Over the waterfall?

Kyorai: Cuckoo, cuckoo, the governor is quite a tasteless fellow.

Oshou the courtesan: Cuckoo, cuckoo, cry at my tomb if I die of love.

—When I visited Matsushima, the beautiful view reminded me of a line of 'the plover be dressed like a crane.'

Sora: If this is the sea of Matsushima, then could you cuckoo dress like a crane?

Basho: Lonesome bird, let the man in melancholy be more sad and sweet.

—The garden in my lodging is small and grassless.

Kyoksui: Young maple leaves are now brown—as though not in season.

—Visiting my mother's grave on the eighth of the Fourth Month;

Kikack: The flowers are arranged; the water mirrors the young leaves.

Zenho in Edo: The leafy shade—there is a peony in bloom in a nice shape.

—Parting with a monk;

Etsujin: It falls with ease—a white poppy flower.
   Kyorai's Notes:
     Kikack and Kyorick said that this *haik* was incomplete, so that Etsujin must have added the preface 'parting with a monk'.

"And yet," said Kyorai, "this is well done as a *haik* of a poppy, especially as a farewell verse."
(The 'monk' is said to be Rotsu; it is said that Etsujin used the word 'monk' instead of 'Rotsu' because he was on bad terms with him at that time.)

Chinseki: It should not be seen by the wise — a poppy in flower in white.

— Visiting Suma and Akashi together with the Old Reverend;

The late Tokock: It's fit for the Village of Suma — a poppy in flower in white.
   (Note) It is said that, in memory of his most beloved disciple, Basho composed this *haik* in the name of Tokock.

Ranran: The white poppy flower — its greenish smell, too, is tasteful.

Hanzan: Morning after morning — cool and pure is the iris beside the well.

— When still half asleep in the morning;

Senka: It pleases me when I have just got up — an iris in flower.

— At the Rakshi-sha, Kyorai's cottage in Saga (two verses);

Boncho: This bean field, that small hut — all looks graceful in Saga.

Sora: The broken hedge — let a little deer pass over.

— At an inn in Nara;

Senna: Nara Town, paulownia flowers in the dark, and who peeps in the room?

Hakshi in Owari: The silks are being rinsed; in the water, persimmon blossoms.

— At the old site of Toyokuni Shrine;

Boncho: The young *take* shoot — to what shall I compare its vigor?
   (Note) Toyokuni Shrine was built in dedication to Toyotomi Hideyoshi, the ruler of Japan before the Tokugawa Shogunate, was later destroyed by the Tokugawa.

Kyorai: The young *take* shoots — there's a mischievous boy in the neighborhood.

Basho: The young *take* shoot — when still a little boy, I would draw and daub.
   (Note) This *haik* is written in *Saga Diary*.

Masahide: They were blown off by a wild boar at night — those hunting torches.

— One night at Akashi;

Basho: An octopus in a trap, its fleeting dream, and in the sky, a summer moon.
   (Note) This *haik* was composed on *A Sentimental Journey*.

Etsujin: His Great Reign — every woman brings a single pan to Tukma Festival.
   (Note) In those days women paid a visit at Tukma Shrine on its festival day, with so many pans as their love affairs.

— At my new house on the third day of Satsuki;

Kikack: The carpenters are setting up the roof, I'm hanging an iris leaf.

Basho: She brushes back a black hair on her brow — a girl wrapping rice cakes.

(Note) According to *Kyorai's Notes*, Basho composed this *haik* for *Salmino* because he thought that the anthology had few verses associative with a tale.

Ganwo in Edo: It is wrapped with a lovely green *take* leaf—that *chimaki* cake.

Shohack: The festal day—it is such a lonely party that we must call out guests.

—In memory of my grandfather, who was slain in the battle in Osaka on the sixth day of Satsuki;

Sengin in Iga: Fifty years ago in Osaka, a summer day I can in no way see.
  (Note) Todo Sengin was a senior vassal in the Iga domain of the Todo, whom Basho once served as a young *samurai*.

—At Takadachi Heights, Far Country;

Basho: Here grows summer grass, here once dreamt the brave hearts.

Basho: You are croaking under the cocoon cot; crawl out, toad.
  (Note) This *haik* was composed at Obanazawa on *A Long and Narrow Road*.

—It says in *The Tale of Genji* that it is so short a distance that you can crawl from Suma to Akashi. And now I know that it is.

Basho: Snail, snail, point to Suma and to Akashi with your two horns.

Boncho: The Satsuki rain—a slug has got away from its snail-shell house.

Boksetz: The Satsuki rains—tasteless is old wheat when we are on a journey.

Fumikuni: The Satsuki rains—we pay as much as those pack-horsemen please.

—The County of Natori, Far Country. Sora and I walked about for the tomb of Lieutenant General Fujiwara-no Sanekata, a great poet of old. People said it is in Kasashima, a good three miles away from the road. It kept on raining. In the sea of mud we gave up visiting there.

Basho: The Satsuki rains, a muddy road—well, then, where's Kasashima?

—On the way up to the Never-Ending Pass, a Yamato-Ki border, they asked pilgrims for donation for road repair. I gave them some money wrapped in a paper sheet—on which I wrote a *haik*:

Kyorai: The Satsuki rains—true, repair of the Never-Ending Pass never ends.

Boncho: The Satsuki rains, a humid season, and the razer rusts overnight.

Basho: The Satsuki rains—the mallow flowers turn toward an invisible sun.

Nun Ukoh:
  The Satsuki rains—the new clothes gather mold before I could wear.

—When a certain old physician was dead, his disciples, all in sorrow, asked me for a verse of lamentation. I replied, I had not known of the deceased when he was alive, so I could in no way think of how I should express grief. And yet they did request for a verse in memory of the physician, who died at seventy—an age rare for men.

Kikack: The Fifth-Month rain—the six-foot palanquin carriers would lose heart.

Kyorai: A song of tea picking, and the plowmen begin to reap wheat.

Masahide: Shigaraki Village—man and wife are going afield to pick tea leaves.

Youriki in Zeze: They are tackling, grappling in the field—those wheat-tall boys.
  (Note) This *haik* is referred as Kyorai's in *Saga Diary*. The change of the poet's name may have resulted from an argument written in *Kyorai's Notes* as below:
  Boncho: "The 'wheat' could be 'flax', I daresay."
  Kyorai: "The 'flax' is all right. The 'mugwort', too, is acceptable. There's no difference anyway. What is the problem?"
  The Old Reverend: "You are always arguing about the choice of a word. Stop it."
  The reader is asked to think of which opinion is good, Boncho's or mine.

—In love with my grandchild;

Nun Chigetz: Rain frog, rain frog, we'll make for you a little straw hut.

Lady Kaco:
  A wheat harvest—the fat year sees them eat fish even in the country.

—Crossing the Barrier of Shirakawa;

Basho: Now in the Far Country—my poetry begins with a song of rice planting.

—At Mogami in the province of Dewa;

Basho: The rouge plant's in bloom, with its stalk and sepals as a brow brush.
  (Note) The rouge plant (safflower), the stuff for rouge, is the well-known produce of Mogami.

—Visited Horyuji Temple when the image of the great Crown Prince Shotock was unveiled to the public;

Senna:
  At the hem of his esteemed garment is a beautiful tinge of noble crimson.

Banco in Iga: It moves from paddy to paddy by way of a bean leaf—that firefly.
  Kyorai's Notes:
  This *haik* was originally composed by Boncho, was amended by the Old Reverend. That happened when Boncho and I were compiling the anthology *Salmino*.
  Boncho: "This *haik* should be excluded from the anthology. This is a commonplace one."
  Kyorai: "I do recommend it as a selection. It vividly describes the sight of a firefly moving over a bean leaf in the dark."
  This Boncho rejected.
  "Boncho throws it down," said the Old Reverend. "I pick it up. Fortunately, Banco has composed a *haik* similar to it, so I will amend and include it in the anthology in his name."

—At Kyoksui's in Zeze;

Kyorai: Fireflies are blown away; and over the lake, a dark stretch of ripples.

—At a firefly-viewing party on the River Seta (two verses);

Boncho: Dark is the night, and out cries a little child on the firefly-viewing boat.

Basho: Amusing is the view of fireflies; yet he's tipsy, unsteady—that boatman.

—When visiting the Three Shrines of Kumano;

Nun Tagami in Nagasaki: The Demon Dale—lovely fireflies too look direful.

Shohack: O white seagull, you know better than to vie with black cormorants.

Hanzan: A nice and flowery face—the lily's looking good in the grass.

—In recovery from a disease;

Kasho in Osaka: Dizzy, dizzy, my head is swimming like a lily in the wind.

Otokuni: It cools the lily sooner than me—a cool breath of air.

—On mosquito incense;

Ranran: It is that children might be crying, and mother bitten by mosquitoes.
(Note) According to Basho's letter, this *haik* was revised by him in imitation of a *waka* of Yamanoue-no Okra:
Now I, Okra, am going home; my children might be crying at home;
And their mother too would be waiting for me at home.

—As a farewell verse;

Rito in Zeze: You've gone in a hurry, with the mosquito net left hung in the room.

—Seeing off a young man who accompanies a certain rich man to Ise Shrine;

Kikack: Short is the night, and I say good-bye to the young attendant.

Joso: It seems to find an opening; the louse comes out from my ear hole.

Ransetz: The leafy shade—cicadas crying in the dark like a larva underground.

Tanshi in Zeze: It pays a visit from tree to tree—the chirping cicada.

Basho: It is soon to die, yet shows no sign of death—the chirping cicada.

Kaishi in Iga: Pity that the blind man should cut hemps full of pearls of dew.

Boncho: Stop crossing the stream; white flowers are waving in the water weed.

Senna: A silk tree sleepily in bloom, the wife of a boat tugger is singing a song.

Fumikuni: The white shower—I've failed to hear the peal of a twilight bell.

—At the lotus pond in Sodo's hermitage;

Ranran: The white shower—the bonze hermit puts up a lotus leaf as umbrella.

Otokuni: It chirps sadly once or twice—a frog in the sunburnt field.

Boncho: So hot a day, it sits on the bottom of a tub—the grasshopper.

Boncho:
    The No-Water Month, a hot, sticky season, we meet again at a tea party.

Masahide: Sunhill Village—even the tongue of an ox looks burning hot.

Boksetz: Hot, simply hot, even in the shade of a hedge my hair feels sweaty.

Yado: Hot, simply hot, even a breath of air from the bamboo bush does feel hot.

Nun Ukoh: It's so hot a lapse of time—a moon-flower party.

Hazan in Edo: So hot a day, so hot a bath, and I'm looking at the green grass.

—Hearing of the death of Kyorai's sister Chine, I wrote to him from Mino;

Basho: She's passed away; her robe would now be aired in the midsummer sun.

Ranran: The No-Water Month—I get up late to enjoy a cool evening.

Soji: Let us lie down at ease—and we will have a cool evening.

  Kyorai's Notes:
    When we were selecting *haik* poems for *Salmino*, Soji came to us with some pieces of his poetry for selection. We, however, were not able to find anything good in them. At evening the Old Reverend said we should lie down and take a rest. Soji answered, yes, if we took our ease we would feel cool. "That is the *haik*," said the Old Reverend. "Make it a verse. That is the selection."

Boncho: A cool morning—dewy bundles of grass are brought into the house.

Senna: Taints of ink on their lips, little boys are enjoying a cool breeze.

Sora: On the festival float sit little boys, a slight makeup in their brow.

Kyorai: The evening glow—there's a chain of bald cloud.

—Visiting Kyoto for the first time;

Shido in Osaka: It is shaped very like Mount Hyea—the cloud in the sky.

Part III Autumn

Anonymous: It blooms in fine spirits—the lotus flower in an autumn wind. (This *haik* seemed to be made by a poet in Edo, perhaps Sodo.)
> (Note) The truth is that the poet was Kaksei in Okazaki. The editor Kyorai wanted to have a *haik* of Sodo's in this anthology. So he had the poet 'anonymous' and commented it was 'perhaps Sodo'. However, the true poet was disclosed by Kakei in his own selection *Waste Land II*, which, naturally, angered Kyorai furiously.

Sampou: I'm shocked, shocked; my tooth falls out in an autumn wind.

Rotsu: They look rather desperate—the *basho* leaves torn by an autumn wind.

Chinseki: It's just like man—the monkey folding his arms in an autumn wind.

—At Zenshoji Temple in Kaga;

Sora:
> The sound of the back hill—I've heard an autumn wind blow all night long.
> (Note) This *haik* is written in *A Long and Narrow Road* with a preface as follows: Sora stayed in this temple the night before, and left this *haik* for me. A one-night distance feels like a thousand miles.

Sansen in Edo: The reed fields—the herons awake all night in an autumn wind.

Boncho: The morning dew—over the turmeric field blows an autumn breeze.

Kyorai: A wild boar may have lain here; the grass getting up wet with dew.

Yado: The great Mount Hyea looks afar, and dewy are vegetables in a cart.

Boncho: The young paulownia—all the three leaves have fallen, all bare.

Basho: Tonight, a night earlier, yet a rather sweet night—Tanabata Eve.
> (Note) This *haik* was composed at Nao-Etsu Town on *A Long and Narrow Road*.

Basho: The two stars meet tonight; do not sleep, silk tree.

Tojack, a boy in Iga: Tanabata Festival—do not hurry, star; you might stumble.

Kyorai: They too live in this elegant town—the *sumo* wrestlers in Kyoto.

Fouback in Iga: The moon flowers in full bloom, a flock of cranes fast asleep.

Kyuken in Zeze: It is bound around by *nukago* vines—that moon flower.

Ranran: The althea in bloom, but neither smiles nor weeps.

Sampou: The althea flower—touched it, passed by it, yet picked it not.

Senna: A lantern hung high at night; yet at noon the pillar looks rather dull.

Fumikuni: The autumn rains—in the ford sounds water ceaselessly.

Tanko: At first it breezes lightly, softly from the grove—the autumn tempest.

Shiyin in Mikawa: A gust of autumn wind—the *susuki* grass will sway anyway.

Nun Ukoh: The silver-grass fields—I feel like a mother of a stray child.

—When visiting Yase-Ohara to compose a piece of writing on a wood vendor;

Boncho: The pole of a vendor swinging; in the basket, blades of grass beckoning.

—When leaving Nagasaki, I parted with Ushichi at the Himi Pass.

Kyorai: The *susuki* grass in flower, you might wave your hand somewhere.

Riyou in Hirata: Grass cutter, you might be hesitant to cut a dewy *hagi* clover.

—In the second year of Genrock I accompanied the Old Reverend on the travels across Far Country and the provinces of Koshi, and then in Kaga I got ill and parted with him in order to go to Ise.

Sora:
  I would fall down dead someday somewhere—where *hagi* clovers in flower.

Basho: Behind the wall calls a quail by a paulownia tree, chirping, chirping.

Boncho: The crimson sunset—there's a shrike shrieking in the Red-Pine Fields.

The late Racgo: Do not light a lamp; wild geese are coming from the North.

—At Katada;

Basho: There's a wild goose asleep at chilly night, there's a traveler sick in bed.
  (Note) See Basho's letter to Shobo in the autumn of the third year of Genrock:
    I came back from Katada by ship last night. How are you all? When in Katada, I caught a bad cold and lay down in bed at a fisherman's hut. A poetic scene, it was true, would catch us when we are in trouble.

Basho: A fisherman's hut—the shrimp are hopping, a camel cricket jumping.
  Kyorai's Notes:
    Either of the two verses—'wild goose' or 'shrimp and camel cricket'—should be chosen for the new anthology, said the Old Reverend. Boncho recommended the latter, saying it was novel and vivid, while I remarked that the former had a very lofty tone. We chose both of them. Afterwards the Old Reverend said it was no use arguing on such different types of *haik*, laughing.

—When Sora and I paid a visit at Tada Shrine in Komatz, Kaga, we saw its great treasures—Sir Sanemori's helmet and a fragment of his brocade tunic. The death of the brave man was a thing of the distant past, but even now such remains did greatly move us.

Basho: Piteous are chirps of a cricket from under the old man's helmet.

Shohack: The green field—among the leaves chirps your insect.

Fouback: A moon night—on the wall chirps your weaver cricket.

—On the way to Ise;

The late Chine: The rainy Leafy Month—avoid the troubled waters of Yabase.

Shido: A crescent night—a shark appeared but soon disappeared.

Hanzan: The millet grows, the moon develops, what a joyous season!

Kyorai: The Fushimi Hills, the citadel, now gone, and the moon we see.
(Note) In Fushimi, south of Kyoto, there used to be a great castle built by Toyotomi Hideyoshi, the ruler of Japan before the Tokugawa Shogunate.

—When the Old Reverend staying with us;

Doho in Iga: A hazy moon night—be burned, pine cones, be burned beautifully.

—Paid a visit to Kamo, where I remembered that, beside the sacred hedge of Tanaco Shrine, the great Saigyo made a *waka* of 'my tears dropping on the sacred rope.' And now I too made a verse.

Fumikuni: I clap my hands in worship in moonlight; on my laps, my shadow.

—When a friend of mine (Ensui) taking the tonsure at Honganji Temple;

Taktai in Iga: The morning moon—he has gone with the haired shadow.

Otokuni: An autumn night, swaying *basho* leaves, and the play of moonlight.

Joso: Monks talking of last year's moon; one from Kyoto, the other from Tukshi.

Boncho: The wind blows alone, yet in the sky, a single moon.

Shohack: It has long hesitated to rain, and at last it rains tonight of all nights.

Sora: A lucky night—my room has a fine view of the moon.

—One moon night—it was in the autumn of the second year of Genrock—I paid a visit at the sacred Kehi Shrine in the port town of Tsuruga, where I learned of the good deed of the ancient great monk Yugyo.

Basho: Pure is the moon shining over the sand that Yugyo once carried in.

—In high autumn, on a full-moon night, the night of my nephew's funeral;

Kyorai: Tonight, the funeral night, the moon is up there as usual.

Shobo in Zeze: It's shining over the tea field beside a temple—the bright moon.

Nun Ukoh: Bright is the moon, and yet they are busy beating clothes.

Shohack: It might be of Prime Priest's mistress—the sound of beating clothes.
(Note) Prime Priest Henjo was a monk poet in the Heian Period.

Boncho: The tide's high, a mail boat making its way in the rough sea of Nalto.

Kyorai: The horse welcoming—they're in rags, the men from distant Ichinohe.

Etsujin: They sway like a man whose horse running away—the ears of millet.

Masahide: They are not eaten even by crows—the sour *kaki* lees in the field.

Ranran: Ouch! Ouch! I've caught a spiny catfish instead of a bull head.

—Not a bird sings; the mountain really quiet (a line of Chinese poet Wang Anshi).

Boncho: There is a sound, there is a scarecrow falling over alone on the ground.

Sora: It's nice to hear—the easy note of country-*kagra* music.

Chiri in Edo: I'm in bed as a traveler; under the eaves, deer butt each other.

Chinseki: The Sour-*Kaki* Woods—in the *soba* field whistles someone like cooing.

Boncho: The clouds in the autumn sky—some are coming low, some going high.

Hanzan: We call it *suzuki* fishing when we fish little *seigo*.
  (Note) A *suzuki* (seabass) is called *seigo* when it is small.

Shohack: A *kick* in bloom, a bordered mat looks chilly in the country-size room.

Kikack: The *kick* flowers are cut and cut, yet there are still good many colors.

Chinseki: Broken bits of cloud—green finches are singing high on the bank.

Doho: A rice harvest in autumn—that is what I think of these days.

Boncho: Children watching, mother's coming with sheaves of rice on her back.

—At the Rakshi-sha;

Kyorai: A persimmon owner I am, and beyond the tree, Arashiyama Hill.
  (Note) One day Kyorai made a contract to sell the fruits of his persimmon tree in his cottage, but all of them were blown down in a storm. He hence named the cottage the Rakshi-sha (The House of Fallen Persimmons). Arashiyama Hill (the word 'arashi' means a storm) is a famous spot of sight in Saga.

Jinsei in Komatz: The white waves beating the bridge; below it, red maple leaves.

Boncho: A chilly day, faintly red maple leaves, and people are cutting *take* trees.

Kanda Festival

Bunsock: It sounds tasteless, it is nothing but country music—The rustic note of drumming in Kanda Festival. (*waka*)

—In reply to the idea that the note is countrified;

Ransetz:
  No, that is the festival of elegant *susuki* flowers and gorgeous *daimyos*.

Joso: Autumn is passing by; the *susuki* grass has drooped four or five days.

Boncho: Stepping out to see autumn sunset, I've found myself catch measles.
  (Note) This comes from a *waka* of One Hundred Poets' One Hundred Poems:
    Feeling lonely, I step out to see the view, but it is much the same
    As that of another place; it is just an autumn sunset.

Boncho: Man and woman are like a tail of a wagtail—busy, fidgety, restless.

Kakei:
  Autumn passing by; there's a piece of salted fish stuck between the teeth.

Part IV Spring

Lord Rosen: The *mei* blossoms smile at me; I should not have got angry.
(Note) Rosen was the feudal lord of Iwaki-daira.

—Accompanying a certain noble man to his villa;

Kyorai:
The fair scent of *mei* blossoms—I'm sniffing around the hill like a hound.

Kucou in Kaga: I go into the sweet scent of *mei* blossoms; in the village, ox horns.

—At a certain garden;

Doho: It comes down on to the sand river—a sweet scent of *mei* blossoms.

Hanzan: Just born, the little butterfly senses a sweet scent of *mei* blossoms.

Senso: The fair scent of a *mei*—the drinker's bill book now blank and new.

Kikack: I'm going toward the *mei* tree; by the wayside, butterbur sprouts.

—Hearing that a *mei* tree in bloom in the backyard of the maiden's house;

Basho: They are pure and lovely—the maidens and the *mei* tree being in bloom.
(Note) This *haik* was composed when Basho visited Ise Shrine on *A Sentimental Journey*.

Senna: It's but a seedy bush—the *mei* tree blooming poorly by the eaves.

Boncho: Ashes thrown away, the white *mei* blossoms look blurred in the hedge.

Shiyou in Zeze: The *mei* blooms in the sun, the burdocks are mostly dug out.

—The scent sails in the dark, the moon low at dusk (a line of a Chinese poet of old).

Fouback: Out rings a bell at twilight, resounding into the scent of *mei* blossoms.

—Half-asleep in bed at an inn on my way to Edo;

Otokuni: A sleepless night, a slightly open window, in the dark, a *mei* in bloom.

—In the beginning of Yayoi in the fourth year of Genrock I paid a visit to Mount Yoshino. The sun sinking behind the mountains, the scent of mei blossoms fairly sweet—which reminded me of my friend Ranso's *haik*: 'No blossoms are seen, yet the sweet scent leads me to a *mei* tree.' I usually regarded this verse as trite, but now it did move me to tears; and in the dream that night, I saw the deceased friend very joyful—O joyful indeed! What a beautiful poetry he had even now!

Ranran: The dream is gone, and at eventide I feel another scent of a *mei*.

Kikack:
>A hundred and eight rings of a bell, and *mei* blossoms astray in the dark.
>(Note) In a Buddhist temple the bell is rung a hundred and eight times to purify a hundred and eight passions of greed.

Kyorai: A lone traveler, I want to stay at a nice inn tonight, a spring night.

Fumikuni: The spring fields — women picking herbs, driving wild geese away.

Ranran: The first fair of a year — in a light snowfall comes a young-herb boat.

Joko: The evening moon low in the west, a song of *nazna* high in the kitchen.

— Thinking of the Old Reverend, now on a journey;

Ransetz: Now in spring he might kneel down to pick a herb — the old traveler.

Rotsu: The young herbs — I can throw away, but won't tread on.

Kikack: The Seven Herbs have been gathered, morning crows cawing merrily.

Joso: I'm picking water parsley, mudfish swimming away at all their speed.

Kikack: A patch of ice on the water; beside it, a few parsley flowers.

Kikack: A hazy spring night — there stands a black pine tree in moonlight.

Kyorai: A hazy moon — the bowl beaters, it seems, have disappeared from town.

Itto in Iga: Flakes of snow fall softly from the hedge — as a warbler perches on.

Keiseki in Edo: A warbler gives a high tweet, and his civil face of triumph.

Kikack: A warbler singing, I'm going a long way to say a Happy New Year.

Boncho: Warbler, warbler, some paddy soil sticks to my clogs.

Gyojitz in Iga: A warbler singing, I'm on moxibustion by the window.

Tangan: The green willow — a sign of spring in the grove in snow.

Boktack in Edo: It would do for a monkey's stool — this knurl of a willow.

Ensui in Edo: A willow behind the hedge — I touch, pinch and fillip its branch.

Shohack: It is too stony to plant willows on the shore — the River Yokota.

Ittan in Iga: The weeping willow — beside it, the water is alive with carp.

Kohack in Iga: Meltwater is trickling; inside, the tub is alive with clams.

Yosui: We used to long for the New Year, and now the moon is on the wane.

— In the country;

Basho: She's skinny from a poor meal, or being in love? — the wife as a cat.

Etsujin: Beautifully, he gives her up all at once — the lover as a cat.
>*Kyorai's Notes:*
>The Old Reverend said in his letter that a man of poetry would make a good poem someday, and now with this Etsujin proved his worth at last.

Kyorai: Bitten by a true love of his, the cat looks up at the sky, his own sky.
  (Note) This comes from a *waka* in the *Kokin-shu*:
    The sky would be a gift from a true love of mine;
    When lost in thought, I would look up at the sky.

—On the chill of spring, a theme assigned for fun by Lord Rosen;

Kiwo: A gust of spring wind—should I take off the coat, or not?

Shohack: Kisaragi—a chilly month when bits of blossom fall from a wild *mei*.

Kiwo: Employees making a move, a roll of straw mat hanging out of their box.

Ransetz: An old memory—I felt sad as a boy when employees made a move.

Boncho: The tree's been cut; no branches, no leaves, yet in bud.

Kikack: A cup of white-fish soup—my servant adds some pieces of laver.

Sampo: It may have been named so after we began eating it—the *sacra* laver.

Ganshi: The spring rain beats the ground, waking up horsetail shoots.

Kakei: A fine spring day—there's a mirage astray above the snow.

Hyaksai: A spring day—there's a mirage afloat above the rough furrows.

Doho: A spring mirage—sand is softly, lightly dropping down on the shore.

Hyoko in Iga: It is afloat about a house under construction—a spring mirage.

Boncho: A spring mirage—there's a vixen leaves her little ones romping about.

Basho: A hazy sunshiny day—a mirage afloat over a silver stretch of grass.

Hairiki in Iga: The shimmers of a mirage—it's time the *udo* began to bud.

Ransetz: A basketful of bracken—ferns are thrown away like odds and ends.

Rotsu: The vernal equinox yet to come; it will be chilly one night or two.

Yasui: You, bagworm, always look like an image of the Holy Buddha lying down.

Boncho: A row of warehouses on the backstreet, and through it flies a swallow.

Takchi in Iga: Wild geese rush northwards, a flock from Ki, then one from Ise.

Ranco: The spring rains—on the roof flowers a little herb.

—On a mountain;

Ensui: The spring rain, a misty mountain, and I go out of the temple's gate.

Basho: It has woken me up from a laze—the spring rain drizzling at ease.

Fumikuni: The spring rain—a loach vendor is walking around Tamino Village.

Nun Ukoh: A spring view—the rain is gone, and on the eaves tweets a sparrow.

Fumikuni: It passes from paddy to paddy—that *suppon* tortoise.
  Kyorai's Notes:

This was written by mistake as 'it passes', not as 'it moves'. Afterwards the Old Reverend complained to me that a difference in wording would give us quite a different impression in poetry. There was a line of an ancient poet: 'a frog chirps, moving from paddy to paddy.' That was, therefore, not only a mere mistake, but you also failed to grasp the poet's idea. You, Kyorai, should have read the verse more deeply. The Old Reverend was full of grumbles.

Shobo: The bamboo framework—there are bees, there are droppings of insects.

Kyorai: Its courtesy—the last year's doll seems reserved in the lower seat.
Kyorai's Notes:
I composed this *haik* very carefully. For instance, I thought my idea would be too clear with a word like 'an old hat' or 'worn paper clothing', rather ambiguous with a seasonal thing, and quite dull with 'regrettable' or 'disappointed'. Then I used the word 'courtesy'.
"Using a word of logic," said the Old Reverend, "would make verses look like an epigram. The word 'courtesy' is not very good, but acceptable."

Tekishi in Iga: The spring wind—keep the wine and cakes firmly, doll carriers.
Kyorai's Notes:
The Old Reverend: "In Iga they make simple verses like this. Fairly attractive."
Joso: "You pretend not to know it, sir, but you caused them to make simple ones."

Nun Ukoh: A hospitable season—a girl is serving branches of peach and willow.

Uso: The peach in bloom; the flowery hedge now useless as a boundary.

Ransui: It looks like a navel fallen from a villager—a mud snail in the paddy.

Hanzan: It has slept overnight on the bud of a leek—that white butterfly.
(Note) This comes from a *waka* in the *Kokin-shu*:
To the spring meadow I've come to pick violets;
So sweet a view that I've slept there overnight.

Toyo in Yamanaka, Kaga: It's gone toward Mount White—a kite afloat in the air.

Enfou in Iga: The pool of water mirrors the sky, and in the sky flies a kite.

Chinseki: The spring sun—parent sparrows peck and perch around the trash.

Doho: A spring day—beside the terrace, on the saddle sits a little sparrow.

Basho: Dark is the night; somewhere cries a stray plover in search of a nest.
(Note) This comes from an old *waka*:
The eventide—somewhere in the misty strand of the River Saho
Cries a stray plover in search of friends.

—On the way from Etchu to Hida, having passed over the dangerous Kago Cross, I made my way across the pathless mountains.

Boncho: The sun setting, and on the bough of a camphor tree, an eagle's aerie.

Sekiko in Iga: A spring sky—beyond the haze appears the head of a cloud.

Sampou: A skylark flies high; his children might be waiting for him at home.
(Note) This comes from a *waka* of Yamanoue-no Okra:

Now I, Okra, am going home; my children might be crying at home;
And their mother too would be waiting for me at home.

Basho: There's a skylark airily trilling, then a pheasant cuts in, shrilling.

—At the Basho-an, a hermitage where the Old Reverend once lived;

Kyoksui: A violet in flower; perhaps he used to wash a little pot around there.

Santen in Edo: Meadows, thistles, *boke* flowers—all tempts me to go afield.

—As a word of respect on a certain picture;

Basho: Yellow roses in bloom; you may sense aroma from the tea roasters in Uji.
(Note) Uji, south of Kyoto, is a noted producer of tea leaves.

Sharai: It makes a lovely camellia look more lovely—a white pearl of dew.

—Being in bad health, I got tired of combing my hair; so I became a nun this spring.

Nun Ukoh: A fallen camellia—neither a comb nor a hairpin does for me now.
(Note) See a passage from Basho's letter to Nun Ukoh:
Having read the preface to your *haik* of a camellia, people told me that you must be a lady of beauty or virtue. I replied to them that you are a nun of poetry.

Mr. Sakagami in Settz: It has fallen down on a slow snail—that *tsubaki* blossom.

Basho: Has a warbler dropped its hat? Nay, that is a *tsubaki* blossom.

Risetz:
The first one blooms, then *sacra* after *sacra*, then here, there, everywhere.

—At Kan'eiji Temple;

Kikack: The *sacra* trees in full bloom, little monks are busy among pine trees.

Shohack: *Sacra* trees bloom on the hill; we should break off some branches.

Boncho: *Sacra* trees on the hill in flower; I hear a rooster crow somewhere.

Joso: First bloom, first fall; that will be that.

Fumikuni:
It looks humble and reserved at dawn—that late-blooming *sacra* tree.

Senna: A spring day—failed to take lunch, felt like a bird among blossoms.

—Passing the foot of the sacred Mount Katsuragi;

Basho: Let me see your face, Lord; your *sacra* blossom is at its height at dawn.
(Note) This *haik* was composed on *A Sentimental Journey*. The God of Katsuragi was said to work only at night because of shyness from his ugliness.

—Long, long ago the people of Flower-Hedge Village in Iga kept that double-flowering *sacra* in Nara by order of a certain noble lady.

Basho: The village might be descended from the flower keeper—might you not?

—My father died young and was buried at Yanaka Cemetery in Edo when I was still an infant of three years old. Before long I left Edo; and it was twenty years later when I revisited Edo. My old mother always told me a *sacra* tree had been planted as a mark in front of my father's tomb, but now in the Cemetery I find every tomb has its own *sacra*.

Enfou:
   I'm wandering from tomb to tomb—like a bee flying from bloom to bloom.

Kyorai:
   The *sacra* trees in bloom; May I not come across someone who knows me.

Boncho: The flowery city—there once lived a monk who loathed *sacra* blossom.

—At a former-*samurai's* house;

Hanzan: A spring night, a flower is put in the arrow bag—be silent, mice.

Chobi in Iga: There bloom *sacra* trees, there is an odor of last night's leftovers.

—Going a long way into the depth of Yoshino in search of *sacra* blossom;

Sora: The Sacred Great Summits—*sacra* in high bloom in the depth of Yoshino.

—At Dokan Hill;

Ranran: Dokan Hill—there once was a stormy day; and now, a flowery scene.

—Seeing a picture of *The Tale of Genji*;

Nun Ukoh: A fine figure—bright bits of blossom fall to the balustrade at night.

—My house was burned in fire in the third year of Genrock;

Hokshi in Kaga: All's burned down; luckily, the *sacra* blossoms had fallen down.

Boncho:
   A temple in spring—the blossoms falling, the monks shutting the doors.

Fuko in Edo: The moon of the night—the red-crab apples now in full bloom.

—At Yamato;

Basho: A pale purple wisteria—fatigued at evening, I'm looking for a lodging.
   (Note) This *haik* was composed on *A Sentimental Journey* with a preface as below:
   I threw away all the burdensome belongings, except for a paper blanket, a raincoat, medicines, a lunch box, an ink-stone, a brush and some sheets of paper. All these borne in my back, I, a poor walker, might fall on my back. My steps were now rather sluggish. My travel always troublesome.

Tangan: A mountain bird is skirting the azaleas, swinging its tail left and right.

Nun Chigetz: The azaleas in bloom, the lake glows red in the setting sun.

Sansen: What with this and with that, the deutzias begin to bud in late Yayoi.

Shikishi in Iga: The call of a bullfinch, and I go on to a mountain path.

—At the mound grave of Lord Kiso;

Otokuni: Where are you, horse? Why don't you become a stone horse here?
   (Note) Lord Kiso, a *samurai* commander in chief, was slain on horseback in battle near Zeze (*The Tale of the Heike*) and buried at the site of Gichuji Temple, a place where Basho's hermitage the Moumyo-an was to be built half a millennium later.

Sora: A spring night—someone staying in seclusion in the holy Hatsuse Temple.

—On the shore of Lake Biwa we made a farewell to the passing spring;

Basho: Friends, let us say good-bye; now in Lake Land spring is passing by.
   Kyorai's Notes:
   One day the Old Reverend said this *haik* had been criticized by Shohack—'Omi (Lake Land)' could be altered to 'Tamba (a mountainous province, northwest of Kyoto)', and 'spring', to 'year'. What did I think about that?
   Kyorai: "Shohack's remark is beside the mark. The mellow, hazy air of the lake would make one fascinated when spring is passing by. And this verse expresses the real feeling of that."
   The Old Reverend: "Verily, verily, the poets of old loved spring in Lake Land as well as spring in Kyoto."
   Kyorai: "Yes, indeed. Could we feel such poetry in Lake Land in the end of a year? Could we, in mountainous Tamba in the passing of spring? The seasons and scenery move us very deeply indeed."
   The Old Reverend: "You are my true friend of poesy, Kyorai."

Part V (Linked Verse)

Kyorai: The first winter rain—a kite is preening its wings;
Basho: A gust of wind, and the leaves are calmed and quiet;
Boncho: And my trousers get wet when I wade across a stream at dawn;
Fumikuni: With a simple bow as a raccoon-dog scarer;
BS: The moon is up at eventide, and on the door creeps a vine;
KR: And tasty are the pears—which he never gives us.
FK: Autumn passing by, I'm making a wild sketch for fun;
BC: Fit and smooth are the knit socks;
KR: All is silent when all are silent;
BS: At noon they blow the conches, going down to the village;
BC: And his straw mat—old, wet and frayed;
FK: Nearby are lotus flowers falling flake by flake.
BS: Drank a soup, tasted a good flavor of Suizenji laver;
KR: And I shall walk another six miles;
FK: A spring day—that servant is still employed by Lu Tong; *
BC: And a hazy moon night—the cutting begins to bud.
BS: Beside the bloom, a mossy wash-basin stoup;
KR: And it's been gone by itself—my anger this morning;
BC: Now then, I shall eat a two-day meal at once;
FK: A promise of snow—across the isle blows a cold north wind;
KR: In the dark a monk goes up to light up a small temple on the hill;
BS: The season is past and gone; the cuckoos have ceased singing.
FK: The woman, skin and bone, cannot wake herself up yet;
BC: So the noble man has his ox-cart parked in her neighbor's lot;
BS: He comes, he comes—guide him here through the thorny hedge;
KR: And now in parting, she holds out his sword;
BC: And yet he's busy combing his hair;
FK: Now, behold this man mad and desperate.

KR: A blue sky, a morning moon, and the day breaks in a haze;
BS: An autumn day, the view of the lake, and frosty Mount Hira;
FK: A pack of buckwheat being stolen, I have nothing to do but sing a verse;
BC: And the windy evening—I've got used to wearing cotton clothes.
BS: Slept among people, set out earlier; I'm a busy traveler;
KR: The sky still glows with crimson clouds;
BC: And the leather-smith makes a saddle string; by the window, a flower;
FK: And the loquat tree—fresh leaves have come out among the old ones.

(Note)
* Lu Tong was a recluse in ancient China.

(Linked Verse)

Boncho: There are scents and odors in the town; in the sky, a summer moon; *
Basho: Some say it's very hot, others say, very hot indeed.
Kyorai: The second weeding is yet to come, yet the rice plants are all in ear;
BC: And he grills a smoked sardine, brushing the ash off;
BS: To my inconvenience they are ignorant of silver coins in these parts;
KR: And that absurdly long dagger is his;
BC: Yet at dark he gets frightened by a frog shooting out of weeds;
BS: And the light goes out while she's picking butterbur shoots;
KR: A pious woman she has been since she was a girl in bud;
BC: Yet at Nanawo in Noto, winter is no pleasant season;
BS: And he has thus got so old as to suck fish bone;
KR: Now ushering in the guest through the wicket;
BC: All the maids so rush to take a peep, the screen falls down flat;
BS: And in the empty bath there only is a bamboo mat.
KR: A gust of evening wind—the seeds of a fennel plant are blown off;
BC: It's somewhat chilly; is that monk returning to his temple?
BS: An autumn moon—the monkey showman's long lived with a monkey;
KR: And as land tax he pays one bushel of rice once a year.
BC: A pool of water—there float some pieces of raw wood;
BS: And my socks get spotted when I walk on the road of black mud;
KR: He's running, a sword in hand, after his master riding a horse;
BC: And a shop boy spills water from the bucket. **
BS: A house for sale—the doors and windows are all covered with straw mats;
KR: And the red peppers have already turned red;
BC: There's a shadow weaving straw sandals stealthily in moonlight;
BS: And an early-autumn night—he gets up to shake fleas off;
KR: Then the mouse-trap door shuts down without a mouse;
BC: The chest is warped, the lid does not fit on.

BS: A life of vagrancy—from hermitage to hermitage, today in, tomorrow out;

KR: And a joy of life—I've got an advice of selection for an imperial anthology;

BC: I have had different shapes and forms of love, though;

BS: And every man and woman ends up as Komachi did; ***

KR: What has made her so sad? She's in tears having a bowl of gruel;

BC: On the wooden floor, a floor a thought broader while the master is out.

BS: The shade of blossoms—let a louse play about on my palm;

KR: A sleepy spring day—there's not a single stir of haze.

(Note)
* When this linked verse was composed, Basho was staying at Boncho's house in downtown in Kyoto.

** *Kyorai's Notes:*
This was originally written as 'a shop boy spills night soil'. Boncho asked the Old Reverend about a word like 'night soil'. Might he use such a word?
"You may," replied the Old Reverend. "But not more than two times in a one-hundred-line linked verse. It would be better to avoid such a word in a thirty-six-line linked verse."
Boncho hence altered the word to 'water'.

*** Ono-no Komachi was a poetess in the Heian Period. It is said that she was beautiful and admired in her day, but died in misery in the end.

(Linked Verse)

Boncho: Chirps of a cricket—the water has ceased trickling down to the lye tub;

Basho: And the autumn evening—to save the oil, I go to bed earlier;

Yasui: New *tatami* mats have been set up, and the play of moonlight;

Kyorai: And a pleasant party—ten cups of *sake* are ready;

BS: We hold a spring feast, decorating the room with various antiques;

BC: And the twitter of a warbler—it snows in large flakes.

KR: Riding in spring—the horse's too excited to keep the reins;

YS: Far away, the peak of Mount Maya is shrouded in a mist;

BC: And a sweet evening breeze blows when I eat sand lance;

BS: Scratching the leech-stuck skin, I feel nice.

YS: Melancholic love—forget it, forget it, take a rest today;

KR: And his impatience—here comes another letter from my lord;

BS: An easy goer, I'm called a dandy *samurai*;

BC: And a lover of a hot bath, I go out under the evening moon;

KR: Downtown, an ownerless house, and autumn goes on;

YS: And what is seen, is dew everywhere.

BS: All ends as a fallen flower; I shall clothe myself in monk attire;

BC: Spring is passing by, they eat vinegared vegetables in Kiso;

YS: Over hills, through woods, titmice are going home;

KR: And they roughly repair the thatched roof.

BC: The winter sky, a north wind, before long it will be stormy;

BS: And the night light is lit for travelers;

KR: Yet it's all been useless—the wit of a clever woman;

YS: A *still-love-you* in flower, a wolf is howling;

BS: And the moonlit evening—he keeps a mausoleum on a grassy hill;

BC: There is a fount of iron-red water, there is a *forget-you* in flower;

YS: Let him boast about, leave him talk things;

KR: Then, let him take a nice set of *sushi*.

BC: Green is the view from the bank; the fields alive with rice plants;

BS: And Kamo Shrine, a good old shrine;

KR: And through the street passes a vendor of a high tone;

YS: As things come and go swiftly, so he races for shelter in the rain;

BS: And it looks peaceful—a blue heron sleeping easy in the light of day;

BC: And a rill sighs and stirs as the rushes sway.

KR: The weeping *sacra* in bloom—I've had a bellyful of blossom; *

YS: Now in Yayoi, late spring, the sky is at dawn. **

(Note)
* *Kyorai's Notes:*
   (Kyorai asked Basho if he might use a word '*sacra*' in a stanza where 'flower' or 'blossom' should be used.)
   The Old Reverend: "What you are saying is reasonable in a sense. Try it anyway. Note that a *haik* of an ordinary *sacra* would be meaningless."
   Then I composed the stanza of 'a bellyful of blossom.'
   "It's a selfish verse," said the Old Reverend, laughing.
** This comes from the opening passage of Lady Sei-Shonagon's *Pillow Book*:
   The dawn in spring. It is getting from dark to twilight, and the sky is tinged with red along the ridgeline, with a streak of cloud trailing in purple.

(Linked Verse)

—To Otokuni, who leaves for Edo;
Basho: The *mei* in bloom, the grass green, and you eat *tororo* soup at Marico; *
Otokuni: The spring day breaks, and a new straw hat I put on.
Chinseki: The cries of a skylark—here comes a season when they plow fields;
Sonan: And rice cakes are given as a gift of good luck;
OK: There's a man with toothache; in the sky, an evening moon;
BS: An autumn day—the guest on the second floor has already departed;
SN: And he releases a quail, seeing it fly out of sight;
CS: A light breeze—the rice plants are waving lightly.
BS: A novice monk, I shall go over Mount Suzka in the first place; **
OK: Who's it calling me so and so?
CS: At dawn the Konishi Corps is in the concave formation; ***
SN: The pine woods silent in a mist;
OK: And verses are written on the cards of *hagi* and *susuki*;
Nun Chigetz: And sparrows cluster at a corner as a shrike shrieks. ****
Boncho: The autumn moon—I have my hands in my warm pockets;
OK: The tide is fickle in the outer sea;
Kyorai: And the flowery sunset—there's a spearman leaning on his spear;
BC: And ash is strewn over the field after the harvest of mustard.
Masahide: A spring day—the desks are put away after sutra chanting;
KR: And the attendants eat in turns in the shop;
Hanzan: At the edge of his face towel, a dark blue stripe;
Doho: And the lovers say a busy good-bye; on the roof crows a rooster;
HZ: Love is firm and daring, I daresay;
DH: Yet he's like wet paper; you cannot pick it up;
HZ: In a word, love's like a round-blade knife in a craft box;
Enfou: And New Year's Eve—a candle is lighted at the family altar.
Ensui: The Suma Beach—here come no letters;

HZ: And the night—I lie down, wrapping myself up in the tunic;

EF: Summer has come; I use a broken fan with its hub bound with a string;

ES: Having set soy sauce in a cask, he looks up at the moon for a while;

DH: And someone gives a cough somewhere in the neighborhood;

EF: The longer I live with him, the squarer he looks.

Ranran: A winter day—I gaze into an abstract picture on the Ayz plate;

Fumikuni: And flakes of snow fall softly on the bamboo clogs;

Yasui: The season coming nearer, yet I have no friends to see blossom together;

Nun Ukoh: And now the Hina dolls sit colorful in a spring breeze.

(Note)
* *Doho's Notes:*
  "When making this *haik*," said the Old Reverend, "I had no special idea. I just hit on it. I felt it was well made, afterwards. I cannot make such a work anymore."
  This is a combination. The Old Reverend first took up the tasteful view of a *mei* tree and green grass in front of him, then a worldly topic—*tororo* soup, a specialty of distant Marico, a town where Otokuni would sooner or later stop at.
** This comes from a *waka* of Saigyo:
  Mount Suzka—I've run away from the world;
  And where am I going? How am I going?
*** This is a scene of the Battle of Sekigahara (in 1600).
**** This linked verse was made at first in Otsu, was suspended at this stanza, and then followed by poets in Kyoto and Iga.

Part VI Life at the Genjou-an

Beyond the Hill of Ishiyama, a little way from Iwama Temple lies Kokubuyama Hill. It is a place where Kokubunji Temple was built in ancient times. Cross a rill in the foot of the hill, then go up some two hundred steps along a winding path, and you will find a sacred Hachiman Shrine. Its principal image is the Holy Amida. Though that would be rather unsatisfactory to a pure Shintoist, yet it seems gracious to me that Buddhism and Shintoism jointly show us charity, mercy and blessing. Usually very few people pay a visit to the shrine, but thanks to that, it is a calm, divine place. Beside the shrine stands a vacant hut, its site thick with mugworts and bamboos, its roof and wall torn and worn-out—that is to say, a good habitation for foxes and raccoons. That is the Genjou-an, or the House of Illusion. Its previous owner, uncle of Sir Suganuma Kyoksui the Brave Man, passed away eight years ago, with his monk name Old Genjou left behind.

   A man of nearly fifty, I have been away from the town for some ten years like a bagworm without a bag, or a snail without a shell. My face was burnt with a hot sun on the seashore of Kisagata in Far Country, my feet hurt on the sandy, rocky coast on the North Sea, and then to Lake Land I came this year. Imagine how reliable a single stalk of reed would be to a nest of a grebe adrift on water. I renewed the eaves, trimmed the hedge, and began living at the hut in the beginning of the Fourth Month. At first I was going to leave soon, but now I wish to live here for a long time.

   Spring has just gone. You can see azaleas still pink with their blossoms, and wild wisterias hanging pale purple from the green pine trees. Cuckoos fly over from time to time, singing, and, once or twice, jays and the gentle tapping of a woodpecker I never mind. An amusing life. I have been very much amused as if my soul were in Wu or Chu, or as if on the River Xiao Xiang or Lake Dong Ting in China.

   The hill facing northeast, and the village a little distant, you can feel a sweet south breeze down from the heights, and a cool north wind up from the lake. You can also see the great summits of Mounts Hyea and Hira in the distance, and underneath, by the hazy lake, the green pine tree of Karasaki—and a castle, a bridge, fishermen's boats. And listen—the voices of woodcutters on their way to Mount Kasatori will be heard, and the song of plowmen planting rice in paddies, and—when fireflies glitter at dark—the nocturnal sound of waterrails beating water. All is beautiful. A perfect world! Among others, Fuji-shaped Mikamiyama Hill reminds me of my old hermitage in Edo, and Mount Tanakami makes me think of some poets of old. Also, you can see the heights of Sasaho, Senjo, Hakamagoshi—and Kurotz Village alive with dark trees, such a famous view as once sung of in a verse in the *Man'yo-shu*.

One day I climbed the back hill to view a wider view, setting up a pine stand and round straw mat, with its name as the Monkey's Stool. But do not think that I want to be like Old Xu, who lived in aronia woods, nor like Old Wang, who had a hermitage in Mount Zhubo. I'm but a lazy country man, stretching out my legs toward the yonder mountains, and spending an idle day on the calm hill. When I can, I draw water from a fountain in the vale and fix a meal by myself; however, I have few cooking tools in imitation of the great Saigyo. The previous owner, too, seems to have lived a nice and simple life, for there remain few pieces of arts and crafts. The hut itself is simple, too: a chamber for prayer, some storage space for bedding, and that is all.

The high priest of Kora Temple in Tukshi is a son of the good calligrapher Mister Kai at Kamo Shrine. When he recently came to Kyoto, through another person I asked him for a piece of calligraphy. The high priest very kindly sent me a tablet written in calligraphy as 'Genjou-an'. It is now an only treasure of my hermitage. Except for it, I need no art works, a man in travel or in seclusion. Beside the bed, on the pillar hangs a Kiso-Cedar hat and a Koshi-Sedge raincoat, and that is all.

Rarely do I have a guest in the daytime. Sometimes the old keeper of the shrine, or some villager, comes and gives a talk novel to me—say, a wild boar ate away some rice, or a rabbit haunts bean fields. And then sets the sun, then falls a silent night, before long appears the moon. I burn a small fire, sitting face to face with the shadow of mine. But do not think I am a lover of tranquility who wishes to seclude himself in the bosom of Nature. I'm but a man of poor health, weary of life and people.

Many years have passed me by. I lived a life of failure, once envying men of high status and ambition, once trying to be a Zen priest; and in the wanderings I devoted myself to making *haik* poems, so much so that I made a living as poet as a result—that is to say, such a man of failure, with no virtues nor gifts, has at last found the way in this sole line. The labor of making verses made Old Du Fu skin and bone, brought the great Bai Latien in agony—even them, even the bards far more gifted than I. But I never mind that. Life's all illusion. We all live in a house of illusion. And that is all. It is time to go to bed.

A life in the summer grove—the acorn tree be my talisman.

Written by Basho.

On Old Basho's *Life at the Genjou-an*

Who says there are no recluses? The wise would have their hermitage in their mind. Who says there's no wonderful nature? Beauty will depend upon who sees it. I have read through Old Basho's *Life at the Genjou-an*. It tells us that a wise, learned man could appreciate the truth and beauties of Nature, and could get along with it. And in praise of the great poet, I make a piece of poetry:

Kokubuyama Hill, south of Lake Biwa;

And the old pine grove—its shade's cool.
There's a simple hut some yards long;
And there lives alone a wise man.
With your verse, the view looks nice and fine;
And the scenery, just like a city of poetry.
It is originally a scenic spot of old,
And now more beautiful with your work.

      Written (in classic Chinese) by Shinken
      in the autumn of the third year of Genrock.

On the Genjou-an

Kyoksui: Cuckoo, cuckoo, you've found his figure in the foothills—have you not?

Yasui: The summer hill—I sneeze and find all is quiet.

Kyorai:
  Water-rails crying, roosters too might be crowing, clucking in the village.

Boncho: The lake and the mountains—it darkens, it is very likely to rain.

Senna: There are red cowberries beside the eaves; do not tread on, monkey.

Chinseki: The summer hill—let me take a rest for a while.

—Sending some sheets of paper;

Yakei: What you care to say, you can put in it.

Rito: A rice offering on a *fuki* leaf—when did you make it?

Otokuni: Pearls of dew on the moss, and there flies a firefly over the floor.

Dosui: Beautiful days—you are just like a white deutzia in a dark thicket.

Tanshi: Dark is the hill, and my clogs tottering, clattering in the Satsuki rain.

Ganshi: They are singing around—lonesome birds of ten or twelve wings.

Deido: The water-rails cease crying at dawn, then woodpeckers begin their job.

Fumikuni: A cool hue of breeze—that cedar hat is swaying on the pillar.

Masahide: The rising moon, the darkening lake, and I'm feeling a cool breeze.

The late Ryuin: Silent is the fountain, and in it, a leaf of a chestnut tree.

Joko: The acorn tree—it's cool having a rice meal together.

—The Old Reverend was absent;

Boksui in Zeze: The chirps of a cicada—you're now singing in another acorn tree.

Shiyin: A cool sight—below us, the lake in a hand-washing distance.

—In a letter;

Hanzan: The cool twilight—in Zeze it would breeze at a rice-plant height.

—A verse and a pack of wheat flour as a gift;

Shido: A pack of new wheat—this is the produce of Toba Field.

—In a letter;

Rocho in Nagasaki: A lover of travel, you are in seclusion in a summer hill.

Kyuken: The late-afternoon shower—I feel a heavy scent of white cedars.

—A view from the Monkey's Stool;

Shohack: It rises from the col of Mount Tanakami—the autumn wind.

—A verse and a straw coat as a gift;

Hokshi: This coat will have dew before long—where do you go with him?

Boksetz: Put off your clogs; you can find a small herb in flower.

—On a package sheet;

Lady Sen in Zeze: A dewy *hagi* clover—I'm sewing a medicine bag.

Nun Chigetz: A rice flower—might I offer it to the Holy Buddha?

Nun Ukoh: I haven't been to Ishiyama; there would blow an autumn wind.

Shobo: The pail is broken by itself, the crickets stop chirping.

Kasho: The eventide, the meal time, the village would now be very hot.

Etsujin: Until when do you chirp, camel cricket? Until the salt pot gets dusty?

—When visiting the hermitage together with Etsujin;

Tosai: As a lotus fruit bursts out, so do we jump into your hermitage.

—When visiting the vacant hermitage next Yayoi;

Ranran: The spring rain, a windy day, and the door is broken.

—And in summer;

Sora: Cool is the hill, yet you have left this nice hermitage, haven't you?

Epilogue

The anthology *Salmino*, or *A Monkey's Straw Raincoat*, represents the best esprit of the Old Reverend Basho. That is not because he was amused at a little monkey clothing a kimono in a temple or wearing a hat in a morning market, but because something, I should say, something moved him into a stir of poetry. And his disciples in Kyoto, Boncho and Kyorai, who had learned *haik* poetry for years under the Old Reverend, began compiling such an anthology that would be a precious one. There came many friends from many places, and many letters from many provinces, which brought good many pieces of poetry and various kinds of prose. Although they were unable to collect verses of some recluses, yet, instead, artless poems of children, women and old people were selected. You may find such pieces of *haik* alive with dialects and colloquial expressions despite poor wording. The anthology, divided in six parts, comprises *haik* poems of the four seasons. The works of other schools are not included. And it was in the mid-summer of the fourth year of Genrock that I happened to meet Boncho and Kyorai at a *haikai* meeting in Kyoto, where they asked me to make an epilogue to the anthology. That is why I'm writing this. Permit me to add another straw raincoat for fishermen in the sea of poetry.

Written (in classic Chinese) by Joso.

Published by Izutsuya Shobei, Kyoto.

A CHARCOAL BAG

After *Salmino* was published in Kyoto, Basho returned to Edo; however, he seemed to be disappointed in the circles of *haik* poets in the capital city. See a passage from his letter to Kyorai:
> In Edo they all have *haikai* games from *samurai* to townsmen, rich or poor, to guards, to monks. The judges are doing good business, but it is a rather deplorable situation. Quite deplorable. Nobody cares for the new style, has any interest in making a simple poem. They all compose decorative verses on vulgar topics, and produce heavy trite ones. I can not understand their manner. But I will not disclose my idea. Should I do so, I would have some new followers, but that would be harmful to my old disciples. Considering this and that, I'm now being silent.

Seeing people regard *haikai* poetry as a mere amusement, Basho deplored that no one had interest in the new style nor in the simple taste. And now, in this part, I should like to show you what style and taste Basho sought for.

Immortality and Modernity

'Sing of things modern, and it will make an immortal piece of poetry.'

Basho is said to have advocated the theory of immortality and modernity. Yet on this subject his own words we can see today are few and fragmented; then, instead, let us see a comment of Doho's written in *Doho's Notes*:
> In the verses of the Old Reverend there are two types of poetry—a poem of immortality and a poem of modernity; and there is a more fundamental factor—true poetry.
>
> If you cannot understand immortality, you cannot grasp true poetry. There are old poems, there are new poems, and poetic taste changes as times change; yet, for all that, there are poems of true poetry. Those are the poems of immortality. Each age has its own style, yet you may feel sad and sweet in some of the verses, whether new or old. Those are the very poems of immortality.
>
> Things change as time goes by. If you continue making poems of the same taste, your poetic style will not change. If you do not change your poetic style, then you are merely seeking for temporary modernity, not for true poetry. If you do not seek for true poetry, you cannot understand the importance of changing a poetic style.

The New Style

'Make a poem of popular taste with a noble spirit.'

Doho wrote a comment regarding the new style, too. See such a passage from *Doho's Notes*:
> The new style is the flower of *haik* poetry. The old style is like a flowerless old tree. The Old Reverend always sought for a newer style, and was very much

pleased when he found someone showed an interest in it. He sought for it and made us seek it.

If you are unable to make a poem of modernity, then you have not yet grasped the gist of the new style. Always seek it, and you can make your sense of poetry one step closer to the new style.

Poem of immortality:

> The bright moon, the misty foothills, and over the fields flows a haze.

Poem of the new style:

> In bright moonlight bloom flowers—nay, that is a cotton field.

In the opinion of Doho the new style seems to be a style of modernity.

Simple Taste

> 'Sing of a pine, see the pine; sing of a *take* tree, see the *take*.'

In his later years Basho thought much of simple taste—the taste that is free from wordplay, showy diction, allusion, and associations with classic works of Japan and China. See a passage from his letter to Kyorai written at the end of the second year of Genrock (1689):

> On New Year's Day, I will compose a simpler *haik*. As you are well aware of it, I am going to do without decorative wording. An elaborate manner, I should say, would make your *haik* poetry rather commonplace after all. Boncho and you are going to continue such a manner?

With the simple taste, it seems, the new style of Basho was completed. But he was the last one to cease seeking for something new. See an episode from *Kyorai's Notes*:

> When the Old Reverend left Edo in the year of his death, Yaba asked him if he should continue composing *haik* poems of the present style.
>
> "The style of poetry will remain unchanged for a few years," replied the Old Reverend, "but it will change in five or seven years."

Poet Basho

> 'A great master would enjoy a risk.'
> 'The benefit of the *haik* is to refine colloquialisms.'

Immortality and modernity, the new style, the simple taste—all these would be Greek to most of the readers. In fact, Basho's *haik* poems are noted not because they are of immortality, of modernity, of the new style, or of the simple taste, but because they are his works. Let us think not about critic Basho, but about poet Basho.

A man of originality and imagination, Basho employed a variety of material.

He used colloquialisms, borrowed words and expressions from ancient poems of Japan and China, and sang of things that had been disregarded by classical poets. He had interest in things old and new, classic and modern, foreign and Japanese. And so on. However, he was not a scholar. He knew the more one gains knowledge, the more one loses poetry. See an episode from *Kyorai's Notes*:

A *mei* in bloom in a village where New-Year dancers have come not yet.

(One day Kyorai gave a minute commentary on this *haik* of Basho's by applying his stock of classical knowledge.) ...But the Old Reverend did not make a reply to that; instead, he said: "When I walked along Fifth Street last summer, my companions found in the front of a pharmacy a sign board 'Very Good for Hakran'. They said it should be written as 'Kakran (heatstroke)', laughing. Then I remarked, it might cure your *hakran* (dilettantism)."

A Charcoal Bag

A Charcoal Bag is an anthology published in the late summer of the seventh year of Genrock (1694), a few months before the death of Basho. It consists of eight pieces of linked verse and a selection of four-season *haik* poetry. It is a collection of simple-taste *haik* poems. And in them there are vivid depictions of daily urban life in those days. The editors were Ko-ok, Yaba and Rigyu, all of them managers at the House of Echigo-ya (now known as Mitsui Group).

Before going on to *A Charcoal Bag*, let me introduce to you two new disciples, Kyorick and Shiko.

Kyorick: Horikawa Kyorick was a high-ranking *samurai* in the domain of Hikone, Omi. Basho thought highly of his sense of art. See a piece of writing *A Farewell to Kyorick* (written by Basho in the summer of the sixth year of Genrock (1693)):

We met last autumn for the first time, and part now in early Satsuki. Before leaving town you have come to my hermitage to say good-bye; we have talked all day.

A lover of poetry, you also like painting. I once asked why you liked painting. Because I like poetry, you answered. Why do you like poetry? — Because I love painting. You thus learned the two things as if learning a single art. A gentleman should refrain from being versatile in talent; what you did, therefore, was a very smart thing. And then you became my teacher in painting, and my disciple in the art of poetry.

Your painting is refined, high-minded and tasteful, far above mine. My art of poetry, however, is useless, unpopular and out of season. Yet some of the *waka* poems of Shunzei's and Saigyo's are fairly tasteful, even if those were made impromptu. "Their poems are real and touching," wrote the learned Emperor Go-Toba. With such an esteemed word in your mind, never fail to keep such a thin, sole line of art.

The Great Priest Kobo said that a calligrapher should seek not for what ancient masters made, but for what they sought for. Saying that we poets, too, should do the same way, I am now seeing you out, good friend, a small lamp in hand as you go out from the brushwood gate of my hut.

Shiko: Kagami Shiko was a poet in monk attire. An editor of *Zok Salmino*. See an episode from *Kyorai's Notes*:

The pear in flower; the horse shakes its ear in the quivering air. (Shiko)

Kyorai: "I can devise such a phrase as 'the horse shakes its ear in the quivering air', but cannot think of such a word as 'the pear in flower'."

Shiko: "It's nothing. I think it's more difficult to compose a smooth verse like yours."

Kyoksui: "Both of you say what you are good at, it's easy to do; what you are bad at, it's hard to. Both your opinions are good. Yet, generally, it's rather hard to make a smooth one."

Kyorai: "You are bad at that, sir."

A CHARCOAL BAG

Foreword

This anthology was compiled by Ko-ok, Yaba and Rigyu, who, in friendly rivalry, had eagerly learned *haik* poetry from poet Basho, as if opening the window of wisdom, or as if dipping water from the fountain of poesy.

It was one frosty, windy, wintry night that the three good men paid a visit at the Basho-an, where they began to burn some pieces of charcoal in the wooden brazier. Old Basho, smiling, said it looked like an ancient Chinese medicine. Then fiddling with such a small piece of burning charcoal with the bamboo sticks, he recited a verse for the three disciples: 'A winter day—fairly old is the pine tree painted in the gilt screen.' That was when, in all ears, all eyes, and full of motivation, the three poets decided to compile an anthology. Thereafter they composed and collected various pieces of poetry—from a spring morning sun to an autumn moon—and at last completed the compilation of a *haik* anthology in two volumes. Look through it, and you will find various pictorial voices of poetry, and strong, steady tunes of oak charcoal.

And why did they name it *A Charcoal Bag*? I did not think it came from the five rules of Chinese poetry, nor the elegance of Japanese classics, nor mere word-play. There seemed to be a certain principle in that. And some days ago—when Old Basho was about to set out on a journey—I talked with him about this anthology. "You might hear," he said to me, "I sang that old poem of oak charcoal beside the wooden brazier that winter night. At that time I said to myself a word 'charcoal bag' was fitting for *haik*. Hearing such a murmur, they thought of compiling the anthology. Could you write a foreword with such a thing in mind?" And we parted. Thinking over his words, I should say the title itself gives an account of his idea. Nothing to add. No more wits I have.

Written by Soryu on the third of Satsuki of the seventh year of Genrock

(Linked Verse)

Basho: Fragrant are *mei* blossoms on the mountain path, and up pops the sun;
Yaba: Somewhere a pheasant calls, somewhere another flies up.
YB: Let's build a house promptly while plowmen are free in spring;
Basho: Rice prices would go up, says a letter from a westerner; *
BS: It rained softly, lightly at evening; and now above the cloud, the moon;
Yaba: So quiet is the autumn night, we can talk over the hedge;
Yaba: And his annoyance — the boss wants my *kick* flower;
Basho: On no account are any men allowed to see my daughter;
Yaba: He's a route dealer to Nara, a small trader like you;
Basho: And the No-Water Month — we have very little rain this year;
Yaba: So I can cross the river to take over my portion of soybean paste;
Basho: Then the shop owner begins to talk of my mother all at once.
Yaba: All night long — she sits up beside a sick old nun;
Basho: And a lot of *konjak* left on the table when the moon party is over;
Yaba: Wild geese flying high, the traveler sets a warm rug on the horseback;
Basho: Then a quick draw of the sword against a drop of dew;
Yaba: And in the shade of blossoms are drunk townspeople;
Basho: Chanter Fair at Mibu Temple — around the gate crowd people;
BS: Alas, the east wind has brought us a smell of night soil;
Yaba: And the sore upper arm — I'm living a lazy life;
Basho: The neighbor is back from Edo — anything interesting?
Yaba: I want to use this mortar, but after you.
Basho: Ten Holy Nights — the temple bells are resounding far and near;
Yaba: High up over the paulownia tree shines a clear-cut moon;
Basho: Shut the gate, slept silent, got a good night; **
Yaba: Picked up money, bought a *tatami* mat.
Basho: The first day of the Ox — I invite the kin of my wife to dinner;
Yaba: Spring has come, yet he's still a master-less *samurai*;

Basho: The flowers in full bloom, the master sets out toward the spa;

Yaba: Then he walks down the path unto a green stretch of wheat;

Yaba: And every house opens the window eastwards;

Basho: And the lakeside village—I've had a bellyful of fish and porridge.

Yaba: The cries of a plover—it's getting colder night by night;

Basho: And the never-ending calculation of taxes payable;

Yaba: And I begin to live with her without the knowledge of the neighbors;

Basho: Behind the screen, a confectionery plate.

(Note)
* In the Tokugawa Period the rice was priced at the market in Osaka in western Japan.
** *Doho's Notes:*
"This *haik* represents the esprit of *A Charcoal Bag*," said the Old Reverend, "but people strangely think much of another verse of mine—'For the lone woman has to hold a memorial service secretly.' They do not seem to understand my idea."

The Three Poets (Linked Verse)

Ransetz: The flowers are in full bloom; Kenco would weave a straw mat; *
Rigyu: And your sparrow-shape *sushi* is ready on a leaf of thistle or *chisa*.
Yaba: A spring day—on my way home, I find the muddy path dried up;
Ransetz: In the square the *sumo* arena is roughly covered with a mat;
Rigyu: And in the evening sky lies a thin and lean moon;
Yaba: Early rice, late rice, all in leaf, all vie with one another.
Ransetz: In the stream stretches a streak of black-dyed cloth;
Rigyu: This job and that task and at noon, a peal of a bell;
Yaba: And from time to time the neighbors ask my wife for some help;
Ransetz: Then they never forget to praise her clam-open knotting.
Rigyu: Okazaki Village, then Shogo-in, then in front of the Hill of Kurotani;
Yaba: All this is to collect receivables of only five hundred;
Ransetz: On the snow, traces of spikes;
Rigyu: On the mountain, dark black pines.
Yaba: Finishing some odd jobs, he unsaddles his horse at dusk;
Ransetz: Now picking up a potato out of the bowl of rice; outside, the moon;
Rigyu: The rain is over at last, and then blows an autumn wind;
Yaba: Sees the cockscomb, then sleeps and snores soon.
Ransetz: A busy day's night—a boy sleeping, another scribbling on his face;
Rigyu: And the baby makes water as she takes him into her arms;
Yaba: Rattling, rattling, clattering—the men are shipping the cargoes out;
Ransetz: Checking the chopsticks, he thinks of what they think of him;
Rigyu: The daughter has married; she keeps house at present;
Yaba: And hence we have no year-end gifts this year.
Ransetz: The bronze statue of Buddha—people touching the holy foot;
Rigyu: And there come all the neighboring birds;
Yaba: Then the tempest—all the millet blows down;
Ransetz: And after the affray the moon shines over the riding square.

Rigyu: My brother has become an independent at last in Edo;

Yaba: As yet, the chief bars him from the village;

Ransetz: And the seller himself tries the drum, drumming;

Rigyu: Then it begins to snow flake by flake;

Yaba: And we send a messenger to Kamakura to get pieces of news;

Ransetz: To whom have I lent the threads?

Rigyu: A spring day—we take out our old mother to see blossoms;

Yaba: And yet blue mold is still on the New-Year rice cake.

(Note)
* Yoshida Kenco was a noted essayist in the Ashikaga Period. He says in *Essays in Idleness*, "Should we see a *sacra* only when it is in full bloom?"

At Fukawaga (Linked Verse)

Ko-ok: On the edge of a wheat field bloom broad beans;
Basho: And on the afternoon creek toddles a crake.
Taisui: The rain is not so heavy as to soak into my garment;
Rigyu: And a peeper would find us drinking;
Basho: Nobody's in bed; outside, the evening moon;
Ko-ok: Then the autumn tempest—the fence falls down flat.
Rigyu: A cricket begins to chirp under the firewood;
Taisui: And she thinks about how to proceed the midnight job;
Ko-ok: To her pleasure, she's going to marry her sister to a gentle man;
Basho: First of all, she sends a letter to High Priest.
Taisui: The wind is narrowed at dawn, the crows cawing around;
Rigyu: Now then, let us go see a site where a house's been washed away;
Basho: A cup of loach soup, and you will be more vigorous than the young;
Ko-ok: And he sells the stock of tea at a bargain.
Rigyu: This spring would probably see less people go see blossoms;
Taisui: That reminds me of the willow, now dead;
Ko-ok: And a hazy evening moon—the snow has been blown off;
Basho: Being lost in thought, she sets aside the bed cloth;
Taisui: The neighbor is quite a bad fellow, no longer my friend;
Rigyu: And she ushers in a poor monk;
Basho: For the lone woman has to hold a memorial service secretly;
Ko-ok: Well, then, where have I left money, my dear?
Rigyu: Slept a dressed sleep, slept a sweaty sleep;
Taisui: And he sees the guest out, a lamp in hand;
Ko-ok: Then she tries measuring the depth of the snow;
Basho: And we are praised for the payment of taxes.
Taisui: His white hair, his good health, a happy old man;
Rigyu: And Tanabata Festival—we cannot stand that heat;

Basho: The full-moon night is approaching—May the potatoes grow;

Ko-ok: And a pack of sweet fish—the vendor pants and puffs;

Rigyu: Nowadays the street is not so bustling as it used to be;

Taisui: And faint is the sound of a gong in the yonder foothills.

Ko-ok: A streak of cloud in the sky; here below, it begins to breeze leaf by leaf;

Rigyu: And the river beach—on a bleached cloth sits a skylark, singing;

Basho: The flowers, the blossoms, and a group of women making their way;

Taisui: And on their way bloom violets, dandelions, and that is all.

A Hundred Stanzas (Linked Verse)

Rigyu: The planting of rice—there's a bare baby, and father in a loincloth;

Yaba: On the bank bloom briers in pure white;

Ko-ok: And after the rain rosary doves coo, coo, cooing;

Rigyu: Then the wind blows westwards through Officer Street;

Yaba: Then a brown pongee's drawn to the end of a pole hanger;

Ko-ok: And people shout as a horse trots.

Rigyu: It stinks in evening moonlight—that green forage;

Yaba: Leaf after leaf falls from the bead tree while I sweep the garden;

Ko-ok: And noisy are little birds when I pick up a red robin;

Rigyu: In monk attire though he is, that fellow is none other than Niheiji;

Yaba: And in Matsuzaka he goes to red-light Yagawa through your back street;

Ko-ok: In the dark she feels sore as a night wind touches her cracks;

Rigyu: And gorgeous are the costumes of some dozen court nobles;

Yaba: And monks trot, trot across the hall.

Ko-ok: Reddish are the sunny sides of *take* trees;

Rigyu: Nearby gushes so clean water that I can rinse my mouth;

Yaba: And I do understand why Omi is called Water Country;

Ko-ok: And a bright crescent—tomorrow will be a fine day.

Rigyu: They are caught and salted at once—the little black-back sardines;

Yaba: Elm fruits fall on the roof, so that it might decay before long;

Ko-ok: And a flowery, cloudy day—a group of girdle vendors returning home;

Rigyu: Around Great Kobo's Day, happy merry days. *

Yaba: My moxa-burned skin scabs and scabs; that is a sign of health;

Ko-ok: And over the table scatter *horo-horo* beans;

Rigyu: With no sleeves to cast, she's lost in thought; **

Yaba: So that she cannot settle herself down to spinning.

Ko-ok: Here comes cargo after cargo from a western *daimyo;*

Rigyu: Yesterday, sunny; today, very sunny;

Yaba: Eaten by worms, all the tobacco plants have fallen to the ground;
Ko-ok: And the garden of a temple—*natto* beans are fermented.
Rigyu: Tried to divert my attention from the ague, but in vain;
Yaba: So the clogs with cane straps feel quite heavy;
Ko-ok: And she's calling her husband rather loudly;
Rigyu: Around the well in the back of the neighbor's house;
Yaba: And the evening moon—here comes a shadow, an old pillar on its back;
Ko-ok: That is a huge ox, by far taller than the tall grass.
Rigyu: Bon Festival is over, the Jodo-Sect temple's quiet;
Yaba: A rush job—the bath is roughly roofed with wooden sheets;
Ko-ok: And they thin the woods of firs and cedars;
Rigyu: A small red shrine—the newer it is, the better it looks;
Yaba: My baggage on his shoulder, the inn's man sees me off to the beach;
Ko-ok: Today, a late-winter day, beggar nuns are chanting a chilly sutra.
Rigyu: It is year after year that he buys a mortar for the making of rice cake;
Yaba: And he again forgets to send an invoice to a merchant in Temma;
Ko-ok: He's a boatman, he's wearing a large-sleeve gown;
Rigyu: Gets up at dawn, pays a visit to the holy statue of Kwannon;
Yaba: Picking up a half-burned piece of wood, she puts it reversely into the fire;
Ko-ok: A good manager, she runs a shop with a fund of some fifteen gold coins.
Rigyu: The moon, the blossoms, the remains of an old fort, and that is all;
Ko-ok:
    Then a whistling gust of wind—a woman is picking seaweed into the pail;
Yaba: And silkworms seem happy in the garden;
Rigyu: It is shortly before noon, the sky's calm and serene;
Ko-ok: And he sits at the edge of the verandah, his swollen leg stretching out;
Yaba: Then he carefully checks an unfinished pan;
Rigyu: Before him spreads an alternative wheat field bordered with stakes;
Ko-ok: That is a calligraphic work of Yorimasa—which the seller knows not; ***
Yaba: What is valued, a woman will care not—if she has children;
Rigyu: Hence she receives another suit of used kimono from a noble lady.
Ko-ok: Tens of steps up from Gioji Nunnery, and you will find Nison-in Temple;

Yaba: And today a very solitary feeling I have;
Rigyu: Then a white scene—it begins to snow lightly, softly;
Ko-ok: And milk white is a lump of cod bowel in the pan.
Yaba: The morning moon—there's a figure threading coins with a straw;
Rigyu: In the shade of a wall you could pick velvet shanks;
Ko-ok: And he has his shrike shriek to drive birds off;
Yaba: Now then, let me hear pieces of news from Mino.
Rigyu: The day of the Snake, a day when we make an offering to the Gods;
Ko-ok: And all the guests can taste a tasty taste of *miso*;
Yaba: There's a girl wearing cotton clothes with a red maple-leaf pattern;
Rigyu: It looks well on her in front of a tea house at the mouth of town;
Ko-ok: Burning Festival—fires, flares, flickers, and skyward, red bits of rack;
Yaba: And a cup of soup with whale and vegetables.
Rigyu: The flowery season—I have moved to quiet Katagi Field;
Ko-ok: A good servant, she's prompt and crisp in response;
Yaba: The sun is setting; in the dark-grey eventide there comes a sound of rain;
Rigyu: And the good tide—now in the Sixth Month the port is alive with ships;
Ko-ok: And the master's room—the women polish the pillars;
Yaba: One argues vehemently, another responds jokingly.
Rigyu: The flood is over; people are clearing sand out of the fields;
Ko-ok: There's a huge chestnut tree—how old is it?
Yaba: Paying caution money, he takes over a house from a bowman;
Rigyu: He's suffered with a skin disease ninety days, though;
Ko-ok: And he throws things roughly, wildly when he gets angry;
Yaba: Often coming to borrow a *go*-game board.
Rigyu: Just in front of town there's a tout rambling for travelers;
Ko-ok: There comes a rich lady—look at the silky stuff around her neck;
Yaba: And abstinence on the first day—who's day this day?
Rigyu: Indeed tiresome are the rainy Hassen days;
Ko-ok: When bales of Sendai rice are packed tightly and carefully;
Yaba: The litigation is over, the bank is now under construction;
Rigyu: And the evening moon—he looks for a physician he knows by name;

Ko-ok: Then he goes home, a package of grilled salmon in hand.

Yaba: The greedy rate of taxation—petitions, complaints, gusts, blasts;

Rigyu: We are too old, too weak to work;

Ko-ok: We also suffer from heat, and the coming of the hottest season;

Yaba: Some months have passed, and now I pass Ausaka Pass;

Rigyu: Unsellable are goods on the shelf of that blacksmith's;

Ko-ok: And hence people discuss the reconstruction of the town gate.

Yaba: They begin to bloom past the equinox—the single-petal flowers;

Scribe: And three men of poetry, three hues of spring.

(Note)
* The Great Kobo was a monk in the Heian Period, the founder of Shingon Buddhism.
** In Japanese 'no sleeves to cast' means 'no money to pay'.
*** Minamoto-no Yorimasa was a noted *samurai* poet in the Heian Period.

Spring

New Year

Basho: The New-Year Decorations—let me hear a good piece of news from Ise.
> *Kyorai's Notes*:
> One day I received a letter from the Old Reverend. "There are many opinions on this *haik*," it said, "What do you think about it?"
> I wrote back: "This esteemed *haik* mentions not your hometown, nor Kyoto, but Ise. Seeing an old-style rite of New-Year decorations, you seemed to imagine an ancient ritual of the sacred Ise Shrine. In short, you were eager to travel again, I presume."
> The reply from the Old Reverend: "It is true that I remembered the sacred Great Shrine at that time. And then I composed the New-Year *haik* in imitation of the great monk poet Ji-en. You are quite right."

Jokshi: The pine decorations—open the door, you will find a red morning sky.

Sampou: A case of lobster—today the cargo would pass the Shirakawa Barrier.
> (Note) Sampou was a merchant dealing in fish and fish products.

Kyorai: Let us celebrate the coming of spring; the deer going back to Tamba.
> (Note) Tamba is a mountainous province, northwest of Kyoto.

Masahide in Zeze: The New-Year morn—if only I could have a follower in sword.

Shado in Osaka: All's busy in spring, sparrows moving about in a brown coat.

Taisui: The nice scent of Kiso—the New-Year Decorations are made of cedar.
> (Note) Kiso is famous as producer of cedar.

Senho: Water Festival—pour the water on that just-married Shin-Sect bonze.
> (Note) Those days the Jodo-Shin Buddhism alone allowed its monks to wed.

Ko-ok: New Year Day—people use rather polite language today.

Rigyu: The New-Year sun—if only I could be a herb picked by a maiden.

Yaba:
> A happy thing at New Year—the boy has taken over the name from father.

Mei

Lord Rosen: There blooms such a *mei* tree as said in *Essays in Idleness*.
> (Note) See a passage from Yoshida Kenco's *Essays in Idleness*:
> A white *mei*, a light-red *mei*, an early single *mei*, a fragrant red double *mei*—all these amuse me.

Kyoksui: So well does the *mei* branch curve, it may fit for the grip of a mortar.

Shiko: The sweet scent of a *mei*, and over there spreads young sunlight.

—At a window;

Doho in Iga: *Mei* blossoms falling, and in the room run thin fragrant sunbeams.

Rigyu: The *mei* tree's in bloom; I've had the bath repaired.

Youto: The *mei* tree's in bloom; I've opened a red-*miso* bottle.

Yaba: Blossom after blossom appears in the *mei*, the way it does year after year.

Sampou: There is a *mei* in bloom in red in the garden; inside, a lovely maiden.
  (Note) This comes from a scene of *The Tale of Genji*.

—Seeing women sing a song as they prepare seven-herb porridge;

Kikack: Herbal sap is spattered, and its green fragrance about her face.

Yaba: Seven-herb porridge—her face half made-up, she is chopping the herbs.

Senjo: They may feel itchy in the feet—the girls picking herbs in the meadow.

—In a letter from Kyoto;

Kyorai: A hazy moon—we are parting step by step.

Monk Joso: Ohara Fields, a hazy moon, and butterflies waltzing around.

Senka: Hazy is the moon, yet it's a little too early a season to take off the hood.

—At a *haik* meeting in Fukagawa;

Rigyu: The calm, serene season—it will be chilly once every three days at most.

Shido: The fifteenth of the First Month—they begin selling used clothes.

Yaba: Mewing, mewing, meowing, the cats begin falling in love.

Kikack: A kitten wrestles with a kitty, and in the air flies a butterfly.

Warblers

Ransetz: It makes me catch my breath at morning—the twitter of a warbler.

Kikack: Warbler, warbler, you are still a poor singer; I give you a pill of music.

Torin: A warble of a warbler, and then sparrows get up, twittering.

Yaba: A warble of a warbler, and a *tofu* vendor raises his voice at the gate.

Rigyu: Careful is a warbler when it gives just a single twitter.

Willows

Koshun: To stop planting a persimmon was to plant the willow, now in green.

Soryu: It stirs on the paper screen in moonlight—the shadow of a willow.

Yaba: My revenues enough for a small family, the willow bowing in the garden.

Ichifou: Short is the tail of a wagtail, long are the branches of a willow.

Rigyu: It's bowing forward the street—the willow in front of town.

Basho: Behind the umbrellas are green willows greeting me in the rain.

Camellia

Ko-ok: People bearing soil, and in the straw basket, a red *tsubaki* blossom.

Koshun: It should not have been cut—the long *tsubaki* branch full of blossoms.

Kyoksui: It's so prudent as to bud early in winter—that camellia.

Ransetz: The camellia in bloom; it's quite a job to saw its branch.

Shiko: Birds are twittering; a *tsubaki* blooms in red beside my house.

Yaba: I've just swept the garden, where there's a *tsubaki* blossom just fallen.

Sacra

—One day I went seeing *sacra* blossoms in the Hills of Ueno, finding people natter, sputter, murmur, shout. Songs, cries, various sounds of things. I took a rest by a pine tree.

Basho: An incomplete set of tableware—I feel so while I see the flowers.

Sampou: I see *sacra* blossoms casually at home; unusually, the *sashimi* is ready.

Joso: An ill-timed visit—I'm in his home while my friend sees blossoms outside.

—Accompanying a noble *samurai*;

Soryu: The *sacra* trees in bloom, the attendants enjoy in their own way.

Kyorai: The *sacra* in bloom; the white-haired flower guards talking in silence.
> *Kyorai's Notes:*
> "Beautiful," said the Old Reverend. "Well can I see a sad and sweet hue in this *haik*."

Ko-ok: Breakfast tea—raising my knee, I'm watching blossoms in the garden.

Keico: Dark is the cloud at dusk, although we see *sacra* blossoms tomorrow.

Sharei:
   Being held up in the arms, the little boy's excited among *sacra* blossoms.

Hokshi: He's rearranging his dark brown vesture—a monk among the blossoms.

Koshun: He too goes seeing a *sacra* when it blooms—the lover of a peony.

Kikack: The *sacra* trees in bloom; I cannot observe the five commandments.

Ransetz: A *sacra* blooms in the garden; May the blossoms not turn into worms.

Nun Chigetz: *Sacra* blossoms falling, a waterwheel turning around on a brook.

Shido in Osaka: The *sacra* blossoms we see, and a black-clad old monk.

Youho: An old lady praying to the late-blooming *sacra*—whose mother is she?

Fuzen in Fukui: It sees a woman leap over a stream—the flowery wild *sacra*.

Rigyu: Kelp broth—a bonze in the kitchen notices a *sacra* blooming outside.

Rigyu: The *sacra* party—let us leave the first menu to the cook's decision.

A CHARCOAL BAG

Ko-ok: A shower of blossoms—the kitchen is decorated with a *sacra* branch.

Yaba: People wine and dine by flowers, have no chance until Summer Festival.

Yaba: Lunch time—everyone gathers at the wild *sacra* tree in bloom.

Spring Festival

Sentock:
  The tide's low, the river flows through the mudflat like a girdle of water.

Torin: The peach trees in full bloom; I get on a punt at Fushimi at noon.

Kikack: Hina dolls sit at night, and where do you think is the God of Katsuragi?
  (Note) The God of Katsuragi was said to work only nights due to shyness from his ugliness.

Joko in Mino: Peach Festival—the wild little boy too has got a piece of rice cake.
  (Note) Peach Festival is held for little girls.

Yaba: A half-day walk, a sunny path, and the peach trees in bloom.

Rigyu: The peach trees in bloom, hemp seeds are trodden as usual.

Ko-ok: The peach in bloom, a horse's rubbing its head with the shrub hedge.

Basho: Now at low tide—the green willow droops on to the muddy riverbed.

Things Vernal

Iyou in Saga: They try to go up the waterfall—the brave little sweet fish.

Basho: The spring rain—a trickle runs down the roof, curving on the beehive.

Shisan: A gust of wind—there remain in the azalea a few pistils and stamens.

Dosui: A couple of swallows nest at the gate; I'm burning trash with care.

Ensui in Iga: The burnt-out fields—a bird flying away, the wind runs a long way.

Senka: The wheat fields—it's nice to see a waving stretch of green breeze.

—As a traveler;

Yaba: The hedge circles the hunting grounds; there would flower purple violets.
  (Note) This comes from a *waka* of Princess Nukata-no Okimi:
    The purple violet fields, a royal preserve, now red at dawn;
    Stop waving at me; the keeper can watch us.

—When this anthology was not yet finished, Ko-ok set out on a journey. Two of us saw him off to Shinagawa Town.

Yaba: A misty, cloudy day—it will be the same view, however far you go.

Rigyu: They say a two-month good-bye—the *mei* and the *sacra*.

Summer

Early Summer

Ransetz: The changing of clothes—hang out salted fish in the sun.

Yaba: The changing of clothes—we could see *sacra* in full bloom ten days earlier.

Kyusetz:
   The changing of clothes—it's busy putting on light clothes on a journey.

Sezshi: The changing of clothes—you look more casual than a sparrow.

Shisan: The blossoms now gone, the *sacra* trees fairly leafy this morning.

Rigyu: The changing of clothes—pure white is the front curtain of a fan shop.
   (Note) See a *waka* of Empress Jito written in the *Man'yo-shu*:
      Spring has just gone, here comes summer, and they look pure white
      —The clothes being aired in the foot of Mount Heavenly Fragrance.

Deutzia

Basho: White are the deutzias, and hesitatingly in the dark stands a willow.

Kyorai: Dark is the night; between the white deutzias there would be a gate.
   Kyorai's Note:
   The Old Reverend said this was an exceptional *haik* of high status. But I think this is just exceptional, not highly made. A *haik* of high status would be a poem of grace. Poems of logic, contrast and comparison are mostly of low status.

—As a traveler;

Kyorick: A white deutzia, my gray horse, and now the sky red at dawn.
   Kyorai's Notes:
   (Kyorai tried to compose a verse similar to this *haik*, but without success; and deplored his lack of a sense of poetry when he read this.) Seeing Kyorick's good arrangement of wording, I remembered a word of the Old Reverend's: "If you cannot make a good tune of poesy, turn your tongue-tip a thousand times."

Shiko: The deutzias in flower, a vendor is tapping on a pail as he walks.

Things Various

Koshun: The song of fishermen—their ships are back to the sound, now cool.

Sodo: Just as Sogi cared about beard, so I'm fond of lotuses in my pond.

Basho: It sings among *take* trees, sighs over senility—the summer warbler.

Cuckoos

Torin: Cuckoo, cuckoo, I had slept on the second floor until you sang.

Kikack: The first bridge, then the second, then daybreak, then calls a cuckoo.

Ransetz: Nightingale, I'm walking on a moonless night, a lamp in hand.

Sampou: I cannot see you, nightingale, though I look skyward with a lamp.

Basho:
    Cuckoo, cuckoo, the tea pickers might hear you calling in the leafy fields.

Soryu: The sky blue, the cries of a cuckoo, and a punt is going down the river.

Rigyu: A cuckoo cries and cries as it blows, then it begins to rain.

Yaba: Cuckoo, cuckoo, the lattice does not allow me to see you.

Wheat

Keico in Mino: Tax-exempt Persimmon Temple—the wheat ears too look greedy.

Sensen: It sways as the wheat ears wave—the great Tsukuba Mountain.

Kyorick: The wheat was reaped, the rice planted, and there fly fireflies already.

—Seeing off the Old Reverend to Kawasaki Town;

Rigyu: On the way, a smell of wheat, and in the town, a scent of new crop.

—At the same time;

Yaba: Field after field appears as we walk, and another patch of wheat.

—And at the same time;

Taisui: It's time to say good-bye; a swarm of flies are gone with the sea wind.

Tango Festival

Kikack: The Satsuki rains—under the umbrella, little paper dolls.

Shado: Hang the iris under the eaves, enjoy the hue of a Satsuki breeze.

Torin: The irises being taken, the pond will be muddy until the fifth day.

Ransetz:
    I've got *chimaki* cakes as a gift, but with neither a letter nor a message.
    (Note) This comes from an episode of *haikai* poet Matsunaga Teitock sending to *waka* poet Kinoshita Choshoshi some *chimaki* cakes together with a letter of verse.

Senka: Commander Miwonoya—his neck would be hard like a helmet.
    (Note) This comes from a scene of the Battle of Yashima in *The Tale of the Heike*.

Soryu: Summer has come; I change the two-piece for a one-piece.

Travelers in Summer

Gako: A line of pines I see, and the heat of town I will soon feel.

Sharei: The heat, the dead trees, the day flowers, and I've had corns on my feet.

Rocho in Nagasaki: The second rooster, then the third, and yet I feel hot.

Ensui: The treeless hill—no way out from the heat of summer.

Basho: A citrus tree in bloom, yet in Suruga all is tea that smells sweet.

(Written in a letter from Shimada Town, Suruga.)

The Satsuki Rain

Soryu: The Satsuki rain—a log bridges to the neighbor across the muddy path.

Torin: The River Yodo and the Yamato—all's a hue of mud in the Satsuki rain.

Yaba: The Satsuki rains—there are little boys taking hold of little fish.

Ranran: The Satsuki rains—the leafy wild burdocks are wet with dew.

(Written in a letter from Torin.)

Taisui: The Satsuki rain—over my face is a book, and another under my head.

Things Refreshing

Basho: The summer river—it's fairly cool sitting on a huge driftwood.
  (Note) This *haik* is not a *haik* of Basho's, but Kowou's. An editorial mistake.

Lady Kana: The shadow of a summer tree stirs, and the leaves in moonlight.

Ushichi in Nagasaki: It looks cool—the *take* tree that has grown behind the fence.

Tanshi: Take the lamp away, and we might feel cool—might we not?

Nun Chigetz: Cool is a breath of lake breeze—bringing us cries of a heron.

Koh-ho in Bizen: It might make you feel cool—a dewdrop from a ladle.

Kyorai: A cool sight—on the sandbank are boys showing one another's catches.

Yaba: A cool evening breeze—we totter, stagger on a riverside rock.

Sodo: The beautiful crescent—I enjoy a cool shadow in my shabby hut.

Things Summery

Sampou: The citrus in season—wonder where my Teika-style desk is.

Masahide:
  Cool is seaweed in a hut in the isle, where a woman shelling abalones.

Rito: To pay taxes, people work among white poppy flowers; that is the life.

Ransetz: They are having rice and vegetables—the girls in the rice field.

—At Kiso;

Kyorick: Women planting rice in paddies—who's Yamabuki? Which is Tomoe?
  (Note) Yamabuki and Tomoe were beautiful women warriors who fought for the *samurai* commander Kiso Yoshinaka. (*The Tale of the Heike*)

Nun Chigetz: It makes a longing face for rain—that day flower.

Hokkon: The leafy hill—nobody cares about green walnuts.

Otokuni: The day breaks; lotus, lotus, burst and wake me up.

Joso: Prayers for rain—a man in borrowed wear would be annoyed if it rained.

Senka: The twilight rain, a water mallow in flower, and there flies a firefly.

Soshu: A hot breath of air — a butterfly is flying around the young grass.

Zanko in Mino: It falls from the plum tree — the shell of a cicada.

Iyou in Saga: There scatter eggplants; all is the fault of wild boar's tusks.

Dofou: The hot air — a round-fan vendor is walking through Samurai Street.

Youho: A big white mountain of cloud — in the distance there's an eagle's aerie.

Senka: Straight is a *take* branch, yet its young leaf is unfit for straightness.

Ransetz: A little boy sucking a *take* sprout — how beautiful his teeth are!
 (Note) This comes from a scene of Lord Kaoru as a little boy. (*The Tale of Genji*)

—A certain one warned his servant not to drink much. One day he held a banquet, showing renowned brands of *sake* to the guests, with his stock of knowledge on liquor. He seemed to feel somewhat awkward, for he made a *haik* as below:

Rigyu: So hot a day, so many a brand of *sake*.

—I visited a certain gentleman's villa, had a friendly talk with him all day, and shortly before dark we looked skyward.

Yaba: The sitting room in summer — we lie down, seeing the clouds going away.

Autumn

('The Bright Moon' is presented as the initial theme, and the others at random.)

The Bright Moon

Koshun: The bright moon up in the sky, I enjoy seeing it all night.

Kyorai: Bright is the moon, and along the verandah scatter husks of millet.

Kakei: Bought a house, moved in, and now saw the bright moon of the year.

Shado: Bright is the moon, yet who's playing the ill-timed dove flute?

Rito: In the shade of a pine, a fish preserve, and up over the sea, a bright moon.

Rigyu: The moon bright, the bridge looks rather low at high tide.

Kikack: A broken house — the garden tree looks chilly in autumn moonlight.

—Seeing a mid-autumn moon in the province of Musashi for the first time in my life, with a line of 'a fine view of Mounts Fuji and Tsukuba' in my mind;

Soryu: Bright is the moon; can we see Fuji Mountain from Suruga Town?

Tanabata Festival

Kikack: The two stars meet; let's set a pillow to the *take* tree.

Ko-ok: The two stars meet; the hem of the mosquito net looks alluring red.

Ransetz: Tonight, a special night, the stars look brighter in the River Heaven.

Bon Festival

Shado: Bon Festival — behind the mealies sways a lantern light like a spirit.
> *Kyorai's Note:*
> Shado: "Rotsu said the 'mealies' could be altered to 'millet' or something, and thereby this was not a *haik*."
> Kyorai: "Rotsu knows nothing about the difference between a word of a theme and a word of ornament. The theme of this *haik* is a lantern light at a poor house on a Bon-Festival night; therefore, 'Bon Festival' shall not be altered. This would otherwise be a *haik* of different taste. In contrast, the 'mealies', a word of ornament, could be changeable to 'millet' or any other better expression according to a scene."

Riyou:
Bon Festival — I'm not drunken, but drunk enough to dance in moonlight.

Yaba:
The Bon-Night moon's up, someone tapping on the door — am I still awake?

A CHARCOAL BAG

Morning Glories

—In seclusion;

Basho: The morning glory—let me leave the gate shut in the daytime.
  (Note) This *haik* is written in his essay *In Seclusion*.

Rigo: In the hedge flowers a morning glory—after the men have gone working.

Koshun: The morning glory—if only it could creep onto that willow.
  (Note) This comes from an ancient *waka*:
    If only a *sacra* could bloom on a willow branch;
    With the fragrances of a *mei*.

Autumnal Insects

Nun Chigetz in Otsu: An autumn cricket—you are aged, your chirps sound weak.
  (Note) This comes from a *waka* of Saigyo:
    A cricket chirping in the chilly autumn night;
    You are getting weak, your chirps gone away.

Joso: It chirps between the words of condolence—that cricket.

Iyou in Saga: The grasped bulbil and the grasping mantis—both had a fall.

Ko-ok: It's driven away with chopsticks—a cricket on the table.

Deer

Sharai: The little deer—one calls, another turns around.

—On request;

Soryu: It's just like a shape of a Mitsune ink-stone—a track of a deer.
  (Note) Okochi-no Mitsune was a poet in the Heian Period, one of the editors of the *Kokin-shu*. See a *waka* of his:
    Are you, deer, calling for a true love of yours? If yes;
    Look at your fields; you can find a *fair lady* in flower.

—As a traveler;

Doho: Lake Land—a little way off the path, a couple of deer standing upright.

Leaves and Flowers

Torin: It's more autumnal than summery—the *hagi* clover in Miyagi Fields.
  (Note) The *hagi* clover in Miyagi Fields (now the Sendai Plains in Tohoku Region) is also called a 'summer *hagi*'.

Yado:
    On the blades of silver grass are sparrows alighting somehow in the wind.

Ensui: Sheaves of rice are aired in the field; and on the mound, a *hagi* in flower.

Joso: The punt in a marsh, the reed ears touch my face in my dream.

—At the port of Naniwa;

Kyorai: The reed ears—chopsticks clack as they are put on the table.

—Seeing women picking mushrooms;

Kikack: It's like a *karta* game; she doesn't notice a mushroom under her nose.

—At a *kick* garden;

Sampou: The misty *kick* garden—there'd be something in the heart of white.

Torin: Today, the ninth day, the wild *kick* flowers are called up, too.

Autumnal Plants

Rigyu: The persimmon tree's full of fruits, and underneath, a flock of children.

Youho: There's a dead crab, there's a chestnut rolling down to the stream.
(Note) The readers are asked to imagine what has happened.

Kihack: A gust of autumn wind, and I find the eggplant well in fruit.

Ko-ok: They have burst by the window—the cotton fruits aired in a basket.

—The red pepper is called a South Sea pepper. That is perhaps because it has been consumed there for a long time. I do not know the details. It is also called a red fruit, a heaven peeper, an illusion, and an eight-bud plant—all these may have been given in a playful mood by such people who liked naming things in their own way. Though such names are not elegant, but it is natural, and it is no use complaining, because it is in fact awkwardly shaped. Once picked, it would be planted happily in a stone pot at the edge of a bamboo shelf. But in a bad case, it would be placed on a cracked mortar or in a bottom-broken well-bucket, at the hem of a roof or at the toe of a second floor or in the shade of a drying place. Not a delicate plant such as a morning glory, it seems not to be treated tenderly. And in the end it would be eaten by a bearded man as a side dish when he drinks, or at best as red spice for *tofu* at times when one has a poor appetite or has no other foods. But do not think all of us take it as a mere seasoning. I know, for instance, a certain gentleman who, on his return from Kitano Shrine, paid a gold coin to a boy for your ripe red pepper. However, he has already passed away; so nobody loves it nowadays, nobody tastes a touch of its bitterness nowadays.

Yaba: First potted, then uprooted, the red peppers are all gone.

Things Various

Ransetz: The hues of autumn—the gorgeous costumes of *sumo* wrestlers in line.

Joso: The end of a thing—a scarecrow is burned under the bath.

Shado: Beating clothes alone, I smell a good smell of the dyed goods alone.

Kakei: The autumn sunset—I feel my flesh being rather light and simple.

Rigo:
The gathering of mushrooms—little boys, be careful not to pick a toadstool.

Shiko: A chilly autumn night—I'm sipping a cup of gourd soup.

Hokshi: The roars of the wind, a sign of autumn, and yet is that all?
   (Note) This comes from a *waka* in the *Kokin-shu*:
      I cannot see a clear sign of the coming of autumn;
      And yet it surprises me — the roaring of the wind.

Monk Yiyi: The autumn wind — be careful, butterfly, you'd be blown to the pond.

Kikack: The cloud hides the moon, darkening the hands of the cook.

Winter

Early Winter

Kikack: The winter blasts—the head land looks more chilly than the offing.

Torin: Cold blasts down from Fuji Mountain; leaves are whirling up in town.

Basho: The roars of the winter sea—on the morning beach lies red sea weed.
  (Note) This *haik* is not a *haik* of Basho's, but Kowou's. Another editorial mistake.

Shiryo: Winter's coming, people are busy covering *sacra* trees with straw mats.

Sharei: The wintry pine woods—cobwebs are blown, broken by the wind.

Tokei: The *soba* wheat has been reaped, the frosty field alive with sparrows.

Zanko: There remains a winter gust in the thicket; beside it, a small hut.

Soshu: The first frost of the season—the cat bristles up in the kitchen.

Hasso: The roars of winter blasts—the cat's blinking repeatedly.

—At Nangou Shrine;

Torin: The roars of winter blasts—there stands a god house among the trees.

Youto: Frosty *sago* palms, broom patterns on the sand—all these look chilly.

Winter Rain

Keico: He would be hungry in the winter rain—that potato lover.

Joso: It runs as the winter rain runs in the offing—the darkness of the sea.

—When the Old Reverend Basho coming to my house;

Sharei: The shabby hut—let it rain today, but without a leak in the roof.

Kyorick: The moon is low at winter daybreak, and it rains once or twice.

—On a journey;

Yaba: The winter night, a rainy night, the neighbor stopped grinding at night.

Long Radish

Basho: People are pulling long radishes, a little boy happy on a saddle.
  Kyorai's Notes:
    Rankock: "What do you like about this?"
    Kyorai: "You should appreciate this as a picture. (...) People are pulling long radishes; not far from them a horse browsing, and on its saddle a little boy sitting happily. If you see such a picture, how do you feel?"
    Afterwards I (Kyorai) heard not Rankock but his brother—not a *haik* poet but a good painter—admired this verse.

Yaba: His headband removed, the long-radish picker looks rather young.

Shado: The Gods have gone with the wind, and a long radish white at eventide.
(Note) In Japan the Gods are said to visit the province of Izmo in the Tenth Month.

Cold Winter

Yaba: Voices pierce town at midnight, which makes me feel very cold indeed.

Shiho: Nowadays we do not exchange greetings without saying it's cold indeed.

Rigyu: A bowl of *soba* without soup—which makes me feel very cold indeed.

Gabi: Cold is winter moonlight, it's white at my feet.

Rito: The fish shop—move up the straw curtain, look up at the winter moon.
(The two verses above were found in a letter sent to the Old Reverend's hermitage in Fukagawa.)

Snow

Yaba: The first snowfall—I shake and nod my head to show the way.

Rigyu: The first snowfall—the horse stands high with its nose high.

Baizan: The first snowfall—white is the ivy over the broken wall.

Yiyi: It snows, it snows, stay with me, winter wren.

Ensui: A snow day—the letters under a light paper sheet look as a blur.

—One winter night at Handoji Temple:

Shiko: The snowy leaves of cedars, and in hazy moonlight cries a night crane.

Hokshi: The snow fields, a red saddle, and would the horse head for Sano?
(Note) This comes from a *waka* of Fujiwara-no Teika:
There's not a tree to halt the horse, nor a shade to clear the snow;
There only spreads a white twilight view of Sano Plains.

Kyorick: It melts at first at the stable—the first snow of the season.

Koseki: It snows and blows, and a charcoal vendor passes through the street.

Otokuni: It snows and blows, and birds crying in the lake and the mountains.

Soryu: A boat on a snowy river, and at its chimney perches a white egret.

Things Wintry

The late Rogan: The withered fields—there's a wedge of sorrow in my heart.

Basho: Beside the grinder is a chilly *kick* flower—white with rice bran.

Kyorick: Ten Holy Nights—an old man in monk attire is wearing new socks.

Nun Chigetz: Burning Festival—crow, crow, never take away the offerings.

Shido: It smells white about the white cedar chopsticks—the white fish.

Joso: The daybreak, the hearth, and a sudden blaze of five or six feet high.

Zanko: Koshin Vigil—I enjoy a *kotatsu* warmer all night long.

Kikack: They too enjoy watching the *kagra* music and dances—the newlyweds.

Kikack: A cloudy day, the sound of waves, and a rain of hail over the sea.

The Sweeping of Soot

Basho: The sweeping of soot—the carpenter is making up a shelf for his home.

Banco: Soot sweeping—the sales manager is in charge of brushing the screens.

Yaba: He's making rice cake cheerfully—that young *samurai* servant.

Ransetz: The Twelfth Month—the ascetics set out gallantly.

Nun Chigetz: Spring is coming soon; in the ice, pieces of rubbish.

The End of a Year

Sampou: Here comes another year-end; everything goes in the same way.

Riyou: The end of a year—there's a man marries without formalities.

Nun Chigetz: Repayment done, the year passing by, in the garden, a warbler.

Ko-ok: The end of a year—the cover of the pot looks loud and showy.

Ensui: The last night of the year—the New Year beans are being prepared.

Yaba: The end of a year—people are being small-minded in money.

—In reply to Old Basho's letter asking me how I am doing in the year-end;

Soryu: Let the year go by; I'm clipping my nails in a temple at vigil.

Koshun: The year passing by; take my letter with you if you go to Kyoto.

Autumn (Linked Verse)

Kikack: A cedar tree on the ridge, and high up above, an autumn sky; *

Ko-ok: And a hawk of late passage flying over the sea. **

KO: A misty morning—the conch shell is blown to call up day laborers;

Kikack: And it hides the moon—the large castle-gate;

KK: Beside it staggers an old man, a wooden brazier in hand;

Ko-ok: In the path lies two or three logs.

KO: A night-soil boat comes to Shimokyo Town from Uji Village;

Kikack: And he looks funny—the baldhead bonze in a straw raincoat;

Ko-ok: Now in the early afternoon—a foot-soldier is baby-sitting;

Kikack: And she comes to herself from heat stroke thanks to the acupuncturist.

Ko-ok: Beside the paddy are bundles of rice seedlings for planting;

Kikack: Nearby, a pilgrim passes by, singing a song of the Woven Hat;

Ko-ok: And she looks for petty money in the drawer below the lamp;

Kikack: While he's taking a nap in moonlight, something on his face.

Ko-ok: The bell is tinkling; salmon will be touching the fishing net;

Kikack: In the river floats a raft—on which sits a wild goose;

Ko-ok: Blossoms at Umedz, maple leaves at Katsura—all sung by Tsurayuki;

Kikack: That you should have a love child.

KK: O money, where have you gone? How have you been spent?

Ko-ok: The Miya crepe is nice—only when it's just-made;

Kikack: She's worn out, she's bitten by a gnat in summer grass;

Ko-ok: And the boy looks vexed at the mention of his pockmarks.

Kikack: Bean-Casting Festival—there scatter tangerine seeds, too;

Ko-ok: Undressing myself, I wait for the water bath to be ready;

Kikack: My house is left all desolate, for you have not visited me;

Ko-ok: I'm on my way home, heavy millet in one basket, light salt in the other.

Kikack: At dusk in autumn sparrows flock around the pine tree of Karasaki;

Ko-ok: Then blows a chilly north wind, and clouds afloat toward the moon;

Kikack: And he brings a few bottles of *sake*, a paper lamp in hand;

Ko-ok: As yet the wall is still not plastered.

Kikack: A sad and sweet night—someone's reading aloud *The Tale of Ogri*;

Ko-ok: There's nothing to do; the ship is not yet ready.

(The remaining four lines were not composed, because Ko-ok left for Kyoto on urgent business.)

  (Note)
  * Kikack says Ko-ok is like a high cedar tree.
  ** Ko-ok replies that he is but a late comer.

A CHARCOAL BAG

Hosted by Mister Amano Torin (Linked Verse)

Torin: Going down the hill, I pick up things for the making of a scarecrow;
Yaba: And an autumn breeze—from paddy to paddy flows water;
Rigyu: The moon is setting, the day's faintly breaking;
Torin: Over the fence spreads a leafy paulownia tree;
Yaba: In the kitchen I ladle plain water from the copper jar;
Rigyu: And the heavy rain stops lightly.
Torin: The melons are in flower; we will be busy from now on;
Yaba: Living in its neighborhood, I've not yet visited Hase Temple;
Rigyu: That is because they watch us the old all night and all day;
Torin: And the early-winter sky—it's rather chilly unusually;
Yaba: Today, this very day, the kitchen is swept clean;
Rigyu: And the happy day has come when she becomes the lady of the house.
Torin: Bright and elegant is the fabric dyed turmeric red;
Yaba: And a spearman alone returning in evening moonlight;
Rigyu: And Bon Festival—somewhere someone's chanting a sutra;
Torin: The fields are all black, a flock of sandpipers playing about.
Yaba: Were it not for payables, we would see blossoms at ease;
Rigyu: Today, the fifteenth day, the middle of Yayoi;
Torin: It's time to put the brazier away from beside the loom;
Yaba: There's a quarrel in the neighborhood, there's no one paying attention;
Rigyu: The rumor says that he suffers a big loss over speculation in rice;
Torin: The swallows are noisy; they would be going south;
Yaba: And a pearl of autumn dew—that drug is good this time;
Rigyu: The moon is low about the treetop of a cedar.
Torin: An old man's talk, the same talk, a never-ending talk;
Yaba: And he's waiting for her in the firewood room—might he be fooled?
Rigyu: Then he tells his fortune by himself, and in his favor at that;
Torin: That is a bad bargain; that does not pay.

Yaba: A summer day—it is too hot to wear a two-piece;
Rigyu: In Kyoto every house's built elaborately;
Torin: And the main dish is grilled fish with Tonda shrimp as a garnish;
Rigyu: Then he slips out again to take a nap;
Yaba: And the Hair Ceremony—I'll give her a pair of sandals as a gift;
Torin: And in the offing there appear a fleet of ships.
Rigyu: A spring day—it's nice to eat out in the shade of blossoms;
Yaba: No wind, not a single stir—a calm, mild day.

Fukagawa, the Twentieth of the No-God Month (Linked Verse)

Basho: Yebis Fair—pitiful is the wild goose in a peddler's basket;
Yaba: And the winter street—it rains, it rains, now off, now on.
Ko-ok: The oak is so knurled, the master is struggling to saw it through;
Rigyu: And up over the half-bare hill shines the moon;
Yaba: Then a gust of autumn wind—he always eats rice cake, his favorite;
Basho: And dew turns into frost in the country where firewood is cheap.
Rigyu: There is a fisherman talking to a boatman as he sets up the net;
Ko-ok: The twenty-eighth night, a starless dark night;
Basho: Being hungry would be fatal—in battle in particular;
Yaba: It snows lightly and softly; everybody is being quiet;
Ko-ok: And at dawn a palanquin bearer blows out the lantern light;
Rigyu: And he applies a plaster on his stiff shoulder.
Yaba: She's chopping dried herb for topping, but her mind is somewhere else;
Basho: For she's going to see a pack-horseman off-duty today;
Rigyu: And the late afternoon—there's a buyer going from door to door;
Ko-ok: The next is the house of a low-pay *samurai*.
Basho: The moon, the flowers, and in this isle even a little devil is pious;
Yaba: Over the warm sand beach grows green grass;
Ko-ok: And a newly tilled field—the manure has seeped into snow;
Rigyu: I'm running in the field; my hat has been blown off.
Yaba: People are scared of the river, the stream is belt deep;
Basho: And in the low land stands a poorly-hedged temple;
Rigyu: In the garden the washing is put toward the sunny side;
Ko-ok: And we unpack the case of salted duck;
Basho: They pinch and save in Kyoto, the way they get along with the world;
Yaba: And his daughter has another baby without his knowledge.
Ko-ok: This is done, that is made, and a peal of Year-End's Bell;
Rigyu: Pointless is the fellow who asks me to write in his place;

Yaba: And friendly are the colleagues; someone's in debt to someone else;
Basho: And a moon night—one's tapping on the wall to keep another awake.
Rigyu: The autumn wind dies down, the seagulls get their hips down;
Ko-ok: The clapper sounding, something touching the net over the carp pond;
Basho: The wharf is getting to be quiet; some going out, some coming in;
Yaba: And they argue on their way to Meguro Temple.
Ko-ok: The nice days in the middle of Yayoi—everywhere alive with blossoms;
Rigyu: And a round charcoal—the dust is blown off by a spring breeze.

(Linked Verse)

Sampou: A snow day—the broken branch of a pine makes me feel more chilly;
Ko-ok: Shortly before sunrise the winter sky is all red;
Basho: On the beach cheap fishes are being unloaded from a fishing boat;
Shisan: *Daimyo's* men are marching, at places, in loose procession;
Torin: And a pale moonlight—there is a soft, silky touch of night wind;
Rigyu: The field looks larger; all the millet has been reaped.
Taisei: The autumn flood—the bank has broken at Kumagai;
Yaba: And some make up wooden boxes to sell dried bonito;
Shisan: Now living at a small hut beside the gate;
Senho: It is on such a narrow street, pack-horses may touch the washing.
Sekigick: Summer has come; they wear new bamboo sandals;
Sampou: And the rice plants are alive in a soft, light rain;
Yaba: And the fall—in the seaside village there's not a single man of fortune;
Rigo: Bon Festival is over, colds are raging.
Yiyi: The evening moon—he would feel melancholy, that carpenter in travel; *
Torin: Now at home he fondles his little child on his back;
Shisan: And blossoms are falling on the tea leaves aired over the straw mat;
Sekigick: And she grills sweet fish fresh from a stream.
Sampou: The morning mist is gone, a pheasant singing happily;
Taisui: In the back of the house, a pathway toward the hill;
Ko-ok: And he looks blue—the lad depressed under his parents;
Sora: Anyway, we have too many vegetable-diet days.
Torin: The rice is polished and packed into bales;
Yiyi: And I go a long, long way to pay my medicine bills;
Senho: When it comes to art, he's crazy about Sesshu, saying Sesshu is Sesshu;
Shisan: Saying so, he fetches a lamp from the next room;
Rigyu: And this morning he again eats a food offered to a Buddha;
Sampou: Suffering a loss many times, he puts a wise look;

Rigo: And over the merchant city Osaka rises a shrewd winter moon;
Yaba: Grandmother is happy; her grandson quit drinking.
Shisan: Sooty is the family altar, its gilt is somewhat worn off;
Rigyu: In the next room someone giggles and chokes;
Sora: He's bitten by mosquitoes when he hides himself as is promised;
Sampou: In the end, shortly before dawn he calls a palanquin.
Torin: It begins raining; people are arguing in the flowery shade;
Taisui: And women plus a man make green rice cakes.

  (Note)
   * This comes from a *waka* of Saigyo:
     A sad moment—the moon makes me feel melancholy;
     So much so that my face wet with my tears.

Compiled by Shida Yaba, Koizmi Ko-ok and Ikeda Rigyu;
Published by Izutsuya Shobei, Kyoto, and Hon'ya Fujisuke, Edo;
The twenty-eighth of the Sixth Month of the seventh year of Genrock.

ZOK SALMINO

In Seclusion

To Basho the sixth year of Genrock (1693) was a depressing year. "It is a matter of regret," he wrote to Nun Ukoh in the First Month, "the fellows in Nagoya have broken the relations with us." In the Third Month he knew the death of Rogan, and saw his son-in-law Towin passed away after a long illness. In the autumn one of his oldest disciples Ranran suddenly died during a journey.

> Pitiful is the mulberry cane broken in the autumn wind.

He seemed to become tired of meeting people. In autumn he secluded himself from his followers for about a month after writing to them a piece of *haikai* prose *In Seclusion*:

> It is desire that Confucius abhorred, that Buddha regarded as the vice of vices, but that one cannot do without. There are not a few people of such a disposition. Far away—in the dark mountains of Krama one might fall in secret love under a *mei* tree; yet were it not for the eyes of a keeper, he would be ruined. And there are many people who play with courtesans; some of them would someday lose their fortune. Yet much more sinful is greed. As one grows older, one becomes greedier, more troubled about gain and money. Such a one may lack a feeling of pity.
>
> And senility. Few people live to be seventy. The prime of life is no longer than twenty years. And then comes the age of forty like a night dream. Then fifty, then sixty, and one gets more senile; sleeping early, waking late, one always wastes time in vain. True, a silly fellow would have odds and ends in mind. On the other hand, a man of art is a man of self-esteem. Such a talent may live a life of competition, and in the end will be caught up in greed and confined to a small world.
>
> The great sage Zhuang said the old should do away with worldly interests and enjoy a calm life free from age. I would talk idly if you came in; and if I went out I would disturb your business. Learned Sun Jing always stayed indoor; the fifth son of the Du secluded himself in his home. Likewise, I should regard friendlessness as a friend, poverty as wealth. And now I am writing this to warn myself, this stubborn fellow of fifty.

> The morning glory—let me leave the gate shut in the daytime.

And afterwards;

> The morning glory—you, too, aren't a true friend of mine, after all.

The Disciples in Nagoya Secede from the Basho School

As said above, Kakei, Yasui, Etsujin and other poets in Nagoya—namely, the poets of *A Winter Day*, *A Spring Day* and *Waste Land*—cut off connections with Basho. See a passage from Basho's letter addressed to Kyorai, who was then angry at Kakei for publishing an anthology of old-fashioned *haik* poetry with its name as *Waste Land II*.

Day after day I hear a lot about the anthology Kakei compiled (*Waste Land II*). It is natural that you are angry with Kakei about his unfair way of business. But think that a little mind always does a little thing. Never mind such a small matter. We are building up a new style of poetry, an immortal enterprise. They are doing what they can. Let them go their way, and they will be old-fashioned after all. In fact, their art of poetry has remained unchanged for the past several years.

In conclusion, the poets in Nagoya refused to follow the new style of Basho; they ended up as pseudo-classical *haik* poets.

It touches me on the swelling—a willow branch swinging in the wind.

The Disciples in Discord

Say something—and your lips will be chilled in the autumn wind.

The disciples of Basho came from a variety of provinces and classes; for instance, Kyorai was born in the city of Nagasaki, the western end of Japan, while Rogan was engaged in dyeing near Hagro Shrine in the far northeastern province of Dewa. Their classes and occupations are: *samurai* (Kyoksui, Kyorick, Fumikuni), former *samurai* (Sora, Joso), merchants (Sampou, Yasui), managers (Ko-ok, Yaba, Rigyu), physicians (Kakei, Shohack, Chinseki), monks (Senna, Riyou), nuns (Chigetz, Ukoh), housewives (Sonome, Kana, Kagetz), hermits (Sodo), actors (Senho, Riho, Baken), craftsmen (Chikco), wanderers (Rotsu) and *haik* masters (Kikack, Ransetz, Shiko). In the age of a rigid class system they kept good fellowship as followers of Basho. Nevertheless, some of them were on bad terms with some others; in particular, several old disciples disliked young Shiko. See a passage from Basho's letter to Kyorai in the fifth year of Genrock (1692):

Shiko left for Far Country in early Kisaragi. Though he's in no respect a shrewd fellow, but regrettably Kikack and others dislike him. Something of a fool—sometimes dancing, sometimes drinking—he must have felt it awkward staying with me. Sooner or later he will go westwards to see you, so I'm writing this to you. Please inform Fumikuni what he is like. See that they have no quarrel with him.

There was another quarrel. In the seventh year of Genrock (1694) Sampou informed Basho by letter that an anthology compiled by Shisan and Torin was criticized by Ransetz. To this Basho replied that the anthology was well received among his disciples in Kyoto and Omi, but at the same time remarked that Yaba and Rigyu complained their verses had been excluded from it.

And still another dispute. In the same year Shado (Chinseki) moved from Zeze to Osaka, where he competed against Shido to win leadership in the circles of *haik* poets. Basho had to go to the western metropolitan city to mediate between them. "Shido and Shado jointly held a *haikai* meeting," he wrote to Masahide. "I acted as go-between, and that is all I did."

Now deep in autumn — then what are you doing, neighbor?

The Last Journey

The early summer of the seventh year of Genrock (1694) saw Basho leave Edo for the west, his last journey. Sora may have had a bad feeling about his *haik* master's state of health, for he accompanied him as far as Hakone Barrier. This time Basho did not write a piece of travel. According to his letter to Sora, he paid a visit to Kakei and other poets in Nagoya. At his visit they seemed to be astounded.

> I stayed at Kakei's three nights two days. He looked pleased. We talked. Yasui and Etsujin joined. Fickle people, they served me very well — breakfast, dinner, night snacks, and a pack of gifts. That was something of a tumult.

In Satsuki he reached his hometown in Iga, and the next month left for the province of Omi. In Otsu Town Otokuni and his sister Chigetz had long awaited him, and one day, to their house came Joso and Shiko in quest of the whereabouts of their *haik* master. They talked. Where had the Old Reverend gone? It was now getting dark. It was raining. And then with a wet straw hat on, and a dripping raincoat on, he came in suddenly — the Old Reverend! What a wonder! What a wonder! The master and disciples were all in a rapture of joy. That happy night they had a joyous talk until midnight.

> I'm travelling, they are plowing, forward, then backward.

> It's a quiet hut; your water rail has visited you not yet.

In the same month he had a stay at the Rakshi-sha in Saga, then at the Moumyo-an in Zeze. And on the summer shore of Lake Biwa, he enjoyed a cool evening with Kyoksui, Shiko and others. They had a pleasant *haikai* party (see the fifth linked verse of *Zok Salmino*).

> Now in the Sixth Month — a cloud lies on the ridge of Arashiyama Hill.

> It glows as if missing summer heat — the giant cloud high up over the lake.

In autumn he returned to Iga, where he began the compilation of a new anthology with Shiko as assistant; but before its completion, he had to leave for Osaka as said above. Being in poor health, the old bard set out westwards together with Shiko and others.

—At Nara;

> Fragrant are the *kick* flowers, silent are ancient Buddhas in Nara.

> Pitiful are the cries of deer — piercing the darkness of the night.

—At Osaka;

> Old clouds, old birds — why do I get older and older this autumn?

Autumn is passing by; there runs through the street an autumn wind.

In late autumn in Osaka he got sick in bed at an inn; before long it was getting serious. In reply to Kyoksui's invitation to a tour of Nara, he wrote him as follows:

> I have had a fever several nights since arrival in Osaka. (...) To make a tour with you, I tried to walk, only to find myself unable to go on even a few miles. I am sorry that I cannot go with you on a journey.

Now at dusk in autumn—there is no one goes on this road.

Zok Salmino

During his stay in Iga, Basho seemed to roughly finish compiling the new anthology *Zok Salmino*, or *Salmino II*. See a passage from his letter to Kyorai:

> I finished the draft of *Zok Salmino*, assisted by Shiko, who had come from Ise. It is a little unsatisfactory for lack of time, but I daresay it can in some extent match the previous one (*Salmino*). Of course, your checking and finishing the draft would be essential before publishing.

You may think Shiko might have completed the anthology at his soonest opportunity after the death of his *haik* master. He did not, however. He was disliked by some of the leading disciples of Basho as mentioned above, which may have caused the nearly-completed anthology to be left unpublished. The details are unclear. Anyway, after several years of deadlock, the *haik* anthology *Zok Salmino* was published, with its draft left unfinished, with no foreword written, and with its editor as 'unknown'. See the publisher's comment written at the end of the anthology.

It consists of five pieces of linked verse and a selection of *haik* poems on six themes.

ZOK SALMINO

(Linked Verse)

Basho: A willow of eight or nine yards high, and the rain waltzing in the sky;

Senho: Spring has come; crows are pecking at the ground, cawing happily;

Baken: And in his favorite costume the pack-horseman loads New-Year goods;

Riho: In the shop the women are busy preparing the evening feast;

SH: And the hue of the moon—the weather has got better since yesterday;

BS: The ferns are dead; it is getting chillier day by day.

RH: They were all blown and fallen—the sour *kaki* fruits this year;

BK: What is more, I have to pay back the money my grandfather borrowed;

BS: So I exchange my travel dagger for a short one;

SH: The soot has been swept; next, rice cakes to be made;

BK: And the peddler comes in, as is promised, with a basketful of little birds;

RH: That is just before I would go out some twenty miles away.

SH: It's amusing—the lane running through *take* woods;

BS: At the gate the sign says, 'Watch overhead!'

RH: A vacant hut, no message left behind, that nephew!

BK: His neighbor says he seems to have gone to Kyoto with his companion.

BS: Beautiful is the morning moon, brilliant are the flowers in late bloom;

SH: And all the rice seedlings are well in bud;

BK: It is an earnest plowman who has won a tender for the vernal lottery;

RH: Being a pilgrim, he sees friends returning from Ise;

SH: The workers are carrying a large chest, reeling, tottering;

BS: A clear sky, crisp air, not a single cloud afloat.

RH: Zen Temple, the sand garden, and I've had a nice and easy day;

BK: And yet the zelkova lumber is too hard to pierce;

BS: Now the bales are delivered by ox to the port;

SH: And the finances—he keeps it secret from his young wife;
BK: Then the moon feast—the company are all present;
RH: In the hedge there are *kick* flowers of various names.
SH: A flock of starlings flock in the chestnut tree, then the nettle tree;
BS: And the attendant monks running alongside the palanquin;
RH: Through the Long-Sword Slope blows a sharp gust of winter wind;
BK: Higher up, there twinkle stars toward my eyes;
BS: And she's made to dance—that graceful woman;
SH: Then she puts a piece of incense softly into the ash holder.
BK: Spring is passing by; all the blossoms have fallen;
RH: A mirage floating upward, the stream running downward.

(Linked Verse)

Baken: There goes every sort of titmouse with a chorus of chirps;
Senho: Amusing is the moon, and red leaves on the shore.
Riho: Bought a house, moved in, and now autumn is passing by;
BK: And a woman watches sweet *sake* simmering;
SH: There are children, five or six in number, eating frosted turnip;
RH: And a traveler washes his feet on the straw mat;
BK: Still vexing is my wrong judgment when I checked a gold coin today;
SH: The fidelity guarantee's accepted, he's busy appealing to his new master.
RH: Today, a fine day, too fine for an early morning;
BK: And he pretends to be a rich man—the guest from my country;
SH: Nothing troublesome, the welcoming of horses ends happily;
RH: The storm has swerved away, the rice ears wave calmly in moonlight.
BK: Now in the fall the kitchen is used as a living room;
SH: That is because his son has become a bridegroom;
RH: And on New Year's Eve he attends a vigil at Karas Shrine in Ise;
BK: So clean is the straw raincoat that there might be no lice in it.
SH: The trees are flowery, the rice bales moist and heavy;
RH: A spring day—a tuft of dyed thread is hung quiet;
BK: There's a line of snow along the warbler's path;
SH: And I'm sick in bed; not that it's fatal;
RH: Year by year I'm getting on worse terms with my family;
BK: What is more, the goods from Misaki and Tsuruga are left undelivered;
SH: And thereby in the market there are lots of eggplants of bad quality;
RH: At any rate the ripe wheat should be reaped in the first place.
BK: The construction of a temple—everyone has his own design;
SH: It is after our lord leaves that we have a sense of loneliness;
RH: Though he has borrowed money, he has not yet begun business;
BK: And down in the garden he takes a rich meal.

SH: The evening moon, an autumn moon, and people double the clothes;
RH: And on the *take* leaves glitter pearls of dew;
BK: Bon Festival—I'm going to hold a memorial service for my mother;
SH: That is because I begin working for the *daimyo* of Shonai, Dewa;
RH: And now in summer all I've got as a gift is a cheap light kimono;
BK: From the young cedar woods blows a breeze that pleases my ears.
SH: A young pheasant flies up from the flowery shade, soon coming back;
RH: And the new rice field—over the dry soil shimmers a mirage.

(Linked Verse)

Riho: The falcon is poised on my arm, being upright in a gust of wind;

Senho: Now in winter the frosty spindle leaves are blown off;

Basho: And the poor soil—the long radishes have grown rough and bony;

Baken: An autumn day—the whole family are having morning tea;

SH: And he makes the rounds of town to collect contributions for a moon feast;

RH: In front of the station are pack-horses passing by glimpse after glimpse.

BK: The rumor runs about that the chief of the Chion-in may be changed;

SH: The *sacra* blossoms have all fallen; the maple leaves grow green;

RH: And he waters the seabass on the chopping board;

BK: Thanks to his good eye of goods he lives a rich life;

SH: And a letter is given to a courier from Suruga;

RH: The shadow on the ground says it's shortly before late afternoon;

BK: The shower is over; in the leafy shade shines clean water in a pit;

SH: Yet the cotton picker gives a worried look to a dark cloud on Mount Ikoma.

RH: A melancholic traveler is like a bird travelling in company with a shrike;

BK: It's getting bright and white; the morning moon is high in the sky;

SH: And there appears a punt lightly from under the blossoms;

RH: There's a gate beside the willow tree;

BK: Being retired, he's living an easy life as a plowman;

SH: On the table are kelp, laver, and some dried fish;

RH: And those the peddler eats, with a few packets of goods aside;

BK: Quite a hot day—there's not a single stir of wind;

SH: Over the sand creep a thorn; on it chirps a cricket;

RH: And it does cry when you say good-bye.

BK: Covered the fire in the *kotatsu* warmer, cleaned the kitchen;

SH: And threshed a bushel of rice;

RH: My eye hurts at times in a certain weather;

BK: And late at night—it gets colder than expected;

SH: In moonlight I smoke tobacco of the year;

RH: Then the early harvest—we thatch the roof with rice straw as is planned.

BK: All my money was used for the dowry, and this time my son is to marry;

SH: What is more, he is planning a tour of pilgrimage;

RH: The flowers are gone, yet the azaleas are soon to bloom;

BK: The temple has moved from the foothill, yet spring comes when it does.

SH: It's getting warmer; in the pond wild ducks flying away wing by wing;

RH: There comes another rain, there blows a mild wind.

(Linked Verse)

Senho: Can't you see a frosty truffle fallen from a monkey's straw raincoat? *
Basho: Chilly is the day, silent is the hill. **
Shiko: There are footsteps in the basin of a waterless pond;
Izen: And a woman with a pack of firewood and bamboo on her head;
BS: The rooster goes up the roost, and then rises the evening moon;
SK: Few passers-by in the autumn street, people shutting their shops.
IZ: Bon Festival, the end of the fiscal year, and they beat down fish prices;
BS: As yet, I cannot get rid of taking a noon-day nap;
SK: And then comes my daughter's husband, who never smiles when he talks;
IZ: He's got a letter from the Middle-West — what says it?
BS: It is an invitation to a feast on the first day;
SK: And yet I've lost my summer coat somewhere — where's it?
IZ: Anyway, fairly refreshing are the green leaves of fir and maple;
BS: And the morning moon — on the mountain, a monastery.
SK: The first storm of the season — plowmen are busy in the field;
IZ: And on the seashore shine a heap of small sardines;
BS: Now in Mi Temple of Ki the flowers are beginning to bloom;
SK: And a long spring day — he's travelling only with a bearer;
IZ: It blows westward, then eastward, and now northward;
BS: He feels his pulse, he's a nervous traveler;
SK: And he's to wed as second wife a waiting maid of a *samurai;*
IZ: If so, the servants should keep their temper.
BS: The sunset, a peal of a temple bell, and there remains two days of service;
SK: And we plow the snow, only to make a path of mud;
IZ: And there come people on horseback, all of them priests;
BS: This year, a fat year in Far Country;
SK: And the moon feast — the *sake* costs more than the meal;
IZ: In the middle of the garden flowers a red cockscomb;

BS: And a girl in love, she tries to calm herself down;

SK: A peaceful dream—her sweat disappears before dawn.

IZ: A blast from pine woods wakes up the birds in the cages;

BS: And the sound of carpentry in the back of the house;

SK: The rice polisher has done his job, going home;

BS: And in the busy street he makes his way empty-handed.

IZ: In these parts there's not a single blossom in Yayoi;

SK: Now still in spring the ducks are still plump.

(Note)
* This is to say there's no poem of a truffle in *A Monkey's Straw Raincoat (Salmino)*
** This is to reply that he could not find truffles on a chilly, silent hill.

(Linked Verse)

Cool is the Evening

The sixteenth of the Sixth Month. The evening. The sky, the lake—all is the same hue. The moon is low over the jagged mountains in the east, and Lake Biwa clothes herself in a tinge of autumn. This evening we have gathered, a free and easy party, drunk but gentle, enjoying a cool breeze here and there, as if being out in a meadow or on a mountain. Some talk, but nobody expects an exciting story, nobody has to be eloquent—a party like duckweed floating on water or fish swimming in water.

It was in early summer that, after four years in Fukagawa, the Old Reverend traveled to the mountainous province of Iga to pay a visit to his parents' tomb. And during the stay at Saga in Kyoto, he visited such cool spots as the Kamo River and Gion Town. I thought he would continue staying at Saga, waiting for the fall to come. However, he may have wanted to enjoy a cool breeze on the Lake, for he walked that hot road several miles unto Zeze.

This evening Sir Suganuma Kyoksui hosts the party, where there are monks, laymen, monk-like laymen. We keep a simple and beautiful friendship like a small pine on a sandy shore. Not deep, not showy, simply plain, yet not tiresome. Imagine that you meet a man who was once friends with you, but has forgot you. It might be before long that he would show a hue of joy in his face. And he would begin talking with you into a time when a rooster crows around and the moon goes westward.

We will be parting soon. The Old Reverend intends to visit his hometown during the Bon Festival, while I think of setting up a hermitage in Ise to invite him in winter. It is as though water birds flied away from the Lake wing after wing. Can they meet again someday? Can they play together someday? This day last year seems like a dream; this day next year is far from us; the party this evening will soon become a thing of the past. And yet the people are merry, jokingly saying a drunk must have another cup of *sake* as a penalty.

Written by Shiko.

Basho: The summer night—the chilled food will be out of shape at dawn;
Kyoksui: In the garden drops a pearl of dew from a lotus leaf.
Gako: The warblers have ceased singing before we could know that;
Izen: So that I put the draft of verse into my old leather bag;
Shiko: The shade of the moon—the dark cloud promises snow;
Basho: And after the job the palanquin bearers split money.
KS: Silly fellows—the wild boar ran away from the hunting fields;
GK: And they bring stones from the hills, with the marking of their names;
IZ: And the stone mason takes out his lunch box and fire sickle;
SK: Listening to a kite crying out—how is the weather tomorrow?
BS: Then, are you making another verse on me? —asks the bridge keeper; *
KS: And the face of the Holy Buddha reflects a red beam of sunset.
SK: The greens grow in the field, where tobacco used to thrive;
IZ: Beside the gate—over the bath blows an autumn wind;
GK: A man leading a horse in moonlight, the street alive with people;
BS: Here comes a day when he makes a comeback with his old name in Owari;
KS: And yet the blossoms this year find him prefer rice cakes to sake;
GK: That is why there's not a point of taint in his formal wear;
IZ: And then blows a spring wind; he's planning construction;
SK: That is a byway to the village through the woods.
BS: The troublesome family—both father-in-law and son-in-law, keen critics;
KS: Yet should anything happen, they would hold an esoteric service;
GK: And now they are carrying their costume case with a stick;
BS: The early-summer fields—thickets of bracken are now dried;
SK: And he sets out earlier—the one-night roommate at an inn in Yagi Town;
IZ: Now in the end of a year he worries about a snowfall.
KS: Nothing is more delicious than a pure and simple *sake*;
GK: Don't worry, my luggage already on board;
BS: And the evening moon—a sealed letter is arrived;
SK: With it appears a lady slowly, elegantly.
IZ: There's an insect cage hung at the corner of Shijo-Kawaramachi; **
KS: And a pack of *tatami* is unloaded from a punt on the Takase Waterway; **

GK: Looking at that for a while, I lose sight of a *daimyo's* procession;

IZ: And then rings the great bell heavily.

SK: The flowers are in full bloom, yet the monks have shut the doors;

GK: And yet stools are set under the wisteria trellis.

(Note)
* The 'verse' is a *waka* written in the *Kokin-shu*:
  The Uji River, a sacred stream of water;
  You are the keeper of the bridge, a good old job.
** The Takase Waterway runs through Shijo-Kawaramachi, a downtown in Kyoto.

Spring

Sacra Blossom

Lord Rosen: The *sacra* begin blooming; the stone warmer no longer needed.

Kikack: The *sacra* begin blooming; I'll see the moon before going to bed.

Basho: The *sacra* begin blooming; if only I could make a verse fresh for my age.

Dobock: The shortcut leads me to a wood, thence to a hill—full of blossoms.

Joso: Funny are the young *sacra* viewers headed by a squarely-shaven guy.

Shado: The *sacra* blossoms have all fallen; I'm seeing *take* leaves at ease.

—Drunk a little at a luxury restaurant, I imagined Lady Wenjun playing the *koto* zither.

Izen: A *sacra* in bloom beyond the window; let me hear the note of a *koto*.
 (Note) This comes from an episode of ancient Chinese writer Sima Xiangru, who fell in love with Lady Wenjun when he heard her play the *koto* zither.

Shiko: The *sacra* feast—it begins to rain, although I bet on good weather.

Sentock: You may mind other minds, may mind more the first *sacra* blossom.

Ensui: A cloudy day—a *sacra* in full bloom, facing north in the meadow.

Yowa: The day of seeing *sacra* blossoms—the women get up very early.

Otokuni: A spring day—all I see, all I think of, is the first *sacra* blossom.

Boksetz: It gives a melancholic look to the blossoms—that old *sacra* tree.

Senka: The spring garden—the *sacra* beginning to bloom, I review its shape.

Shisan: Here comes the second dish; on the nose of the fish, a flake of blossom.

Tactai: Bagworms are beginning to appear, and then bloom the *sacra* flowers.

—In the country;

Riri: The *sacra* trees in bloom—then what *konjac* dish do you recommend?

Toshu: The *sacra* tree begins to bloom; my stipend is no more than fifty-*kock*.

Itto: Beside the gate of a temple is a *sacra* tree—with tremendous hips.

Josetz: Below the falls, a fallen tree; over the basin, a carpet of *sacra* blossom.

Kikack: The *sacra* trees in bloom—who would look good in a flower hat?

Ichiro, a boy: The *sacra* in bloom, I set up a fine display of flowers in the room.

Tactai: Still wet is the recoated wall; beside it, a *sacra* tree in bloom.

Senho: A *sacra* tree in bloom in the temple; before long they will invite people.

Senho: The double *sacra* in bloom; you can have Nara tea-porridge in Kyoto.

Young Herbs

Ransetz: A spring day—on the verandah, soil-stained *nazna* herbs.

Kyoksui: The owl has ceased hooting; in front of the cliff, a young herb.

Ko-ok: The sea rippling at evening, someone's chopping *nazna* herb in a ship.

Bito: The peony seems chilly, the young herbs look happy.

Mei and Willow

Basho: Spring is being put into shape—the moon hazy, the *mei* trees in bloom.

Yasui: Now in Kisaragi—the Daikock altar, too, is ornamented with a *mei*.

Kikack: Wild yams are sold on the roadside, the side job of a *mei* guard.

Shobo: The *mei* tree in bloom; I hear a millstone creaking in the town temple.

Ryobon: The flower arrangement—a *mei* in company with butterbur sprouts.

Sora: The *mei* in full bloom, a sick monk is sweeping the garden with a broom.

Banco: The *mei* trees in bloom, the new bamboo blind looks chilly.

Gyojitz: A light snowfall—there remain footsteps toward the *mei* tree.

Sensen: There are shabby huts, there blooms a *mei* tree rich in white.

Daitan: The *mei* in bloom; I'll shut up its fragrance in the bed room.

—At Tenjin Shrine;

Youshi: The *mei* trees in flower, I make a wish in fragrant air.

Senna: A hazy moon night—every *mei* and willow stands in its own shape.

Igen: Leaving its branches in a stream, the willow resists the flow at times.

Riyou in Koto: Old though it is, the willow is the very mark of a shortcut.

Kyusetz: The horse acrobatics—try passing through under the willow tree.

Hajo: Swift is the horseman—riding along a row of willows.

Birds and Fishes

Kikack: The long sword is put on the beam, a warbler singing among blooms.

Fumikuni: A warbler's singing outside; inside, I've just had a bath.

Nun Chigetz: The twitter of a warbler, and I take a pause in the kitchen.

Basho: Behind the willow, before the grove sings a warbler once or twice.

Kyorai: It sounds high in the roars of the falls—the sharp cry of a pheasant.

Shado: The spring rain—pack the cries of a pheasant into your straw coat.

Sanka: It looks left and right on the heights—that robin.
Choko: It goes well with the knocks of a silversmith—the cries of a robin.
Yado: It makes a turn behind the horse—a swallow flying over the field.
Horan, a boy: It squeezes itself in the nest—that parent swallow.
Kaishi: Sparrow, sparrow, this doll box is a gift from big sister.
Kahyo: I'm trying to swatter flies; my little sparrow keeps quiet.
Choso: They seem reluctant to leave the strand—the wild ducks in east wind.
—At the Nishigau Falls, Yoshino;
Doho: They may be scared before the roars of the falls—those little sweet fish.
Hosui: A mirage shimmers in the air, and in the water glitter sweet fish.
Shisan: The pause of tide—in the water, a crowd of white fish.
Sanho: A white fish is white, so white, you may forget to talk of its whiteness.
—At Fukawaga;
Kikack: The four-hand fishing net—white fish are all caught.

Spring Flowers

Masahide: They are cut, mown, yet grow more—the spring grasses.
Shikin: They should go to a pine—a procession of ants among the young herbs
Nun Ukoh: I've had a skin-eruption in the spring mead—what weed did that?
Ensui: The stagnant stream—beside a reed sprout are bubbles taking a rest.
Anshi: The evening rain has sprouted horsetails, some long, some short.
Sharai: Brilliant is a *sacra* tree in bloom, tasty is a *yomena* herb in green.
Kojack: In the green bloom wild roses in white, and thorny thistles in red.
Baken: Stumbled and fell from the bank; before my nose, a violet in flower.
Sekko: Strode over a gap on the bank; in it, a butterbur sprout.
Nairyu: It flowers as is trampled—the trampled long radish.
Masahide: Young bracken—here comes a wood-vendor from Mount Kasatori.
Sekica: It must have grown that three-leaf dropwort—the odor of *miso* paste.
Itto: The sunny fields—there's a cat scratching out an *udo* sprout.
Hohack: There flower dandelions cheerful, yet their leaves rather dull.

Cats in Love; Butterflies

Tangan: He's crying at his shadow—the lover as a cat in moonlight.
Shiko: He can't bear hunger, he sneaks a bite, he's a cat in love.

Kihack in Mino: He can't give her up, he cries in her village, he's a cat in love.

—On a calm day;

Ryubai: Alighting on a flower, it's still fluttering its wings—that butterfly.

Izen: Put on one more wing; you, butterfly, looks chilly in Kisaragi.
(Note) The word Kisaragi (Second Month) means 'wear one more'.

Anshi: A butterfly waltzing in the air—watch a falling camellia blossom!

Jouko in Dewa: The wind has risen; a little butterfly's now a good dancer.

Sesso: A butterfly's busy among flowers; it must have taken a nap.

Spring Deer

Takchi: An antler on the ground—a deer may have dropped it on its way.

Plowing in Spring

Boksetz: A spring day—we seed the field with hemp for the autumnal service.

Shikin: The evening moon—you can see seedling tags in the fields in Kasanui.
(Note) See an old *waka*:
The rainy evening—a traveler shakes water off his straw raincoat;
And takes an inn at Kasanui Village.

Ichiro: The great Naniwa Plains—people plow thousands of furrows.

Peach and Camellia

Torin: The white peach, its fresh flowers, and their hue of dew.

Kaiga: The peach trees are beginning to bloom, the cumquat still in full fruit.

Secci: Far away—*momo* bloom among *nanohana* flowers; that will be Fushimi.

Sui-oh: It goes between a fragrant *mei* and a brilliant *sacra*—a lovely *momo*.

Kikack: The *momo* tree is in bloom, calling a *sacra* like a side actor at Kabuki.

—Riyou in East Lake Land held a memorial service for his grandfather, then holding a *haikai* meeting with 'The Holy Lights of Amida' as its first topic.

Kakjo: Shine, gem camellia, on his simple monk robe.

Zanko: The graft is dead, yet the camellia blooms when it does.

Dobock: A fallen *tsubaki* blossom—picking it up, I give a look at its navel.

Yaba: A *tsubaki* blossom so simply fell, I try fixing it to the calyx.

Yellow Rose; Azalea; Wisteria

Anshi: The yellow rose's in bloom, a straw raincoat hung on the fence.
(Note) This comes from an episode of Ota Dokan, a noted *samurai* commander in the Ashikaga Period:
One day Dokan took shelter into a shabby house from a sudden shower, and asked for a straw raincoat. Inside, there was a girl, who, silently, held out a branch of a yellow

rose to imply an old *waka*:
> The yellow rose's in full bloom, in high bloom;
> But I'm sorry to find there's not a single fruit in it.

That is a pun—'*mi*', a fruit; '*mino*', a straw raincoat; that is to say, I'm sorry, but in the yellow rose there's not a single fruit (say, in this house there's not a single straw raincoat); however, the rough, tough *samurai* failed to understand that. He may have stood there without a word, utterly bewildered. Afterward he knew what, in a graceful manner, the poor girl had wanted to say. Being ashamed of himself, the *samurai* began learning poetry and in later years became a celebrated man of verse. A rather good story.

—In the country;

Shado: The vernal feast—on the shark *sashimi*, a flake of *yamabuki* blossom.

Secci: I'm digging out an azalea, the ant colony is in confusion.

Keico: The grove, the field, and a wisteria vine creeps down to the wheat.

The Spring Moon

Rocho in Nagasaki: It looks as though leaning on Mount Hico—that spring moon.

Spring Rain; Snow; Frogs

Keico: The misty spring rain—blades of grass look somewhat feeble.

Nairyu: A rainy spring day—we are having a chat in good tune.

Youto: The spring rain—there comes a rooster in the kitchen.

—Visiting Noh actor Shume at his inn in Edo;

Shiko: The spring rain—he's napping with a pile of scenario books as a pillow.

Toshu: The spring rains—the hammer of a blacksmith has lost gloss.

Fouback: Spring has come; light snow on my straw hat disappears in the rain.

Fousui: There's a frog jumps once, twice, then sits on a stone.

Low Tide

Kyorai: The isle of Awaji—there's a sail stuck in the calm.

Anshi: The seashore of Shinagawa—no shadow of Mount Fuji at low tide.

Things Vernal

Kyorick: The changing of a job—people are asked for donations.

Fousui: Young are the spring leaves, and I try striding over a baby paulownia.

Doho: It has grown very well—the young green pine tree on black soil.

Hairiki: It looks like a sitting man—a mirage afloat about the rock.

Banco: The outskirt of Nara—in front of a blacksmith blooms a white spirea.

Taiso: Voice after voice runs in the market—as they sell *udo*, then *tocoro*.

Kinsui in Mino: Sparrows hide among leafy trees; people sneak out for Ise.

Masahide: A spring day—someone's singing a pop song in the tea field.

Senka: The spring pond—there jumps a carp of some three feet long.

Shiro: The spring paddies—people picking pond-snails among birds of passage.

The Third Month

Shiko: Spring going by; a white-*sake* vendor looks regretful in hazy moonlight.

New Year

Busen, a boy: The New-Year water—beautiful is a sheet of ice on my palm.

Hyaksai: It might appear over the nobleman's path—the first haze of the year.

Shohack: From village to village sings a warbler—as we taste New-Year soup.

Hohack: The New-Year decorations—if only we could use a spiral shell.

Sampo: The clothing ceremony—she's surprised at the crest of the distaff side.

—My old father wrote me that it says in a Chinese verse that you should check your costume over and over.

Sensen: The New-Year night—I'm looking inside and outside my costume.

Basho: Nobody would see it, yet on the backside of the mirror blooms a *mei*.

Kikack: New Year Day breaks; the mice will be glad to be called 'my wife'.
  (Note) Those days a mouse was called 'my wife' on a New Year Day. Also, see a poem of Bai Latien:
    Don't wither, rose, don't die;
    My garden is alive with things spring.
    I'm a bachelor, a lonely man;
    When you flower, you will be my wife.

Ransetz: The green vines, the Daphne decorations, and now, Ze-ami Festival.

Kyorai: The New-Year dances—they're ready left and right under the pine tree.

Doho: Here comes a warbler, flapping—look here, see the citrus decorations.

Fousui: New Year Day—courteous in greeting, you going back quite quickly.

—My grandchild was born last winter.

Ensui: New Year Day—the *mei* tree's not yet in bloom enough.

Chodah: The opening ceremony of a warehouse—the head is the eldest boy.

Yado: A spring day—take a look at the flowers in my back.

Kosetz: It is packaged with green ferns—the seabream of a good shape.

Saryu: It looks as though warming the salmon weir—the New-Year sun.

Zensen: Another New Year has come; I've become so old as Nun the White.

(Note) Nun the White, a legendary woman, is said to have lived eight hundred years.

Sharei: The loquat leaves shine green, and the first haze of the season.

Sampo: A thing contradictory: the infant but bearded God Yebis.

Ninko: It looks wet and fresh—the big earthen cup in the New-Year sun.

Chikco: New Year Day—where should I put the cat's bowl?

Zerack: New Year Day—the New-Year rice cake is offered to the wig.
(Note) This seemed to be a ritual in the actors' homes those days.

Senho: The New-Year decorations—the chestnut looks soft on the rice cake.

Hokack: It is like airing in summer—the opening ceremony of a warehouse.

Summer

Cuckoo

Kikack: Cuckoo, cuckoo, are you calling for hail now at dawn?

Joso: A cuckoo's calling somewhere; the lake water looks somewhat muddy.

Sora: Cuckoo, cuckoo, you may find no shade in the White Beach.
   (Note) This comes from an old *waka*:
      I've fallen in love like a cuckoo in the hills;
      Can't you hear it singing in the leafy shade?

Shiko: Mount Asama white at dawn, and yet no cries of a cuckoo.

Josetz: Cuckoo, cuckoo, you are crying in Naltaki, vying with a roar of falls.
   (Note) The word 'Naltaki' (northwest of Kyoto) means a roar of falls.

Rohon: Cuckoo, cuckoo, the sky's alive with swallows.

Anonymous: Cuckoo, cuckoo, will you sing not on the Yodo but on the Seta?
(This is said to have been sung by a pilgrim in front of Ishiyama Temple, Seta.)

Senho: Cuckoo, cuckoo, why don't you take a rest at the Kasai Woods?

Trees and Flowers

Anshi: The summer grove—the sour oranges are sunburned indeed.

Yateki: The summer grove—every village has its own view.

—At a garden (two verses);

Shikin: The persimmons are in bloom—then which is the oldest?

Sensen: True, it's fruitless, yet alive with young leaves—the old *kaki* tree.

Soryu: It seems as if keeping up a princess lily—the thread of a web.
   (Note) This comes from a *waka* of Saigyo:
      A skylark is flying high over the wasteland;
      And lonesome is a princess lily alone in flower.

—On a lily in the garden of a cottage;

Shiko: Over the hedge sails a lily—being in flower like a white cloud.

Bito: The forest fire—afterwards I found an iris in flower on the waterside.

Senho: An iris in flower, I'm drinking a cup of chilled soup.

Utanoichi in Iga: Irises in flower on the strand, a nice thing for the blind!

Sekko: The summer *kick* flower—earlier, eggplants would be in flower.

—At the Basho-an;

Senho: The day flower—cloudy, yet in full flower.

Basho: Deep drunk, I look outside; by the window, a moon flower.

The late Ranran: The moon flower—I woke up half-naked past midnight.

Zanko: They have been blown to the sound—the seaweed flowers.

Shikin: The rushes in flower, and a stretch of muddy water.

Haksetz: The lotus leaves seem uneasy; the water is low in the pond.

Ryobon: By the lotus pond stand host and guest—fanning flies away.

Gourd

Basho: The summer morning—cool is a dewy gourd with a bit of soil on.

Shigyo: It's not so heavy—the princess gourd in my sleeve pocket.

Peony

Fougen: The peony is gorgeously in bloom, a poor meal should not be served.

Rice Planting

Ushichi in Nagasaki: I'm going to Kyoto; the girls, to home after rice planting.

Anshi: Girls are planting rice—shall I tie up the string of your straw hat?

Gyojitz: She looks somewhat slow in planting—that somewhat plump girl.

Jouko: The song of rice planting—the girl begins to sing in earnest.

Hokshi: A fine day—from paddy to paddy flows water with a sweet melody.

Shiko: Village people are planting rice in a row, a little boy grasping a swallow.

Fireflies

Kyorick: Mosquitoes are smoked out; for company, the fireflies too driven out.

Yateki: The crescent in the sky; the fireflies get up in the grass, glittering.

Enjoying Cool Air

Hanzan: The cool air—I tread along *take* trees, touching their trunks.

Izen: The fig tree, its big leaves, and cool is the evening.

—When staying at a certain hermitage in Fukagawa;

Fumikuni: A windless morning—yet the *basho* leaves make us feel cool.

Bosui: Cool is the air—getting out of the palanquin, I walk along rice fields.

Bonen in Nagasaki: A cool evening—by the back gate, in a rill, a dark sleeper.

Banco: The shallow water—swinging its tail, the ox seems to feel cool.

—As we please (three verses):

Shado: The ladder—it's fairly cool sitting on the middle of it.

Shiko: It's fairly cool sitting and swinging the legs on the verandah.
Secci: It's fairly cool feeling a breeze that blows off intoxication.
—When the Old Reverend Basho visiting me;
Youto: Through the crack of the wall, fortunately, comes a cool breeze.
Youto: A summer day—it's fairly cool slipping out of a mountain of jobs.
Kyorai: A summer day—it's fairly cool walking among busy people.
Masahide: I feel cool on a rock, perplexed when passers-by greet me with eyes.
Doho: He enjoys a cool breeze at dusk—that craftsman in a light kimono.
Gabi: A breath of air—it's fairly cool wearing a summer coat.
Riho: Cool is the night, and across the street, a shop in moonlight.

High Summer

Yateki: The midsummer sun—in the garden, at a corner, a dried oxalis.
Banco: It looks quite hot—the dust about a pile of plums in a shop.
—In reply to your good physician;
Masahide: Indeed your advice is good, but it was so hot a night, I caught a cold.
Otokuni: In a roughly thatched house is a swordsman on practice in hot air.
Dofou: The sun is high, and it looks quite hot—the sooty ceiling in the kitchen.
Soran in Owari: It looks quite hot—the roughly trimmed thorn hedge.
Gaho: A hot day, my shabby hut, and then a cool breeze returns with the moon.
Intai: Quite a hot day—I fan myself to find my hand rather skinny.
Tactai: It makes me feel all the more hot—a stack of *tatami* mats.
Rito: So hot is the night, the abalone has got mushy.
Senho: Drop in a blacksmith; you would feel burning indeed.

Take Tree

Kasei: It's stitched with *take* roots—the crumbling flank of the bank.
Kyoksui: The young *take* trees—out from the kitchen window, a pillar of smoke.

Satsuki Rain; Summer Shower

Fugyok in Dewa: The Satsuki rains, a green season, yet the egrets still white.
Basho: The Satsuki rains—silkworms suffer sickness in the mulberry fields.
Senho: The Satsuki rains—I can walk on the shore without a flick of mud.
Sekko: The afternoon shower—I happen to have a sunshade with me.
Taiso: The afternoon shower—there's a reed dabbing a lotus leaf in the pond.

Gyowou: The afternoon shower—here and there lie *take* sheaths.

Hosui: The shower—I could borrow an umbrella, but a hundred yards ahead.

Cicada

Masahide: After the afternoon shower, the chirps of cicadas like a shower.

Coco: It came, sang, and flied away—that summer cicada.

Otokuni: The chirps of cicadas in the woods—some cool, some hot.

Gyowou: Cicadas chirping at eventide, and at the window, a weaving girl.

Bonito

Yoshu: The first bonito of the season—seawater dripping from the basket.

Things Summery

Sampou: He seems to be napping; he has stopped fanning.

Keico: It's rich in worms, is poor in summer greens—the field of a temple.

Joshin in Ise: I've got skinny in summer, though it has been one of my wishes.

—On a river;

Buncho: Let's burn wheat husks, let's grill willow minnows.

Chodah: It grows proudly in the garden—a purple perrila among the weeds.

Sui-oh: They'd know why a ball of cedar sprigs is hung—the evening fireflies.
(Note) A ball of cedar sprigs is hung at the front of a *sake* shop as the sign of new *sake* being put on sale.

—Living with my old mother at a small house;

Baken: A summer evening—it is a sort of happiness fanning to grill fish.

Bosui: The sun goes west; the peeled *mei* fruits are moved to the sunny side.

Yado: The rain is over, and I find an arrowhead facing another direction.

Sui-oh: A cool breeze—a snail draws back its horns as the wisteria rustles.

—Envying the ancient Chinese poet Yuan Ming for his cool and easy life;

Basho: The cool mat of straw—let me have a nap on the bed by the window.

Izen: A summer day—I'm taking a nap, covered with a starchy light robe.

—Being a poor monk, I can by no means avoid a wintry chill; but in summer I do enjoy cool air in public, with a fan in hand.

Shiko: Summer clothes—five hundred is enough money for my wishes.

Autumn

The Bright Moon

Basho: The bright moon, the misty foothills, and over the fields flows a haze.

Basho: In bright moonlight bloom flowers—nay, that is a cotton field.

(This year the Old Reverend stayed for some time in the mountainous province of Iga, then making these verses at a *haikai* meeting on a bright moon night. "Which do you think is better?" the Old Reverend asked me. But I was unable to answer that.

'The misty foothills'—it reminds me of a *waka* of Monk Saigyo: 'Now the cloud is going away from the summits; The winter rain might have seen me waiting for the moon.' And 'over the fields flows a haze'—a view where flows a haze, runs a stream, and spread rice fields—it makes me imagine a scene of Old Du's poem: 'All is mist and water as far as I can see.'

'A cotton field'—it is a simple word, but flowery in vision. A new style of poetry. It also reminds me of a *waka* in the *Kokin-shu*: 'Now in the fall—*katura* fruits shine in moonlight; Shining brightly just like strewn blossoms,' and of a line of Su Shi: 'The flower has a scent; the moon, a shade.' You can well say it follows faithfully the good old poetry of Japan and China.

The former, I should say, has a sad and sweet hue; the latter, a sense of esprit. How can I say this is better, or that is more beautiful? Let us wait until, in future, a wise man will give us the right answer.

Written by Shiko.)

Shado: A bright moon up over the isle of Tamino, and here comes a chill of sea.

Joko: A bright moon—were it in the west, I'd see it from inside a mosquito net.

Lord Rosen: All things shine in moonlight, which makes me think of Nature.

Nun Chigetz: A bright night—we would argue should there be two moons.

Anshi: Bright is the moon, someone's walking along the shadow of a row house.

Ryoyo: Here comes the bright moon, here comes a guest from Sarashina.

Fugyok: Bright is the moon, there's no shade to tap off ash.

Hairiki:
    Tonight, a moon night, I've found by the middle gate a pear tree in fruit.

Saryu: Bright is the moon, and in the leafy shade, a white flower.

Hosui: Bright is the moon, there's no one at the Watcher's Pine.

Sampo: Tonight, a moon night—whether you're pious or not, it is a holy sight.

Foukock: Bright is the moon, and gates are open where family are still awake.

Jusho: Bright is the moon, and there are four or five men on a punt.

Jouyou:
    Tonight, a moon night; being an old man, I see the moon from my house.

Deikin: Bright is the moon, and yet I'm sorry we can see no stars.

—When staying at Yamada in Ise, I thought of setting up a hermitage.

Shiko: The moon is bright; I've come to Futami Beach in search of a good site.
    (Note) Saigyo lived for some time in Futami Beach, Ise. See a *waka* of his:
        What has brought me here—Futami Beach? And all night long
        I see the moon, with my sleeves wet with sea waves.

Kouga: Let me seed the field with poppies, let me see a bright moon.

Joshin: Here stands a *kaki* tree; and high up in the sky, a bright moon I see.

Sohi:
    The moon is up over the ridge, and yet the mountain fowls are still awake.
    (Note) This comes from a *waka* of Kakinomoto-no Hitomaro:
        Long is the trail of the long tail of a mountain fowl;
        Yet still longer is the night when I sleep alone all night long.

Bokshi:
    The bright moon—the firewood alone represents the living of the village.

Rigo: Tonight, a moon night, and in the garden you might weave a straw mat.

Tanpou: Bright is the moon, and there are a gaggle of women.

Yateki: Bright is the moon, and I have failed to pick things up on the road.

Masahide: The bright moon—we clap our hands to welcome a sudden guest.

—When living by the River Yodo;

Joso: Bright is the moon, and I step aside for a boat tugger.

Keito: The evening moon, a graceful moon, and a courier running in moonlight.

—Remembering that my father Shogen once gave me some secret instructions on the Noh dramas of old ladies;

Senho: It has risen from the darkness—the moon over Mount Obasute.

Baken: The moon has set; the roof of the wall wet with dew.

Rito: The young moon in the sky, and to the treetop creeps a creeper.

Bokdo: The sound of sea, and up over the long corridor shines the moon.

—On a punt at Five Pines, Fukagawa;

Basho: You're up the river, I'm down here, and up over both of us, the moon.

Basho: The sixteenth night—it has got a little closer to a dark-night darkness.

Ensui: The sixteenth night, the white *soba* flowers—no chance of darkness.

Tanabata Festival

Izen: It's been getting darker; the rice paddy mirrors the River Heaven.

Ryoyo: Crow, crow, you've watched the two stars meet; let me hear, let me hear.

Tocho: It might go between the couple of stars—that ship-shaped cloud.

Senho: Princess the Weaver—what kind of goddess are you?

Otokuni: A morning wind—the maid might be fanning Princess the Weaver.

The Coming of Autumn

Rosen: A windy autumn morning—millet dregs are at a corner in the garden.

Saji: Autumn has come; a giant cloud is blown in the firmament.

Autumnal Herbs

Ryubai: Pure and clear is the morning dew—glistening on a violet bellflower.

Zuiyou: It beggars all arts and crafts—the bellflower in bud.

Jokshi: It's still in flower in young spirits—that old *fair-lady*.

Baken: A *fair-lady* in flower—don't be beaten with the stick of Ousaka.
(Note) Those days in the festival of Ousaka Shrine women were patted in the hips with a stick so many times as their love affairs.

Uritz: It is alive with various colors of flowers—the pathway to green fields.

Shiro: A *formal-coat* in flower, it is time to take the bow from the fixing tool.

—A *haik* sent to the Basho-an

Fouback: Life's short, the lilies are gone, lotus blossoms yet to come.

Fumikuni: A *touch-me-not* in flower—like a lovely Princess Sayo in the country.
(Note) Princess Sayo was a legendary woman in ancient Japan.

Banco: It looks sad—the cockscomb flowering in red, but its leaves getting dead.

Basho: The seasonal honks of wild geese, yet the cockscombs still burning red.

Shigyo: The cockscomb still in flower in the fall; when are you going to fall?

Secci: A swaying reed taps on the shutter, from time to time, a tap-tap.
(Note) This is a line of linked verse followed by Basho's: 'And now, where are you, pine cricket?'

Kakei: The autumn wind is blowing, all the ivy leaves dancing.
Kyorai's Notes:

The Old Reverend once said, "A *haik* should not say every detail like this." Shiko seemed to be highly impressed with that word at that time, for he recently said to me, "At that moment I understood what a *haik* is." But I remembered nothing about that, though I must have heard the same word at the same place at the same moment. What a dull brain!

Toyo in Yamanaka, Kaga: A logger napping on a bough—vine, vine, bind him!

Sanka: They vie in length in every touch of wind—those hanging vines.

Morning Glory

Nun Tagami: A hazy moon night—I'm counting the buds of a morning glory.

Anshi: A willow branch hangs downward; on it creeps a morning glory upward.

Fouback: I pour water in the flat vase—sit up, morning glory, sit up straight.

Kikack: It's like a graceful woman—the morning glory feebly in flower.

Insects and Birds

Lady Kana: It chants a sutra beside the plantain lily—that autumn cricket.

Hokshi: It jumps at me as I open the closet—a little cricket.

Masahide: The insects get lost as the wind blows out the fire, then chirps of fire.

Sui-oh: The autumn night—dreams, snores, and chirps of a cricket.

Tojack: Bagworm, bagworm, you are looking good in moonlight.

Tangan: A dragonfly on the tip of a pole—what are you tasting?

Chodah: A mantis on a stone—are you cooling your stomach?

Shiho: A lotus fruit or a cicada shell—which is lighter?

Joso: An autumn cicada—you are dead beside your shell, aren't you?

Baken: It shakes as the wild geese honk—the small cot on the shore.
   (Note) This comes from a *waka* of Fujiwara-no Teika:
     Looking around, I find neither *sacra* blossoms nor red maple leaves;
     Only seeing a small cot on the shore at dusk in autumn.

Hyoko: It nimbly runs out of sight—a wagtail on the white sand shore.

Shiko: A chirping quail—you are looking up at the millet ears, aren't you?

Basho: Titmouse, titmouse, don't you know you are called Old Tit?

Autumn Wind

Youto: An autumn wind—it's time we should ferment tobacco leaves.

Shikishi: An autumn wind—you, little sparrow, have grown into a black-beard.

Shiko: An autumn wind—everything is in dry and cool fashion.

Foukock: It whistles through thin pine needles—the autumn wind.

Ho-en: The grasses droop as they get older, and here comes a typhoon.

Kyusetz: He keeps his feet against the typhoon—that tough log vendor.

Ensui: Raging, raging, roaring, the typhoon runs over to the sea.
   (Note) This is a line of linked verse followed by Basho's: 'And a crane lifts its head up in the millet field.'

Lightning

Itto, a boy: Frightening is lightning—when you stay home alone.

Sohi: Over the sea are dark clouds—being fringed with flashes of lightning.

Doho: The day breaks, and up to the edge of a cloud runs a flash of lightning.

Basho: There runs a flash of lightning, and in the darkness cries a heron.

Fruits and Mushrooms

Iyou: A chestnut drops on the stone statue of Holy Jizo, bounding up, and away.

Genko: A letter to the charcoal burner—I add a request for some *kaki* fruits.

Shado: A blue sky, red *kaki* fruits—not that it's unusual weather.

Bosui: They run out one by one from under the broom—the fallen hackberries.

Senho: A bowlful of fresh mushrooms—we should have added salt, though.

—When visiting the Old Reverend in the mountainous province of Iga;

Izen: A basketful of pine mushrooms—the yonder hills look like those of Kyoto.

Basho: An autumn day—to the pine mushroom sticks a nameless leaf.

Maple

Hokkon: In the backyard are red maple leaves worn out beside the fence.

Deer

Fousui: Now at dawn—the cries of deer fade away in the wind.

Isshak: I turn over in my sleep, clanging the clapper, and away run deer.
   (Note) This comes from a *waka* of Saigyo:
      It surprises me, is surprised by me—that deer;
      Calling friends right beside my hut in Oyamada.

Farming

Shayo: Although there are no plowmen, yet a patch of *soba* in flower in white.

Baizan: Under the tree appears a raccoon dog, the place of rice offering.

Josetz: The path on a paddy—it's nice to see well-grown rice being in my way.

—In reply to Tojou in Ise, who asks me by letter how my hermitage is;

Basho:
   The country life—to host you, the buckwheat flowers in white at present.

(Note) This comes from a *waka* of Saigyo:
 It might host the moon in the sky—that cloud;
 Coming and going from time to time.

Nairyu: A busy day—having reaped the early rice, the plowman looks relieved.

Tojou: The frosty rice fields—somewhere chirps a wild titmouse.

Shiko: A place of comfort—the green field is alive with siskins.

Shiko: A chilly morning, light frost, and the taros are roughly pulled out.

Izen: A chilly day—autumn has begun with red stalks of buckwheat.

Boksetz: It would be a small margin of profit—a rich harvest of red peppers.

—Seeing a grandson of famous drinker Tarutsugu at the Daishi Shore;
Senho:
 It will grow to a vine, to a flower—the watermelon seed of a great drinker.

Chrysanthemum

Chodah: It blooms firmly in the typhoon—the old man's flower.

Jokshi: A white *kick* is called Gem Peony; not that it is its child-in-name.

Shiko: A chilly day, a white *kick* flower, and the boiled cotton is dripping.

—As title of a certain picture;

Koho: Dewy *kick* flowers—a *samurai* trudges unto a trail with a foot cover on.

Joso: I talk about a *kick* flower when I talk about a hermitage I want to rent.

Late Autumn

Yasui: Pond Hirosawa, an autumn evening, and I go back to town with solitude.
 (Note) Pond Hirosawa is a sight spot in Saga, northwest of Kyoto.

Otokuni: Autumn is passing by, and a sorrowful note of fiddle strings.

Basho: Autumn is passing by, and a chestnut bursts open its prickly fist.

Things Autumnal

Shido: It has costed me fifty or sixty shrimps—that single goby.

Dan'you: The pine forest—let's try building a little cot with husks of millet.

Keishi: A chilly night—I give a look at the cage of a rough falcon.

Shiyou: The autumn rains—there appears a mosquito when I forget one.

Tekishi: From the arrow bag drop dewdrops as the archer shivers with tension.

Banco: Late at night, a peal of laughter—they seem to be threshing rice.

Monk Soha: The *susuki* chopsticks—let's eat grilled *miso* paste on a *kaki* leaf.

—Visited Noh actor Homma Shume. On the wall of the stage there was a picture of skeletons playing a Noh drama with flutes and drums. Just as the living enjoy their lives, so do the skeletons play about. Once upon a time, resting his head on a skull, a certain sage learned that life's like a dream; and now the picture tells us ours is just the same.

Basho: A flash of lightning—there stirs an ear of silver grass about the skull.
   (Note) This comes from an old tale: A certain traveler dreamed a dream of Lady Ono-no Komachi chanting a *waka*, with an ear of *susuki* grass about her head. Afterward in wasteland he found an ear of *susuki* grass about a skull on the wayside.

Winter

Winter Rain and Frost

Yaba: The first winter rain, a light rain—knots are wet in the hedge.

Hokshi: It rains not, yet blows in a good tune in the pine forest.

Basho: The first winter rain—let us get a day older today.

Lord Rosen: Here comes another winter rain, here comes another somber sky.

Baken: The first winter rain—I'm watching taros being boiled in the pan.

Yamei: The first winter rain—the rice field of five acres is darkened all at once.

Anshi: Here comes a firewood vendor, here comes another winter rain.

Kouga: The first winter rain in Yoshino—then where's a cup vendor?
(Note) Yoshino was famous for its production of lacquer ware.

Iyou: The winter rain in the mountains—the bears might go back to their dens.

Keico: It's reflected in the mirror late at night—the cold winter rain.

Yateki: It's wet in the winter rain—the incense burner left on a garden stone.

Rosen: The winter rain—the villagers cannot dry *kaki* fruits in the sun.

Riho:
　It rains up in the mountains, then down in the village, and it's time to sleep.

—The west wind has driven your floating clouds away; Off the shore shines the sun, yet it is soon likely to rain (an old *waka*).

Senho: The winter rain—off the shore the west wind brings the morning sun.

Hokkon:
　The first frost of the season—on the whitened soil, claw marks of a dog.

Shiko: The morning frost—the single-leaf ferns are whitened leaf by leaf.

—The sixth year of Genrock. One early-winter day I visited Sodo to join a *kick* party to be held in his garden. It was a month later than *Kick* Flower's Day; but a month before, the chrysanthemums did not even budded yet. The ancient Chinese poet Su Shi said a *kick* party should be held when they flower. Also, *kick* parties of old were put off at times. And on this day, a winter day, we gathered to sing of autumnal *kick* flowers.

Basho: The nice scent of *kick* flowers—there's a broken shoe left in the garden.

Kikack: The *kick* flowers have awoken, and the dewdrops in deep yellow.

Torin: The *kick* flowers bloom beautifully—deep fragrant in the garden.

Senho: Hassen Day, a rainy season—the *kick* flowers are wet with dew.
  (Note) Hassen Day is a day of abstinence in the Chinese way of Yin and Yang.

Sora: The beautiful meal—to what fish should we attach a *kick* flower?

Baken: The *kick* garden—the guests are about to crawl out of the round mat.

—A Chinese hermit of old, Tao Yuanming enjoyed seeing *kick* flowers and playing a string-less *koto* zither. Nowadays people love larger *kick* flowers, but selective breeding is against Nature. I have so far left my *kick* flowers growing. Not that I had such a *koto*. And recently my old friend Hitomi Chikto kindly sent me a simple *koto*; since then, mornings and evenings, I have enjoyed its tunes, sometimes without a tune, sometimes in harmony with the wind. A rather pleasant life of music.

Sodo: It goes well with a wild *kick* flower—the *koto* with no coat of lacquer.
  (Note) The seven verses above were composed at a party at Sodo's *kick* garden.

Plants

Kyoksui:
  Look through the crack of the wall; there's a daffodil blooms in the sun.

Hyoko: It flowers rather neatly—that leafy daffodil.

Izen: There flower daffodils in the weeds that used to be someone's garden.

—The eldest son of Fan Li, the title of a *waka* of Saigyo written in his anthology the *Sanka-shu*;

Basho: The *kick* flower freezes—as though it would never drop any drop of dew.
  (Note) Fan Li was a sage in ancient China. His eldest son failed in a certain mission due to stinginess.

Shayo: A sasanqua in flower on a Little Spring day; now in its season, though.

Doho: A winter day, the note of a bird, and there are a few *mei* blossoms.

Roritz: *Tsubaki* flowers have fallen on snow—and what about sasanquas?

Dead Leaves; Winter Blasts

Sentock: The sky speckled with many stars; here below, many leaves falling.

Lord Rosen: A chilly starry night—leaves are falling over fish in the river.

Izen: The winter river—dead leaves lie black between the rocks.

Kifou: Going up from the foot to the heights, I feel a nice touch of leaves.

—When visiting the Honryu-bo, Sohi's hermitage;

Ichido in Ise: First pick up a fallen leaf, then go into your hermitage.

Sampou: A frosty day—Alas, the withered *fair-lady* has lost grace.

Tosui: An ox is going on a path, and ahead spread dead fields.

Nairyu: The withered fields—I stand alone where my friend stood last year.

Rigyu: The withered fields—that snipe will not fly up even if I clap my hands.

Shiko: The withered fields—the cranes need not raise their heads now.

Nun Chigetz: The winter blasts cannot be seen, cannot be strewn.

Foukin: The winter blast—the ox is blown in the back, mooing.

Izen: The winter fields, a cold blast, and a pool of water is iron red.

Jinsei: The winter blast—pieces of straw are whirled out from the ox horn.

Yebis Fair

Basho: Yebis Fair—today a vinegar vendor too dresses in formal wear.

Rigo: Yebis Fair—a duck sells at a goose price.

Birds and Fishes

—Seeing the sea at Noto;

Kukou: They go, they come, day in, day out—a flock of plovers on Dust Beach.

Chodah: It stumbles as it chases hailstones—the running plover.

Joso: The cries of plovers—we wine and dine on a roofed boat on Koshin Vigil.

Anshi: The winter sound—at the wooden mark of an anchor cries a plover.

Basho: It will feel warm—a wild duck wearing its feather down over its feet.

Sakbock: Wild ducks are flying away, a dog is running on the causeway.

The late Risetz: It might come in when you draw seawater—a sea cucumber.

Shayo: It's been taken together with jelly fish—this dull sea cucumber.
   (Note) A jelly fish floats in water, while a sea cucumber lies on the bottom of sea.

Taisui: The winter beach—through thin ice can we see the flounder have roe.

Sampou: A snow day—let's eat the first icefish of the season with a pinch of salt.

Sekko: A shower of hailstones—there lie mantis fish with their stomach up.
(A mantis fish is as large as a puffer fish, sometimes lies on water with its stomach up. It lives in rivers in the North provinces.)

The Wintry Moon; Bedclothes

Riho: The winter moon—a food vendor walking around in town.

Joso: The winter moon—out from under the eaves runs a rowdy cat.

Shoshun: The paper blanket—the chill will be gone when you get asleep.

Shiko: The moon night, a daffodil, and in front of the gate runs a river.

Glow of Embers

Basho: The glow of embers—the wall reflects the shadow of the guest.
  (Note) Basho composed this *haik* at Kyoksui's lodging in Edo when the *samurai* poet was living there on official duties.

Tosen, a boy: It looks somewhat poor—a night blanket over the *kotatsu* warmer.

Dobock: With the *kotatsu* warmer aside, I can easily see the moon.

Snow

Kikack: The eventide, the first snow, and in front of the gate, a white bridge.

Kikack: The red-light town—a morning moon, white snow, and the *sake* weak.

Sekikick: Winter days—every snowfall and hailfall has its own chill.

Youho:
  There's a chirp of a winter wren, there's a patch of snow at the end of town.

Chodah: The snowy hedge—some may say it's a shield of frost.

Shiko: A snow day—even a two-year-old child is ready to put on straw sandals.

Hogin: Over the uncoated wall, over the straw bales fall white flakes of snow.

Joso: A snow view—I've chanced to see the front and the back of Mount Hyea.

Yowa: It's like a shaven head of a monk—the snowy Mount Hira.

Hairiki: Over Iga, over Yamato—the mountains are covered with flowery snow.

The Kagra

Fumikuni: The *kagra* music and dances at night—I grit my chilly teeth.

Bowl Beater

Roso: They are always coming in supper time—those noisy bowl beaters.

Baken: The beating of bowls—a dried-salmon vendor is asked for donations.

Kyorick: They passes by the newly-weds' house—those bowl beaters.

Senho: They would drive wolves away—those bowl beaters.

The Sweeping of Soot; the Making of Rice Cake

Zanko: The sweeping of soot—chase the mice into the box tree.

Koitz: The sweeping of soot—I cover my head with a sheet of Minato paper.

Baken: So kind is the neighbor's wife—as to help us sweep the soot.

Anjo in Mino: They'll come when we are sweeping soot—those bowl beaters.

Izen: The sweeping of soot—I have trampled on a meal tray.

Taisui: The making of rice cake—a woman wakes the men up.

Ranran: People making rice cake, the rooster cowers under the roost.

Babutz: He too helps make rice cake—that ascetic boy.

Year-End; Beggars; New Clothes

Sora: The Busy Month, a busy market, and a street of mud.

Rito: The Busy Month—I spread sand in front of my house before washing hair.

Soshi: It sits in the garden at the end of the year—the stone I've sold off.

Sharai: The end of a year—a monkey is leisurely sitting on a bough.

Banco: The end of a year—father and son are carrying a bale of something.

Riyou: The end of a year—there's a man marries without formalities.

Kikack: The Year-End market—who are you calling, gentleman?

Masahide: The Year-End market—someone has spilt *azki* beans.

Tekishi: The end of a year—I'm packing coins of silver.

Ensui: The end of a year—the loop of a pail has been renewed.

Izen: The end of a year—I've been looking for my velvet purse all day long.

Rogan: The end of a year—I've at last got that reed brush of Ise.
(This *haik* was composed by Rogan in the end of a year when he stopped at Ise on his way to Kyoto. With this left in our memories, he passed away.)

Basho: The year is passing by; saw a thief one night—which I remember.

Shiko: Let the year go by, I'm in bed in satin damask at someone's house.

Doho: A busy day—I have somehow finished bed-making within this year.

Shohack: They have gone to their hut by the woods—the beggars worn-out.

Togo, a boy:
   They're perplexed—the New-Year dancers in front of a vacant house.

Sampo: New clothes are given; a little child is pleased with a patch of cloth.

Rigo: The rooster crows out the Old Year; then nothing but silence.

Things Wintry

Sharei: A cold day—I'm making tea in the shade of a folding screen.

Doho: It runs to the path through *take* trees—the cold blast of river wind.

Rika: A cold day—so cold that the well water may feel warm.

Senjo: They chant on the long and wuthering bank—those ascetic villagers.

Hosen: Frost columns have formed on the ground—have you done that, mole?

Secci: A cold night—I'm clinging to the *kotatsu* warmer until midnight.

Kocock: The shade of a hill—a monkey's scratching its hips in the winter sun.

Senho: A chilly day—on the chopping board are chips of chopped carrot.

Sampou: The *kick* flowers are all cut, piles of firewood are put instead.

Buddhism; Memorial Services; Dirges

Nirvana

Senho: The holy image of dying Buddha—even the red mounting is not showy.

Basho: Nirvana Day—there're sounds of beads in the wrinkled hands of the old.

Futetz: The temple on a hill—the holy image of dying Buddha is kept by a cat.

Sampo: The holy image of the dying Buddha—all are sorrowful, rich or poor.

Buddha's Birthday

Kyoksui: Buddha's Birthday—azaleas are put in a row on the roof of a well.

Fugyok:
  Flowers falling; two or three days have passed since Buddha's Birthday.

Shido: Buddha was born this day, Devadatta was his cousin.
  (Note) Devadatta was a disciple of Buddha, but later disobeyed him.

Bon Festival

Ransetz: Bon Festival—all tastes weak that we eat.

Kyorai:
  Bon Festival—it would be saddening to see the other bed now ownerless.

Senho: Bon Festival—there's an ascetic calling in a bonze.

—The summer of the seventh year of Genrock. I was staying in Otsu Town when I received from my elder brother a letter saying that I should join in a memorial service at Bon Festival at my hometown.

Basho: We are visiting our graveyard, everyone gray-haired, a stick in hand.

—Two dirges to little ones:

Izen: Sorrowful are men's-size chopsticks put in front of the tomb.

Shiko: It is blown by an autumn wind—the tomb of a son of my friend.

—At Takiguchi Temple, Kamakura;

Boksetz:
  It's just before he'd be slain—that the sword was struck with lightning.
  (Note) This comes from an episode of the great monk Nichiren, the founder of Nichiren Buddhism.

Shiryo: The cemetery—a streak of lightning flashes on the water in the pail.

Nichiren's Death Anniversary

Senho: Holy Nichiren passed away this day; they offer citrons and persimmons.

The Day of Buddhahood

Kyorick: The Day of Buddhahood—my stomach and bowels full of *natto* soup.

Joko: Whose day today? —This day, a windy day, the great Tendai's Day.

Things Buddhist

—When the holy image of Zenkoji Nyorai was unveiled at Shin'nyo-do Temple, eastern Kyoto;

Kyorai: The sonorous chanting of a sutra—the hills are filled with cool air.
> *Kyorai's Notes:*
> The 'cool air' was originally written as 'crisp air', which was altered by the Old Reverend to 'fragrant air' because "a mild expression is better for a verse on Buddhism," thence to 'cool air' when this *haik* was selected to *Zok Salmino*.

Nun Chigetz: There are two poppies in the vase: one's in bloom, the other not.

Otokuni: It looks like a holy mass—when the poppy flowers have all fallen.

Bosui: They ask a *samurai* the depth of the river—the pilgrims to Mount Fuji.

Yaba: A summer day—someone's chanting an evening sutra in the cool morning.

Shiko: The eventide—outside the refectory chirp sparrows in a winter shower.

Travel

Parting

—It was in the summer of the seventh year of Genrock that I saw off the Old Reverend Basho.

Kakei: The smell of wheat bran, and I say good-bye in front of a rice-cake shop.

Izen: It's time to say good-bye; I'm eating *kaki* fruit at the top of the slope.

—When Kyorick setting out toward Kiso;

Basho: Chestnut tree, show your white flowers for the traveler of noble spirit.

Farewell

—When Izen leaving Kyoto for his home country;

Joso: Mouse, mouse, you did eat some farewell potato.

Basho: Farewell, farewell, the little sweet fish are seeing off tiny ice fish.

—When visiting Minobu Temple in the province of Kai, I passed along the winding road of Utz.

Boksetz: Being an old man, I ride on an ox on the ivy pathway.

Etsujin: Mount Suzka, flashes of lightning, and thus do we go round the world.
   (Note) This comes from a *waka* of Saigyo:
     Mount Suzka—I've run away from the world;
     And where am I going? How am I going?

Yakei: There's a traveler at an inn, there's a cicada flies away quickly.

—When passing a borderland into the northeastern province of Dewa;

Kowou: The sound of beating clothes at night—there used to be a marshland.

Kyorick: An autumn wind—your Ten Dumplings somewhat small nowadays.

Kyorick: Chilly is the night—when I sleep alone in a room for a prince.

—On the way to Kumano;

Sora: Bon Festival—they serve tea for travelers even on a steep mountain path.

Ensui: The mountain path in Kiso—the swallows are building earthen nests.

Gaho: The citrus blooming in white in the dark, the traveler is ready at dawn.

Fumikuni: Hot is the sunny sandy road—when I go on horseback across Hara.

—When arriving at Ise after a long travel;

The late Rogan: Opening the fan at desk, I could feel a cool autumn wind.

Senho: Chilly is a night on a journey, and they give me a coverlet at the inn.

—One evening—somewhere in Ashi-Arai in the province of Hitachi—I asked for a night's lodging at a certain house, but they declined because they were to hold a vigil. I spent that night under the eaves after all.

Shiko: A night on a verandah—the *mei* fragrant, and the *azki* soup tasty.

Shiko: A sick traveler I am, yet beside my pillow is the first gourd of the season.

—In the winter of the fourth year of Genrock I left Awaz for Edo, and on my way I visited Mister Tsukamoto at Shimada Town.

Basho: Being a traveler, I must give my name aloud in the winter rain.

Zok Salmino is an anthology made and compiled by the Old Reverend Basho and his disciples. The editor is unknown. Since the death of the Old Reverend the draft had been kept by his elder brother at Ueno Town in Iga. And after several years of our entreaty, the elder brother gave us the draft this spring, then allowing us to publish it. The draft is not a finished one; in it there are many deletions and insertions. We should therefore like to publish it as it is, without any additional amendments.

        Written by Izutsuya Shobei in Satsuki, the eleventh year of Genrock.

EPILOGUE

EPILOGUE

The Death of the Bard

The early winter of the seventh year of Genrock (1694) saw the condition of Basho getting worse. Kyorai, Masahide, Joso, Izen, Otokuni, Boksetz—they all hurried to Osaka at the news that the Old Reverend was critically ill. In a cold rain there came Kikack, too (he happened to be on a trip near Osaka). Requested by their master sick in bed, they made several verses. Basho praised one of them: 'Chilly is the night—when I sit right beside the medicine box. (Joso)' — "It's a sad and sweet one. Very nice." He acted as *haikai* master even in this fatal condition. And his last *haik*:

There's a traveler sick in bed, there's a dream running about in wasteland.

And the twelfth of the Tenth Month. In the chilly sunny early-winter afternoon the great *haik* master Matsuo Basho passed away at an inn in Osaka, with his disciples in sorrow at his side.

The remains of the poet was carried to Gichuji Temple, Zeze Town, Omi, where there was his hermitage the Moumyo-an. The funeral was attended by more than three hundred people from Zeze, Otsu, Kyoto and Osaka. The remains, wearing a white robe sewn by Nun Chigetz and Lady Kagetz (Otokuni's wife), was buried at a corner in the temple, a place from which you could see the beautiful views of Lake Land the poet loved—green hills, rice fields, far mountains, and the great Lake Biwa. And thus ended the golden age of *haik* poetry.

The Disciples

After his death Basho was worshipped as sainted *haik* poet. The Basho School became all the more prosperous.

Kikack and Ransetz lived as popular *haikai* masters in Edo; however, they showed no interest in the new style of Basho's. What they liked was his early style with wits, urbanity and classical taste. People too followed such a manner. The new style of Basho's seemed to be unattractive to pleasure-loving townspeople.

In contrast, Shiko became a leader of simple-taste *haik* poetry. Based in Mino, his school gained great popularity mainly in rural areas in Western Japan.

The death of Basho shocked his disciples in Omi. Masahide lost the motivation to go on to a further *haik* style. Monk Joso dedicated the rest of his life to memorial services for Basho. Meanwhile, Kyorick played an active role as a *haik* poet and critic; for instance, he compiled an anthology of the *haik* prose of Basho and others. Otokuni, too, did a lot for the Basho School: *A Sentimental Journey* was published by him.

Kyorai was the faithful follower of the new style. Yet he was more of a critic than a poet. He criticized Kikack for deviations from the new style, argued with Kyorick about immortality and modernity, and then wrote *Kyorai's Notes*—a collection of his irreplaceable memories about Basho. When seeking for what is highest in poetry, he was always drawn back to the past.

Kyoksui, a *samurai* poet called the Brave Man, died in that way. To save the domain of Zeze, he put a certain wicked officer to the sword on his responsibility; and by way of compensation, he killed himself promptly by *hara-kiri*, the end of the *samurai*.

Sometime before the death of Basho, Boncho had a hard time. He was put in jail. The reason is not clear. After release the talented poet lived in poverty and died in poverty; until his death, however, his wife Nun Ukoh was always with him.

Sora continued a wandering life. One year—sixteen years had already passed since the death of Basho—he participated by chance in a governmental mission going westwards to Kyushu. He thus traveled to the far western provinces, which his *haik* master could not visit. On the way, however, he fell seriously ill at Iki Island in Kyushu. The mission went on further. The sick old man was left behind. Imagine a rainy, windy night—a moonless, starless night; alone in bed in a village in the isle far from his hometown, the dying old man might have heard the raindrops whispering a sad and sweet tune of poetry, and the sea wind softly singing verses of *sacra* blossoms, young green leaves, a lovely autumn pink, a cold winter rain, and travel—those hard but joyous travels of *A Long and Narrow Road*: how beautifully that moon shone, how lively that summer grass stirred, how solemnly that red hot sun set sparkled, and how sadly that silk flower smiled; but all's over, all past, all gone with time and tide, leaves of words left in wasteland—and like his *haik* master, Sora too died on a journey.

It is said that there are more than 30 statues of Matsuo Basho in all over Japan. This is one of them erected in Soka-city.

Soka was first put on the map by Matsuo Basho as Soka City was the place Basho began his journey to the northern parts of Japan.